Caring for Jewish Patients

Joseph Spitzer

General Practitioner
Honorary Senior Clinical Lecturer in General Practice and Primary Care
Barts and the London, Queen Mary's School of Medicine and Dentistry,
University of London

Radcliffe Medical Press

Radcliffe Medical Press Ltd
18 Marcham Road
Abingdon
Oxon OX14 1AA
United Kingdom

www.radcliffe-oxford.com
The Radcliffe Medical Press electronic catalogue and online ordering facility.
Direct sales to anywhere in the world.

British Library Cataloguing in Publication Data

A catalogue record for this book is available from the British Library.

ISBN 1 85775 991 5

Typeset by Aarontype Limited, Easton, Bristol
Printed and bound by TJ International Ltd, Padstow, Cornwall

Contents

Preface

Rabbi Tarfon used to say: 'You are not required to complete all the work yourself, but nor are you free to desist from it.'

Avos 2:21

At the outset, it is important for me to make clear where I stand on the spectrum of Jewish religious practice. I would describe myself as being an orthodox Jew.* Naturally my text is based on Jewish practices as seen from my own perspective and viewpoint. However, I have tried to balance this stance to encompass other Jewish groups, especially as the Jewish patients that readers may meet might include those whose affiliations are with other sections of the community and whose practices may differ considerably from those of the orthodox.

Almost from my first day at medical school, I found myself being asked questions about Jews and Judaism. I am obviously a practising Jew, I wear a *cappel* (skullcap) at all times, eat a kosher diet and observe the *Shabbos* and *Yom-Tov* laws. I became used to people approaching me and asking 'I hope you don't mind, but can I ask you about . . .' and then enquiring about some aspect of Judaism that had puzzled them! I am now a general medical practitioner (GP) and am still frequently used as a source of information about Judaism. My practice is located in the Stamford Hill area of north London in the heart of the largest strictly orthodox (mainly Chassidic) Jewish community in Europe; this group accounting for some 65% of my patients.

Teaching medical students is an important part of my professional medical life, and when I started teaching I again found myself responding to students' questions about Judaism. Much of the basic information in this book originated from those discussions with my students and my responses to their interested enquiries. There are two rabbinic sayings that come to mind in relation to my love of teaching and encapsulate my feelings about my own teaching (and writing this book). The first is from Rabbi Akiva (c. 130 CE) to his favourite pupil Rabbi Shimon bar Yochai: 'My son, more

---

* The term 'orthodox' was first used to describe authentic Judaism by the early reformers as a label for their more traditional opponents and as such the term, although now in universal use, is not one that comes comfortably to orthodox Jews themselves. A better term would be 'authentic Judaism', implying the practice of Judaism through adhering strictly to the principles and practices of biblical and rabbinic law.

than the calf wishes to suck, does the cow yearn to suckle' and the second is from the great teacher Hillel (c. 40 BCE): 'I have learned much from my teachers, but most have I learned from my students'.

In 1996 I produced a booklet entitled *A Guide to the Orthodox Jewish Way of Life for Healthcare Professionals* jointly with my practice nurse Nicky Vyras (who is not Jewish). As part of her course work for the Health Education Certificate at The College of North East London, she had previously produced a short pamphlet for her peers, giving brief information on the orthodox Jewish way of life. Having worked closely for many years with the Jewish community at my north London general medical practice she felt that it would be appropriate for her to share her experiences and produce a leaflet for other health professionals also working with this community, giving useful information about some aspects of orthodox Jewish life. Members of the Chassidic Jewish community choose to lead an insular existence and not many avenues are open to enable an outsider to explore their rich culture. Ms Vyras felt that having worked within this community and having established a relationship of trust with many patients over the years, she was in an ideal position to share her information and insight. In her original course work she was closely advised and guided by me. I felt that, instead of being left to gather dust, the work should be rewritten, expanded and circulated, as its contents would be of value to other healthcare professionals working within the orthodox Jewish community. So we produced *A Guide to the Orthodox Jewish Way of Life for Healthcare Professionals* for our professional colleagues, in an effort to inform them about the orthodox Jewish community and thereby to increase understanding and awareness of this group. The first edition was a joint reworking and expansion of the original very concise pamphlet. The booklet was published by The Department of General Practice and Primary Care at St Bartholomew's and the Royal London School of Medicine and Dentistry, and the East London and The City Health Authority.

The first edition of *A Guide to the Orthodox Jewish Way of Life for Healthcare Professionals* was very well received. Copies were distributed to healthcare professionals not just in my practice area but elsewhere in the United Kingdom in places with orthodox Jewish patients. The text formed the basis for several other publications by various authors and organisations who (with permission) have adapted it to their own requirements. The booklet attracted a great deal of comment and suggestions. I published and distributed second and third revised and expanded editions in 1999 and 2002 respectively, as sole author.

Shortly before the publication of the third edition of *A Guide to the Orthodox Jewish Way of Life for Healthcare Professionals* I was approached by Radcliffe Medical Press to write this book, following the success of *Caring for Muslim Patients*, the first volume in this series. My previous books form the backbone of this work but they have been greatly modified and expanded to fit Radcliffe's requirements.

All the case histories, although written for the purpose of this book, are loosely based on real situations. Details and names have been changed and many are amalgamations of several scenarios. As such, none should be interpreted as relating to a specific patient.

I acknowledge God's generosity in affording me the opportunity and ability to produce this work: 'Thanks be to the Lord for He is good and his kindness endures for ever' (Psalms 118: 1). I am grateful to my wife Esther for her forbearance during the months of writing, when even more than the usual amount of caring for our family fell on her shoulders: 'The wise amongst women builds her family' (Proverbs 14: 1). My children are my most critical students; hence, according to Hillel's aphorism quoted above, they are also my greatest teachers. Writing this book must have been at the cost of the paternal attention which they deserve and I hope that they (both God and family) will forgive me for having neglected them at times during the preparation of this book.

Joseph Spitzer MB BS MRCGP DCCH DRCOG
General Practitioner
Honorary Senior Clinical Lecturer in General Practice and Primary Care
(Barts and the London, Queen Mary's School of Medicine and Dentistry,
University of London)
May 2003

Email: j.spitzer@doctors.org.uk

Man's thoughts are his own – but God gives him the words to express them.

Proverbs 16: 1

Acknowledgements

With grateful thanks to:

Dayan AD Dunner
Mr and Mrs S Desser
Rabbi J Dove
Dr I Ellis
Dr L Flancbaum
Mr MM Guttentag
Rabbi D Hulbert
Mr E Kahan
Dr AL Levy
Professor Kate M Loewenthal
Mr AP Rose
Mrs Esther Spitzer
Mr MD Spitzer
Dr Emma L Teper
Ms Nicky Vyras
Mr SM Winegarten
London School of Jewish Studies Library
Royal Society of Medicine Library

Introductory remarks

Now Israel, what does God ask of you? Only that you are in awe of God your Lord, to go in all His ways and to love Him, serving God your Lord with all your heart and all your soul; to keep God's commandments and His decrees that I am prescribing for you today, for your benefit.

Deuteronomy 10: 12–13

Of the several themes running through this book one will be repeated several times where relevant; that is the reminder to the reader of the enormous variation in Jewish religious practices. It is essential that when meeting a Jewish patient a healthcare professional does not assume a level of religious observance – the rule is that it is always better to ask than to assume.

In relation to the variation in religious practices I have generally taken the approach of describing the practices of the orthodox and so called ultra-orthodox as being an example of one end of the spectrum of religious practice, even though those groups comprise a relative minority of Jews. This should enable the reader to understand that practices will be less extreme the further his/her patients are away from that end of the spread of adherence to religious practices and rituals. One problem of this approach is that it may give the reader the mistaken impression that Judaism is an austere and restrictive religion, full of constraints and negatives, and that this might be reflected in the patients they meet. This is far from being the case! Judaism is a positive joyous religion with a very rich communal life and its practices and adherents reflect this.

Having accepted that Jews observe the commandments because they are God's word, one may wish to delve into their purpose a little deeper, looking for explanations for each. Unfortunately detailed discussions of this fascinating aspect of Judaism is outside the scope of this book's title.[1]

In this book the reader will encounter some examples of the practical aspects of the practice of Judaism such as details of the observance of *Shabbos*

---

[1] A full Bibliography is provided at the back of the book for readers who might wish to pursue this aspect of Judaism further. A good starting point is *Masterplan, Judaism* (1991) by Rabbi A Carmell.

(the Sabbath) and festivals (Chapter 9), *Kashrus*, keeping the kosher laws (Chapter 10), and adhering to the Laws of Family Purity (Chapter 11). These are concepts which contain laws which seem restrictive and which may appear to be out of place in the modern world. There is however another side to each of these examples.

Although a description of *Shabbos* by necessity includes details of the activities forbidden on that day, the positive aspects of the joy of celebrating the *Shabbos* far overshadow these seemingly negative aspects. *Shabbos* is a period providing a total break from the hurly-burly of the workaday world; it is a day for reflection, prayer, rest and above all it is a day devoted to the family. It provides a complete break from the pressures of daily life and is as invigorating for the mind as it is for the soul.[2]

Observing the kosher laws enables the thinking Jew to appreciate what he puts into his mouth, to consider all the effort that has gone into its preparation and gives him the opportunity to thank God for what he enjoys. Reflecting on this for a few moments, whilst saying the *brochoh* (benediction) before eating, makes eating all the more pleasurable.

When discussing the laws of family life, a simple description does not immediately convey the positive aspects of observing these laws which to a modern healthcare professional might seem archaic and hard to understand. The period of physical separation enables a couple to relate to each other on terms of mutual respect without any sexual pressures and the resumption of sexual contact each cycle rejuvenates the marriage and keeps the relationship fresh and alive. At its core, these laws strengthen the family which is the focus of Jewish life.

These are just a few examples of the positive aspects of following a Jewish lifestyle and adhering to these practices gives the observant Jew a structured existence, a sense of purpose, a closeness to God and a feeling of inner peace.

When caring for Jewish patients the reader should bear in mind that the essence of Judaism and the true underlying theme and spirit of Jewish religious practice is encapsulated in the words 'Serve God with joy' (Psalms 100: 2).

---

[2] It is precisely for this reason that I have used the Hebrew word *Shabbos* throughout instead of the English Sabbath, as the latter doesn't truly capture the unique essence and nuance that the word *Shabbos* conveys to the practising Jew.

Heal me O Lord, that I might be cured; save me that I might be saved, for You are my hope!

Jeremiah 17: 14

Medical practice is an important introduction to intellectual and ethical pursuits and to understanding God and to achieving true success; thus will the physician's study and ambition become one of the great occupations, unlike weaving or carpentry.

Maimonides, The Eight Chapters
(Introduction to his commentary on Avos) 5

Through my flesh will I recognise my God.

Job 19: 26

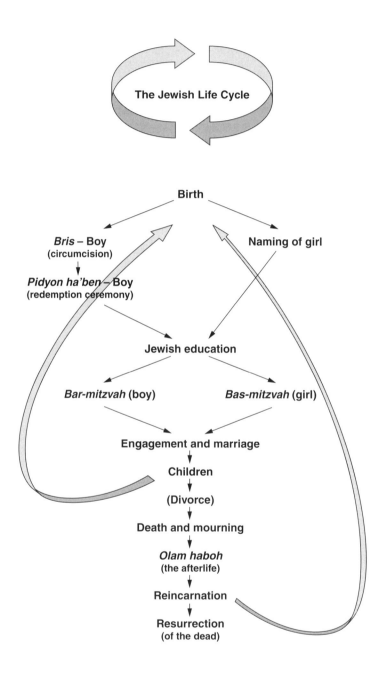

The Jewish Life Cycle

Birth

Bris – Boy
(circumcision)

Naming of girl

Pidyon ha'ben – Boy
(redemption ceremony)

Jewish education

Bar-mitzvah (boy)   *Bas-mitzvah* (girl)

Engagement and marriage

Children

(Divorce)

Death and mourning

Olam haboh
(the afterlife)

Reincarnation

Resurrection
(of the dead)

PART I

Jews and Judaism

CHAPTER I

Judaism, Jews and Jewishness

One God; one people

Hear O Israel, The Lord our God, the Lord is One.   Deuteronomy 6: 4

The *shema* (declaration of belief in God)

What is Judaism?

Judaism is a monotheistic religion, the single most important principle of which is a belief that everything in the universe is under the direct control of the one God. Man's purpose on this world is to recognise and serve God, live justly, perform good deeds, study the *Torah* and live life accordingly. Jews believe that the soul is immortal but Judaism concentrates very much more on the practical aspects of creating a just world for the living, rather than on meditating on aspects of the afterlife.

Monotheism

God is one, neither two nor more, but a unity, unlike other unities in the universe which may have many parts or like a body which is divided into parts. So the unity of God is quite different from anything else in the world. If there were many deities it would mean that they had body and form because individuals only differ from one another in bodily form. If the Creator had a body and form He would have an end, a ceasing. It is impossible to imagine a body that does not end and whose strength does not wane. Our God – blessed be He! – has strength to which there is no end and does not falter because the sphere continues to revolve for ever by His force which is not a bodily force. Because He is incorporeal, none of the happenings which occur to parts of a body can be attributed to Him, so it is impossible that He should be but one. The understanding of monotheism is a positive commandment, as it is written 'the Lord our God is the one and only God' (Deuteronomy 6: 4).

Maimonides, *Mishne Torah*, Book of Knowledge, Foundations of the *Torah* 1: 7

All aspects of Judaism, whether relating to belief, philosophy, religious or civil law, have their basis in the *Torah*, the Written Law (often referred to as the Biblical Law of the Bible or Old Testament), as interpreted by the rabbis throughout the ages in the Oral Law (often called the Rabbinic Law). The practice of Judaism involves performing the *mitzvos* (the commandments) which can be thought of as the acts that Jews perform because God requires it of them. The Written Law contains the basic 613 *mitzvos*, which are listed in rudimentary outline in the divinely written *Five Books of Moses* (the Pentateuch) which the rabbis in the Oral Law expand in considerable detail.

A life-giving medicine

The rabbis taught: it is written 'you shall put the words of my *Torah* into your hearts' (Deuteronomy 11: 18). The letters that make up the Hebrew words 'you shall put' can also be read and understood to mean 'the perfect medicine' (i.e. they are homonyms, so the verse could be understood to mean 'the words of my *Torah* are the perfect medicine'), because the *Torah* can be compared to a life-giving medicine; as in the following analogy:

A man once hit his son causing him serious wound. He put a dressing on the wound saying 'my son, so long as the bandage is covering the wound, you may eat and drink what you desire and bathe as you wish and need have no fear that you will be harmed by these activities. However should you take off the dressing, the wound will suppurate'.

So, the Holy One Blessed be He said to His people the Jews, 'My son, I have created the evil inclination and I have created the *Torah* as the antidote for it. If you engage in *Torah* matters you will not be

> overcome by the power of the evil inclination. But if you ignore the
> *Torah* then you will be overcome by the power of the evil inclination'.
>
> Based on *Talmud* Kidushin 30b

The Written Law is never understood literally in isolation by Jews but is always read together with and interpreted through the Oral Law, which in orthodox belief was also given to Moses on Mount Sinai at the same time as the Ten Commandments were given, but which was not written down until very much later. The main repository of the Oral Law is the *Talmud*, a vast encyclopaedic work (third to sixth century) covering all aspects of Judaism and Jewish law (*Halochoh*). The *Talmud* and its many commentaries are regularly studied in great depth by orthodox Jews and it forms the basis of religious authority in traditional orthodox Judaism. Almost all subsequent Jewish legal works throughout the ages are based on the *Talmud*, which remains the cornerstone of Jewish law to this very day. The main post-Talmudic works on Jewish law are the *Mishne Torah* (literally 'the repetition of the *Torah*'), where Jewish law is systematically organised and comprehensively codified in a clear, lucid style, written by Maimonides (1135–1204), and the *Shulchon Oruch* (literally 'the laid table'), where the details of Jewish law are clearly laid out (often paraphrased in English as 'the code of Jewish law'), written by Rabbi Yossef Caro (1488–1575). Both the Written and Oral Laws are seen as being inseparable, and indeed are regarded as being one unit, which together are often also collectively referred to as the *Torah*.

The actual practice of Judaism requires observance of the *mitzvos*, the commandments, the religious obligations incumbent upon all Jews. Judaism predates Christianity and Islam, the other so called Abrahamic religions. Jews do not venerate Jesus or Muhammad, nor do they celebrate any of the Christian festivals such as Christmas or Easter.

The *mitzvos* (the commandments)

Man can approach God only by doing His commandments.

Rabbi Yehuda HaLevi (1075–1141) in *Kuzari*

Judaism is not so much a religion as a way of life governed in all its aspects by the meticulous observance of the *Torah* and the *mitzvos* (the religious duties required to be performed by Jews). Curiously, and in contrast to other religions, Judaism concentrates on practice rather than on theological concepts and a system of beliefs. It is possible to be a 'good Jew' without much knowledge of Jewish theological principles, or Jewish ideology, so long as he or she performs all the relevant *mitzvos*. In fact when a convert applies to an orthodox religious rabbinic court (*Beis Din*) to become Jewish, he or she is firstly required to adopt a Jewish way of life and to observe the practices of Judaism. The examination prior to acceptance of converts also concentrates mainly on knowledge and acceptance of the practices of Judaism and the keeping of the *mitzvos* rather than a deep knowledge of the philosophical or theological concepts of Judaism. This indeed is fully in keeping with the very essence of Judaism. The traditional belief is that Judaism originated at Mount Sinai, when God offered the *Torah* to the Children of Israel seven weeks after their miraculous liberation from Egypt. When the Jews were given the *Torah* at Mount Sinai, they accepted upon themselves to embrace the *Torah* unquestioningly as God's word, undertaking at the same time to keep all the *mitzvos*. It is stated in Exodus (24: 7) that when accepting the *Torah* the Children of Israel said 'all that God has said we will do (first) and (then) understand'. This statement marks the very moment of the birth of Judaism. The Jews agreed to follow God's word – 'we will do' first and foremost, before even attempting to try to understand the basis for God's will – 'we will understand'.

Freewill – choosing good or bad

Freewill is granted to every man. If he wishes to direct himself toward the good way and become righteous, the will to do so is in his hand; and if he wishes to direct himself toward the bad way and become wicked, the will to do so is likewise in his hand. Thus it is written in the *Torah*, 'Behold, the man is become as one of us, knowing good and evil' (Genesis 3: 22) – that is to say, the human species has become unique in the world in that it can know of itself, by its own wit and reflection, what is good and what is evil, and in that it can do whatever it wishes.

Maimonides, *Mishne Torah*, Book of Knowledge,
Laws of Repentance 5: 1

The belief that the Jews were given the *Torah* by God at Mount Sinai is one of the basic fundamental beliefs of Judaism (*see* the Thirteen Principles of Faith, pp 11–12). This includes the belief that the *Torah* that God gave to the Jews at Mount Sinai consisted not only of the Ten Commandments but also of the entire Written Law together with the Oral Law, which were all given over as an inseparable unit. The Written Law itself contained the basic 613 *mitzvos*, of which 245 are positive commandments (the 'Thou shalls'), and 365 are negative commandments (the 'Thou shall nots'). The Oral Law was transmitted verbally and given over for the rabbis of each successive generation to apply (hence the alternative name 'Rabbinic Law'). Traditional Judaism regards the Written Law as being only the bare bones of God's word; the Oral or Rabbinic Law adds the details of the *mitzvos* and adds many more Rabbinic *mitzvos*, both positive and negative. Orthodox Jewish teaching accepts the Oral/Rabbinic Law as having almost equivalent stature to the divinely given Written Law.

The Thirteen Principles of Faith

1   I believe with complete faith that the Creator, Blessed is His Name, creates and guides all creatures, and that He alone made, makes, and will make everything.

2   I believe with complete faith that the Creator, Blessed is His Name, is One, and there is no oneness like His in any way, and that He alone is our God, Who was, Who is, and Who always will be.

3   I believe with complete faith that the Creator, Blessed is His Name, is not physical and is not affected by physical phenomena, and that there is nothing at all comparable to Him.

4   I believe with complete faith that the Creator, Blessed is His Name, is the very first and the very last.

5   I believe with complete faith that the Creator, Blessed is His Name – to Him alone it is proper to pray, and it is not proper to pray to any other.

6   I believe with complete faith that all the words of the prophets are true.

7   I believe with complete faith that the prophecy of Moishe (Moses) our teacher, peace be upon him, was true, and that he was the father of the prophets, both those who preceded him and those who followed him.

8   I believe with complete faith that the entire *Torah* now in our hands is that which was given to Moishe our teacher, peace be upon him.

9   I believe with complete faith that this *Torah* will not be exchanged nor will there be another *Torah* from the Creator, Blessed is His Name.

10   I believe with complete faith that the Creator, Blessed is His
     Name, knows all the deeds of people and their thoughts, as it
     says, 'He Who fashions their hearts all together, comprehends
     all their deeds' (Psalms 33: 14).
11   I believe with complete faith that the Creator, Blessed is His
     Name, rewards with good those who observe His command-
     ments, and punishes those who violate His commandments.
12   I believe with complete faith in the coming of the Messiah, and
     even though he may delay, nevertheless I await his coming
     every day.
13   I believe with complete faith that there will be a revival of the
     dead when the Creator so desires, Blessed is His Name and
     exalted is His mention, forever and for all eternity.

These Thirteen Principles of Faith are based on the Commentary to
the *Mishne* (Sanhedrin, Chapter 10) by Maimonides (Rabbi Moishe
ben Maimon (1135–1204), the great Rabbi and Physician).

Jews

According to Jewish law (the *Halochoh*) anyone born to a Jewish mother is
de facto Jewish. One is Jewish only if his or her mother is Jewish, irrespective of the status of the father. Thus, someone born of a Jewish father to a
non-Jewish mother is not a Jew. Having been born a Jew, Jewish law
regards that status as continuing throughout life, and it is automatically
passed on to a Jewess's offspring and cannot ever be renounced. Having
been born a Jew one is regarded in Jewish law as being a full Jew. Jewish
law does not recognise the concept of being 'half Jewish'; one is either
Jewish or not!

Judaism does not seek to convince or convert the rest of mankind to its
own views and there is no missionary or evangelistic element to Judaism.
Jews regard Judaism and its practices as being only for those born as Jews;
indeed those who seek conversion are actively discouraged. Judaism does
not regard adherents of other monotheistic God-fearing faiths as being in
error but believes that everyone, Jew or Gentile, has their place and role
in this world, and by leading virtuous lives can earn a place in the world
to come.

In rare circumstances it may be possible to become Jewish by conversion,
a process which can be lengthy and difficult. To be accepted by mainstream orthodox Judaism as a genuine conversion the procedure must be

carried out by a recognised rabbinical court (a *Beis Din*), following which the convert (*ger*) becomes fully Jewish in all respects and is required to observe all the commandments (*mitzvos*); a sincere convert is held in high esteem. Conversion is an irreversible process and children born to a woman after her conversion are also automatically Jewish. Authorities, other than strictly orthodox rabbinical courts, also perform conversions, and their requirements are generally less stringent than those of the orthodox rabbinical authorities. Such converts may however find that the status of their conversions, any subsequent marriages and the Jewish status of their children will not be recognised by orthodox rabbinical authorities.

Variation and variety

Jews are found in almost every country in the world. Jewish history has been a story of almost constant movement. Migration, expulsion and dispersal, for social or economic reasons but more often on account of religious persecution, have been a feature of the Jewish way of life, since the days of Abraham. Some communities stayed but briefly in their locations, whereas others could trace their settlement back through many centuries and even millennia. More recent Jewish history has been no different, and the last century has been marked by the disruption and destruction of communities that had previously been undisturbed for many generations, with their dispersal and redistribution all round the world.

Modern day Jewry can be divided into two main subgroups, Sephardim and Ashkenazim. In broad terms, Sephardim include Jews whose origins were in North Africa, Southern Europe, the Levant, the Middle East and the Orient. The Jews who were expelled from Spain in 1492 were Sephardim and, of these, some settled in Holland, accounting for the small number of Sephardim of North European descent. Ashkenazim originate from Northern, Central and Eastern Europe. Culturally, Sephardim are much more diverse than Ashkenazim; for instance, Jews of Yemen have very different customs and practices from those originating from Morocco. Ashkenazim subdivide into two main groups, Chassidim ('the Righteous (or Pious) Ones') and Misnagdim (literally 'the opponents', i.e. those Ashkenazi Jews who are not Chassidim and who do not share all their philosophical views) (*see* p 27 for the historical background). However, since the major upheavals and resettlement of the Second World War, distinctions between the various groups, especially amongst Ashkenazim, have begun to blur.

Today, Jews are to be found all over the world and there is considerable variation amongst Jews themselves – for example, there are European,

Oriental and African Jews, there are white and black Jews, there are American, Indian and British Jews. There are Jews whose entire 'Jewishness' goes no further than their merely having been born of a Jewish mother. (Although they may regard themselves as being Jewish in name only, Jewish law nevertheless considers them as full Jews.) Many Jews do not affiliate with any recognised Jewish movements or synagogues. Non-affiliated or even agnostic Jews are still considered to be full Jews according to Jewish law. For most people affiliation to a particular Jewish movement or synagogue is less a matter of ideology and theology but rather more a sense of community or belonging. For many, affiliation to a synagogue is related to belonging to that synagogue's burial society (see p 151), something which has always been regarded as important, particularly by British Jews. There are also Progressive, Liberal and Reform Jews who may be selective in their religious observances, whereas at the other end of the religious spectrum are the very strictly observant Jews often termed 'orthodox' (or 'strictly-orthodox' or occasionally even 'ultra-orthodox'), whose entire way of life is inseparable from their being Jewish. They adhere strictly to Jewish law, conducting their lives according to the dictates of the *Torah*; they regard themselves as being the only Jews practising genuine, authentic Judaism. Each group may have subgroups, for instance there are Sephardim of Moroccan origin and Sephardim of Afghanistani origin, and Ashkenazim of Lithuanian extraction may have customs and practices quite different to those of Dutch origin. There are non-orthodox movements including Reform, Liberal and Masorti branches. The strictly observant orthodox include the Chassidim, the Misnagdim and some Sephardim. There is considerable overlap between these divisions and in recent decades, with ease of travel, distinctions are in many places starting to blur, with marriage between the different groups becoming commonplace, especially in Israel.

Orthodox/Reform 1

When a Jewish communal organisation set up a committee to look at the housing needs of the Jewish community, they invited Rabbi Rothstein to represent the orthodox community. However, when he heard that the committee would include a representative of the local Reform synagogue, he withdrew, as he refused to sit on the same committee as 'one of those blasphemers who don't accept the divine origins of the *Torah* as given by God to Moses on Mount Sinai'.

Religious practice

Orthodox

Strictly observant Jews have been termed 'orthodox' (or even 'ultra-orthodox') Jews (*see* p iv). The best known and most conspicuous subgroup of orthodox Jews are the Chassidim (or Chassidic Jews). Apart from the Chassidim, there are sizeable communities of orthodox Misnagdim and Sephardim. There are certain differences in practice between Chassidic and other orthodox Jews and these have been highlighted where appropriate.

Orthodox Jews do not regard Judaism as 'just a religion', but more as a way of life. They do not compartmentalise their lives into religious and secular portions and times. To them, Judaism is an all-encompassing way of life based on the *Torah*. Fundamental to orthodox belief is the divine origin of the entire *Torah* (both the Written Law and the Oral Law) and the divine inspiration of the rabbis who interpreted the *Torah* in their expansion of the Oral Law. Other fundamentals are summarised in the Thirteen Principles of Faith as defined by Maimonides (*see* the Thirteen Principles of Faith, pp 11–12).

Chassidim

The title Chassid (the 'ch' is pronounced with a hard, guttural 'ch' as in the Scottish loch; the word can be transliterated either as Chassid as used in this book, or as *Hassid*), plural Chassidim, literally means 'the Righteous (or Pious) One(s)'. The Chassidic movement was started in seventeenth-century Poland by the followers of the famous rabbi, the *Ba'al Shem Tov* (the 'Master of the Good Name'; the acronym BeShT is often employed in written works) and was spread rapidly throughout Eastern Europe by his disciples. The main philosophical characteristics of the Chassidic movement are great enthusiasm for performing the *mitzvos*, ecstasy in prayer and great personal devotion to the individual leader or rabbi known to Chassidim as a *'rebbe'*. Chassidic philosophy has its roots in mysticism and *kabbolah*, and many Chassidic practices have deep mystical significance. In contrast the Misnagdim (literally 'the opposers') were vehemently against the use of mysticism and *kabbolah* in their practice of Judaism and were much more pragmatic and rational in their practices, basing everything on a logical analysis of *Halochoh*. The Chassidic movement split into many branches each led by its own *rebbe*, the leadership being passed down, often in dynastic fashion, over many generations. Prior to the Second World War many Chassidim lived in rural environments, leading a secluded way of life, isolated from all the influences of the Gentile world outside.

Following the destruction of their traditional way of life in the Holocaust, the remnants of the Chassidic movement settled in several centres around the world, most notably in New York, Israel, Belgium and London, where they slowly began to recreate their traditional way of life, regrouping themselves around their various *rebbes*.

Chassidic communities are generally very insular, keeping themselves to themselves and trying to lead a self-sufficient lifestyle. Understandably they may occasionally give the impression of resenting interference from outside agencies. However, they do live in the secular world, thereby coming into daily contact with non-Jewish society and the environment around them. Healthcare workers such as health visitors or district nurses should bear this in mind when calling on orthodox Jewish or Chassidic families, and should be careful to explain their roles clearly.

Orthodox *Sephardim*

Amongst the Sephardim, like the Ashkenazim, there is a wide spread of religious observance. A significant and growing proportion of Sephardim are strictly observant, and in many communities throughout the world they are the major orthodox force. They retain the varied practices and customs of their places of origin and have formed synagogues upholding these traditions. Many Sephardic customs and practices, like those of the Chassidim mentioned above, are founded in mysticism and the *kabbolah* and carry mystical significance.

Progressive Judaism

There are various groups of Jews who come under the umbrella description of Progressive Judaism; these include the Reform, Liberal and Masorti. The Reform movement dates back to the eighteenth century when European enlightenment was at its peak. Groups of Jewish intellectuals joined the enlightenment movement which had its base in German-speaking middle Europe. Emancipation was the catchword of Reform Judaism, whose philosophy can be summed up in the concept of being 'a Jew at home but a good German outside', thereby facilitating entry into the culture of the world outside the ghetto. One of the results of emancipation was that, for the first time in Jewish history, secularisation and then assimilation became rife, as Jews started to mix freely in a more liberal non-Jewish world. By the early nineteenth century, more secularised Jews had begun introducing reforms into the synagogue. Prayer services were shortened and Hebrew was largely dropped in favour of the vernacular. Congregational singing to organ accompaniment was introduced, in effect modelling Judaism on the Lutheran Church. The movement towards enlightenment spread rapidly from Western Europe to the large Jewish communities of Eastern Europe, where it became known as the *Haskalah* movement. Reform Judaism allowed Jews for the first time to be able to regard themselves as being Jewish without having to meticulously observe the minutiae of Jewish law, which the Reform saw as old-fashioned and irrelevant to the modern world. By the second half of the nineteenth century an even more radical wing emerged, calling itself Liberal Judaism. This called for changes to many of those fundamentals that defined traditional Judaism, such as the dietary laws and the *Shabbos* restrictions. Whilst the Liberal movement accepts the divine origins of the *Torah*, it believes that it was mediated through human intellect. Liberal Judaism maintains that the keeping of the *mitzvos* (commandments) is a matter of individual choice. In the case of children born of mixed marriages, Liberal Jews regard Judaism more as a matter of upbringing and education rather than sticking rigidly to the orthodox's halachic matrilineal definition. The Masorti movement claims to offer a style of Reform Judaism with an orthodox flavour, for instance using the regular orthodox prayer book, but they also do not accept the truth of Divine Revelation, when God gave all of the *Torah* at Mount Sinai.

A long-term and often very bitter schism arose between the orthodox and Reform right from the latter's inception and continues to this very day. Marriages, divorces or conversions performed by any of the various branches of the Progressive movements may not be recognised by orthodox authorities.

Variation in religious practice

The majority of Jews in the world today are not orthodox, are non-observant, and lead a lifestyle that is to a large extent almost indistinguishable from that of the indigenous population amongst whom they live. They may observe none or perhaps just a few selected Jewish practices or rituals. Nevertheless many non-observant Jews feel intensely 'Jewish' in spite of the fact that they do not practice Judaism in a traditional orthodox Jewish way. The majority of Jews that readers of this book might come into contact with are likely to be from the majority and more widespread but less observant group than from the strictly orthodox community. I shall attempt to balance my description to apply to and encompass all Jewish groups. The strictly traditionally orthodox tend to live in quite clearly delineated close-knit communities, and it is only those healthcare workers who live close to these centres who are likely to meet large numbers of them. Nevertheless there will be occasions where orthodox patients may be admitted to specialised units in hospitals away from their home areas. Otherwise most hospitals and GPs may have a sprinkling of Jewish patients across the whole spectrum of Jewishness and observance in their practices.

Orthodox/Reform 2

Sadie was 82 when she was admitted to hospital. She asked to see a Jewish chaplain but was upset to find that the official Jewish hospital chaplain was an orthodox rabbi. Although she had rarely attended, she had been a lifelong member of a Progressive synagogue. She felt that she could not relate to an orthodox rabbi.

It can be difficult for non-Jews to appreciate the wide variety of Jewish practice and observance. Practices that are acceptable to one group of Jews may be anathema to others, and healthcare workers must be wary in extrapolating what they see in their non-orthodox and less strictly observant patients as applying equally to their orthodox ones. For instance, ward staff in hospital may become confused when, for example, one Jewish patient would quite happily accept a cup of tea, served in a hospital cup with milk from the ward kitchen, whereas another Jewish patient would firmly decline to do so, insisting on using only a disposable plastic cup or one brought in from home, and drinking only kosher supervised milk.

Different practices

When Mr Henry Stern, a non-observant secular Jew, was admitted to hospital, he was surprised to find that the staff only served him black coffee without milk. When he asked for milk the staff expressed their surprise saying that they thought he was Jewish and they assumed all Jews would only take kosher supervised milk. He explained that those Jews who were particular about kosher milk were in fact in the minority. He said that most Jews, whom he described as 'normal' Jews like him, would use any milk and even after a meat meal. The staff were confused by the wide spectrum of religious practice amongst people all described as Jews.

An example of an area where an understanding of a patient's Jewish religious practices may be of relevance to healthcare professionals is in the presentation of conditions such as early dementia, confusion and many psychiatric conditions. Here the patient's aberrant behaviour may be manifested in inappropriate religious or ritual practices which might only be apparent to someone who fully understands the patient's religious, social and cultural background. For instance, whereas praying several times a day is part of the normal daily ritual of the orthodox Jewish male, saying the special *Shabbos* prayers on any other day of the week should give rise to concerns about that person's state of mind. Similarly a Jewish housewife who lights her *Shabbos* candles at any time other than at sundown on a Friday evening would raise similar concerns.

Conclusion

Jewish religious observance and practice runs through a very wide spectrum, from the extremely devout orthodox whose entire way of life is governed by Jewish law and their meticulous adherence to its tenets, to the other extreme where there are those Jews who are entirely secular, observing none of the practices so rigorously observed by their co-religionists. In between are all shades of religious practice and observance. When describing attitudes, ideas, philosophies and practices that healthcare workers may observe in their Jewish patients, it is tempting to describe the norms of the strictly orthodox as 'extreme' and then to extrapolate from this to say 'others may do similar or less'! I shall attempt to explain practices specific to each group where possible. However, in dealing with individual Jewish patients it is usually far better to ask each one about their individual practices and preferences, where appropriate, rather than to make assumptions.

Summary

- All Jewish beliefs and observances are based on the God-given *Torah* which encompasses both the Bible (Old Testament), 'the Written Law', and 'the Oral Law', the Rabbinic Laws, both of which were given to the Jews together as one unit at Sinai.

- The practice of Judaism involves the observance of the *mitzvos*, God's commandments.
- Jewish law defines a Jew as anyone born to a Jewish mother.
- Central to Judaism is the belief that everything is under the direct control of the one God.
- Amongst Jews there is a very wide spectrum of Jewish religious practice and observance from the totally secular non-observant through to the very strictly observant minority.
- When looking after Jewish patients it is recommended not to assume their level of religious practice and observance; when in doubt it is always best to ask.

Further reading

Aaronson A (2000) *The Foundation of Judaism* (2e). Targum/Feldheim, New York,

Blech B (1999) *The Complete Idiot's Guide to Understanding Judaism*. Alpha Books, Indianapolis.

Carmell A (1991) *Masterplan, Judaism: its program, meaning, goals.* Feldheim, Jerusalem/New York.

Cohn-Sherbok L and Cohn-Sherbok D (1997) *A Popular Dictionary of Judaism.* Curzon, Richmond.

Cohn-Sherbok L and Cohn-Sherbok D (1998) *A Concise Encyclopaedia of Judaism.* Oneworld, Oxford.

Cohn-Sherbok L and Cohn-Sherbok D (1999) *A Short Reader in Judaism.* Oneworld, Oxford.

Forta A (1995) *Judaism.* Heinemann, Oxford.

Forta A (1996) *Judaism: a dictionary.* Nelson Thornes, Cheltenham.

Fuller JHS and Toon PD (1988) *Medical Practice in a Multicultural Society.* Heinemann, Oxford.

HaLevi J (1964) *The Kuzari: an argument for the faith of Israel* (trans H Hirschfeld). Schocken Books, New York.

Hirsch SR (1994) *The Nineteen Letters on Judaism.* Feldheim, Spring Valley.

Kaplan A (1992) *The Handbook of Jewish Thought.* Maznaim Press, New York/Jerusalem.

Qreshi B (1989) *Transcultural Medicine.* Kluwer, London.

Robinson G (2000) *Essential Judaism – a complete guide to beliefs, customs and rituals.* Pocket Books, New York.

Roth C (ed.) (1972) *Encyclopaedia Judaica.* Keter, Jerusalem: 16 vols (also single vol concise edn and junior edn) with yearbook and decennial updates.

Sacks J (2000) *Radical Then Radical Now: the legacy of the world's oldest religion.* HarperCollins, London.

Solomon N (1996) *Judaism – a very short introduction.* Oxford University Press, Oxford.

Spitzer J (2002) *A Guide to the Orthodox Jewish Way of Life for Healthcare Professionals* (3e). J Spitzer, London.

Telushkin J (1991) *Jewish Literacy: the most important things to know about the Jewish religion, its people and its history*. William Morrow & Co, New York.

Wein B (2002) *Living Jewish: values, practices and traditions*. Artscroll, New York.

Wouk H (1992) *This is My God – the Jewish way of life*. Souvenir Press, London.

Wouk H (2000) *The Will to Live On: this is our heritage*. HarperCollins, New York.

CHAPTER 2

Jewish history in a nutshell

A basic concise outline

Remember the days of old, consider the years of each passing generation, ask your father and he will tell you, your elders and they will inform you.

Deuteronomy 32: 7

In His hand is the soul of all every living thing and the spirit of all mankind.

Job 12: 10

Everything has its time and there is a time for everything under the sun.

Ecclesiastes 3: 1

Introduction

Jews have a very strong sense of history; they are an ancient people with a powerful feeling for its origins and its traditions. It is important to realise that traditional orthodox Jews believe in the divine origins of the *Torah* (the Old Testament) and believe that the details contained in it are historically accurate and are taken to be the detailed historical records of the origins of the Jews and indeed of many other peoples and nations.

Early beginnings: the Patriarchs, Moses, the *Torah*

Judaism traces its origins back to Abraham (*Avrohom*) as do Islam and Christianity – together known as the three Abrahamic religions. God promised Abraham (in 1761 BCE) that 'I will make you into a great nation,

I will bless you and make your name great' (Genesis 12:2). Abraham's two sons, Isaac (*Yitzchok*) and Ishmael (*Yishmael*), went their separate ways, and Islam traces its origins to Ishmael. One of Isaac's sons was Jacob (*Yakov*) and the three, Abraham, Isaac and Jacob, are known as the three Patriarchs (*Ovos*). Jacob had 12 sons from whom descended the Twelve Tribes of Israel. One of the youngest sons was Joseph (*Yossef*) who was sold into slavery in Egypt. In time Joseph became viceroy of Egypt and the rest of Jacob's family, totalling 70 individuals, joined him in Egypt in 1523 BCE.

Initially the Egyptians welcomed the Israelites, as the descendants of Jacob now became known (based on God giving Jacob the alternative name of *Yisroel*/Israel), and they grew rapidly in number. However when a new power assumed rulership of Egypt the Israelites were enslaved and were treated with great cruelty by the new regime, an oppression which continued for 210 years. God, in fulfilment of his promise to Abraham, took the Israelites out of Egypt under the leadership of his prophet Moses (*Moishe*, known universally in Jewish literature as *Moishe Rabenu*, Moses Our Teacher). The eventual exodus from Egypt in 1313 BCE occurred in a most dramatic and miraculous manner, and was followed a week later by the no less miraculous crossing of the Red Sea with the concomitant destruction of the mighty Egyptian army. This is described in detail in Exodus, the second of the Five Books of Moses (Pentateuch). Seven weeks after the dramatic exodus from Egypt the *Torah* was given to the Jews at Mount Sinai in the most spectacular and unique display of Divine Revelation. The acceptance of the *Torah* by the Israelites marks the real beginning of practical Judaism.

The Land of Israel, the Temples, the Babylonian exile

Forty years after leaving Egypt in 1313 BCE, the Jews, under the leadership of Joshua, entered the Land of Israel (*Eretz Yisroel*) or the Promised Land (the land that God had promised Abraham that he would give to his Jewish descendants). They conquered the land and having secured it, Joshua and his successors shared it out amongst the twelve tribes. The Jews were initially led by a series of Judges and then Prophets until a monarchy was established with the appointment of King Saul (*Sho'ul Hamelech*). Later on King Solomon (*Shlomoh*), a son of King David (*Dovid*), built the great Temple in Jerusalem. The building of the Temple marks the start of the era often described as the golden age of Jewish history. The Temple stood for 410 years until destroyed by the Babylonians in 423 BCE, who also took many Jews back with them into exile in Babylon. The Babylonian exile lasted 70 years and ended with the building of the second Temple on the same site as the previous one in Jerusalem. The second Temple stood for 420 years until its destruction by the Romans in 70 CE. The leadership of the Jewish people during the time of the second Temple continued under the Men of the Great Assembly (c. 540–300 BCE), and then for the next 300 years by the *Zugos* (the Pairs), the two sages who were joint leaders of the *Sanhedrin*, the Supreme Court, one with the title *Av Beis Din* (Head of the Rabbinic Court) and the other *Nosi* (Prince). They built the framework for the future of Judaism by settling the final text of the Books of the Prophets (*Nevi'im*) and Holy Writings (*Kesuvim*) and established the basics of Rabbinic Law. The period of the second Temple was less lustrous than the previous golden age of the first Temple. The leaders around the time of and immediately following the destruction of the second Temple were known as *Tanno'im* (the Teachers) (c. 311 BCE–240 CE). They were the great sages who were the first to commit the Oral Law into writing by publishing the *Mishne*, the basic outline of the Written Law, completed around 188 CE.

The final exile, dispersal (Diaspora), the *Talmud*

Following the destruction of the second Temple in 70 CE the present era of Jewish history began. To this day, the current period is known as The Roman (Edomite) Exile (*Golus Edom*). The Romans dispersed many of the Jews who survived the bloody wars in Israel, mainly throughout the Mediterranean basin, but also in smaller numbers to the corners of the Roman Empire (the Diaspora). Some of the population remained in the towns and villages of Judea and Samaria (Palestine being the name given to the region by the Romans), notably in Jerusalem, Hebron and Safed. Until the establishment of an independent Jewish state, the State of Israel, almost two millennia after the destruction of the Temple, the Jewish population remaining in the Land of Israel comprised small impoverished communities largely supported by the charitable foundations of their brethren in the Diaspora.

For several hundred years there were large Jewish communities in Babylonia (*Bovel*) with great Jewish Academies (*yeshivas*) and centres of learning. It was here that the Oral Law was committed to writing lest it be entirely forgotten. The great Babylonian *Talmud*, based on the *Mishne*, resulted from this effort and was completed in the three centuries following the completion of the *Mishne*. The *Talmud* is a vast compendium forming the basis of all subsequent Jewish law and knowledge. Thus the basis of all post-biblical Jewish literature that comprises the foundation of the Oral Law was committed to writing in the five centuries following the destruction of the second Temple. The sages who compiled the *Talmud* were known as *Amoraim* (the Interpreters) (c. 240–500 CE). Following the completion of the *Talmud* the great academies flourished in Babylonia and neighbouring countries for many more centuries initially under the leadership of schools of rabbis known as *Savoraim* (the Ponderers) (c. 500–690 CE), named thus because they pondered over the final version of the text of the *Talmud*. The period following that of the *Savoraim* became known as the period of the *Geonim* (the 'Brilliant' or 'Majestic' scholars) (c. 690–1040 CE), until petering out some thousand years ago with the crumbling of the final vestiges of the eastern Roman Empire and the rise of Muslim culture.

The Middle Ages: persecution, expulsion and migration

About twelve hundred years ago Jews began to migrate from the Mediterranean lands, north-eastward throughout Europe, fleeing constant persecution. The Jews who remained in the Mediterranean and eastern lands became known as Sephardi (literally 'Spanish') Jews and those who migrated through Europe became known as Ashkenazi (literally 'Germanic') Jews. Over a period of hundreds of years Ashkenazi Jews spread further east through Europe, building communities wherever they settled and developing their own language, Yiddish, based on early medieval German but incorporating much Hebrew and elements of other local languages. This era is known as the age of the *Rishonim* (the 'first' or 'early' leaders) (c. 1040–1440 CE), who were the spiritual leaders of that age and who left a rich literature of commentaries on the Bible and Jewish law. Although this was a period when Jewish scholarship flourished greatly, no community was safe from persecution for long. Jews had to flee from persecution in almost every generation. The Crusaders wreaked havoc amongst the Jewish communities of Europe, decimating many and causing others to flee time and again. Pogroms and expulsions were recurrent themes of European Jewish history for most of the medieval period. Paradoxically, however, expulsions were occasionally balanced by invitations to Jews from governments anxious to utilise their ability and commercial skills, this accounting to a large extent for the enormous growth of Polish Jewry in the sixteenth century. Tragically, vast numbers of Polish and Ukrainian Jews were murdered in the Cossack massacres of 1648–49. The era of the *Rishonim* was said to end around the middle of the fifteenth century and subsequent Jewish leaders (from about 1440) were then called the *Acharonim* (the 'later' leaders), a line which continues to the present day.

Fifteenth to eighteenth centuries: false messiahs, *Chassidim* and *Misnagdim*

In the fifteenth, sixteenth and seventeenth centuries the spirit of Eastern European Ashkenazi Jewry was generally at a low ebb, their lives made wretched by grinding poverty and pogroms at the hands of lawless mobs encouraged by anti-Semitic governments. Perhaps most destructive of all were the false aspirations given by several 'false messiahs', the best known of whom was Shabtsai Tzvi (1626–76) who initially brought great hope that the miserable exile was at an end, only for these aspirations to be dashed when he was denounced as a fraud.

At the dawn of the eighteenth century a new era of hope was born in many of the Jewish lands and communities of Eastern Europe. Rabbi Yisroel Ba'al Shem Tov ('the Master of the Good Name') established the Chassidic (literally 'the Pious Ones') movement based on the philosophy of love of God and one's fellow man. He gave hope to the ordinary Jew, elevating him through spiritual growth and prayer. The movement revitalised much of Eastern European Jewry and continues as a powerful movement to this day. Initially there was bitter opposition from other groups of Jews, notably led by Rabbi Eliyohu of Vilna ('the Gaon (genius) of Vilna') whose followers were known as the *Misnagdim* ('the Opposers') in view of their vehement rejection of Chassidic ideas. In time, the two groups came to live side by side accepting each other's differences as alternative aspects of serving God each in their different ways: 'Elu velu diverei Elokim chayim' ('these and those are the words of the Living God').

Eighteenth and nineteenth centuries: enlightenment and reform

In Western Europe the pattern was somewhat different. The standard of living amongst Jews was higher, especially in Germany where Jewish communities, mainly centred in the large towns, were well organised. In 1789

the French Revolution brought major changes to Western European
society. The old structure of society broke down, and this, together with
the industrial revolution, brought with it the emancipation movement
which swept through Western Europe. The barriers between Jew and Gentile began to crumble and Jews became involved and more accepted into
wider society. These changes also reached Eastern Europe but took much
longer to do so and in the event made relatively little impact. Emancipation
resulted in major changes in Jewish life, and in Germany many assimilated
Jews began to adapt Judaism to their more enlightened way of life and in
time the Reform movement became established. Their schools introduced
secular subjects and the arts and sciences were taught. Synagogue services
were altered and modelled on the Lutheran Church. Many fundamentals of
Judaism were challenged and many practices abandoned. This caused a
bitter rift between the traditional orthodox groups who saw reform as
a threat to fundamental Jewish beliefs, particularly the central belief
of Judaism that the *Torah* was divinely given by God and could not be
adapted at man's whim. Indeed the rift continues to this day, and the orthodox tend not to recognise marriages, divorces or conversions performed by
non-orthodox rabbis.

The *Sephardim*: from the Golden Age to expulsion and dispersal

In the centuries during which the *Ashkenazim* were spreading and becoming established in Europe, large and important communities had become
established in the Sephardi lands. Spain was a major centre of the Sephardi
world, where Jews became established in the world of finance, the arts and
in the royal courts. To Jews this period became known as the Golden Age of
Iberian Jewry. There were also flourishing Sephardi communities right
round the Mediterranean basin and as far away as India and other parts
of Asia. However, this was not to last, for from the middle of the fourteenth
century there began a regime of stark terror for Iberian Jewry unrivalled in
its evil until the advent of Nazi Germany. The Catholic Church established
the Inquisition, a murderous machine, ostensibly intended to cleanse
the church of any manifestation of 'heresy', but dedicated in fact to state-
sponsored anti-Semitism. This culminated in 1492, with the total expulsion, at short notice, of the vast Jewish community of Spain, who were
compelled to flee to various parts of the Sephardi world as well as to the
Middle East. Penniless and destitute, they took their most important posses-
sions – their profound scholarship and rich culture – with them to their

places of refuge, re-establishing great centres of Jewish learning. A group settled in Holland where they established their own successful community, from which, in 1656, came the merchants who responded to Oliver Cromwell's invitation to re-establish a Jewish community in England, the Jews having previously been expelled by Edward I in 1290. Smaller numbers fled to Eastern Europe where they were absorbed into the local Ashkenazi communities.

The twentieth century

The end of the nineteenth and first half of the twentieth century were marked by a massive emigration of Jews from mainly Eastern Europe, driven by persecution and extreme poverty. Over two million Jews left for North and South America, South Africa, Great Britain and a small number to *Eretz Yisroel* (what is now Israel, then part of the Turkish Ottoman Empire). Wherever they settled they established new communities. With the outbreak of the First World War (1914–18), many European Jewish communities were again torn apart and most did not really recover before the great destruction during the Second World War (1939–45).

The Holocaust

Modern Jewry's darkest era started with the rise, in Germany, of Adolf Hitler in 1933. He was a dictator who had two main aims: one was to establish a mighty empire of world supremacy and the other was the total destruction of world Jewry. He set about the latter immediately upon his appointment and persecuted German Jewry in a methodical, ruthless way, causing many tens of thousands to flee. Following a major pogrom throughout Germany on the infamous Kristallnacht (the Night of Broken Glass) on 9 November 1938, German Jewry faced the reality that there was no future for Jews under Hitler. For many it was too late, and following the start of the Second World War with Hitler's invasion of Poland in September 1939, much of European Jewry was doomed. By the end of the war in 1945 some six million Jews had been murdered, bringing to an end more than a thousand years of Jewish life in Central and Eastern Europe.

Sephardi Jews were affected to a much lesser extent by the events in Europe and they continued to live in the (mainly Arab) lands of North Africa and the Middle and Far East. With the establishment of the State of Israel in 1948 an increase in anti-Jewish feeling in many Arab countries started an exodus of Jews from many of the well-established Sephardi communities, some of which could trace their origins back through more than two millennia.

Israel

The establishment of the State of Israel in 1948 ostensibly gave Jews their first official secure homeland for almost two thousand years. However, the years since its inception have been anything but peaceful with frequent wars and hostile unrest between Israel and its Arab neighbours. Israel today is in many ways much like other modern democracies, with its infrastructure of government, industry, agriculture and healthcare facilities. But, above all, for Jews it holds a special significance, for it is, uniquely in the modern world, the only independent autonomous democratic Jewish state.

Judaism, Zionism and Israel

Judaism dates back some four thousand years with its roots firmly planted in the biblical Land of Canaan or *Eretz Yisroel* (the Land of Israel). Zionism is a modern political movement founded in the late nineteenth century which regards the modern State of Israel as the Jewish homeland.

It is in relation to attitudes to Zionism that much of the division and wide spread of the spectrum of Jewish views and opinions can be seen.

Zionism sees the Jews as a nation with a country and state of its own, to which all Jews have a right to belong, by virtue of their having been born Jews. This encompasses all Jews irrespective of levels of religious practice. It sees the practice of halachic Judaism as being separate from the secular aspects of statehood and nationhood. The traditional orthodox camp are, by contrast, unable to separate religious practice from being Jewish. To them, Judaism and the practice of *Halochoh* are one and the same. They therefore regard Zionism as a secular substitute for religious practice. Many of the very strictly orthodox regard Zionism as anathema to religious practice, and indeed there are many Zionists who feel that being loyal to the Zionist cause and ideals is a perfectly adequate way of expressing their Judaism without having to observe practical Jewish law by keeping all the *mitzvos* (commandments) as well.

There are many of the strictly orthodox who do not regard the present State of Israel as being their rightful homeland, as it is not *Eretz Yisroel* (the Land of Israel), the utopian country of the future which will be based entirely on *Torah* law. They believe that this will come about when the Messiah (*Moshiach*) comes and gathers all of Jewry back to the Promised Land and rebuilds the third Temple in Jerusalem. Devout Jews pray several times each day for the coming of the Messiah, the rebuilding of Jerusalem and the Temple as of old and the restoration of the *Torah*-based state. Many feel that the present State of Israel has no relevance to that utopian state for which they pray. There are others who feel that although the eventual goal is the coming of the Messiah and the rebuilding of *Eretz Yisroel*, the establishment of the State of Israel is one of the first steps heralding the impending arrival of the Messiah.

Of course there is a wide spectrum of opinions between these views and modern Jewish society represents a spread of views between these polarised extremes. There are also many religious Zionists aspiring to the ideals of both Zionism and *Torah* observance at one and the same time.

The final chapter: *Moshiach* (the Messiah)

Jewish tradition believes that the final chapter in the present phase of Jewish history will be written with the coming of *Moshiach*. The belief in the coming of *Moshiach* is enshrined in the writings of the prophets of the Bible, and is one of the fundamentals of Jewish belief (*see* the Thirteen Principles of Faith, pp 11–12). Jews believe that this exile, the final exile, will end with the arrival of *Moshiach* and the building of a third Temple in Jerusalem on the site of the previous two. This, it is believed, will herald an era of universal peace and spiritual life not only for Jews but for all of mankind.

Summary

- Some 3500 years ago Abraham was the first to recognise and publicise the One God; his grandson Jacob's grand children were presented with the *Torah* after their liberation from enslavement in Egypt.
- There followed a period of about 1000 years (with a 70 year gap) when the Jews lived in the land of Israel with political autonomy and a monarch. For the most part, life was based on the *Torah* and centred around the Temple in Jerusalem.

- Following the destruction of the Temple the Jews were exiled from their land and dispersed throughout the world. There followed a 2000-year repeated cycle of settlement, persecution, expulsion and migration culminating in the Holocaust in the twentieth century.
- With the dispersal came diversification of Jewish groups, initially the *Sephardim* and *Ashkenazim*, the latter spawning the Chassidic movement in the seventeenth century and with the start of the enlightenment movement the founding of the Progressive movement in the nineteenth century.
- The State of Israel was established in the second half of the twentieth century but the majority of Jews still live in the Diaspora.
- Jews believe that at some time during the continuum of Jewish history the *Moshiach* (the Messiah) will arrive and there will then follow a new age with an in-gathering of the Diaspora and a new Temple in Jerusalem.

Further reading

Blech B (1997) *The Complete Idiot's Guide to Jewish History and Culture*. Alpha Books, Indianapolis.

Cohn-Sherbok L and Cohn-Sherbok D (1994) *A Short History of Judaism*. Oneworld, Oxford.

Gilbert M (1987) *The Holocaust: the Jewish tragedy*. HarperCollins, London.

Gilbert M (1993) *Atlas of Jewish History* (5e). Routledge, London.

Gilbert M (2002) *Letters to Aunt Fori: the 5000-year history of the Jewish people and their faith*. Weidenfeld & Nicolson, London.

Roth C (1942) *A History of the Jews in England*. Oxford University Press, Oxford.

Wein B (1990) *Triumph of Survival – the history of the Jews in the modern era 1640– 1990*. Shar Press, New York.

Wein B (1993) *Herald of Destiny – the story of the Jews 750–1650*. Shar Press, New York.

Wein B (1995) *Echoes of Glory – the story of the Jews in the classical era 350BCE– 750CE*. Shar Press, New York.

Wein B (2001) *Faith and Fate – the story of the Jews in the twentieth century*. Shar Press, New York.

CHAPTER 3

World and British Jewry

Growing in numbers around the globe, but falling numbers in the UK

God blessed them (Adam and Eve) and God said to them: Be fertile and become many; fill the earth.

Genesis 1: 28

He (God) took him (Abraham) outside and said 'look at the sky and count the stars. See if you can count them.' (God) then said to him, 'This is how (numerous) your descendants will be'.

Genesis 15: 5

Introduction

It is estimated that there are just under 14 million Jews in the world, constituting about 0.2% of the world population. Of these about 300 000 live in the UK, with approximately two-thirds of those living in the Greater London area.

World Jewry

Since the destruction of the second Temple 2000 years ago Jewish history has been a story of constant movement. Migration, expulsion and dispersal, for social or economic reasons but more often for reason of religious persecution, have been constant features of Jewish life. Some communities stayed only briefly in their locations whereas others could trace their roots

---

back through many centuries and even millennia. More recent Jewish history has been no different and the last century has been marked by the disruption of communities that had been established for many generations, and their dispersal and redistribution right round the world.

As detailed in Chapter 1 (*see* p 13) modern Jewry can be divided into two main groups, based on their geographical roots, the Ashkenazim (originating mostly from Europe) and the Sephardim (originating from the Mediterranean basin and the Middle and Far East); both groups having many subgroups. Since the major upheavals of the Second World War differences between the various groups, especially amongst the Ashkenazim, have started to become less distinct.

Today Jews are to be found all around the world, but there is considerable variation in the extent to which they identify themselves as Jews, and as to whether they affiliate to any formal Jewish groups, organisations or synagogues. The largest concentration is in North America, some 6 million, followed by Asia (including the former Soviet Block) with 4.25 million, and Europe which has about 2.5 million.

A good place to live

A city which does not have the following ten, is a place where a wise man should not dwell: These are: a physician, a surgeon (to perform circumcisions), a bath house, a privy, a source of running water such as a river or spring, a synagogue, a teacher for the young, a scribe, a collector for charity, a court of law for the administration of justice.

Maimonides, *Mishne Torah*, Book of Knowledge, Discernment 4: 23

A *Torah* scholar should not live in a city that has no physician.

Talmud Sanhedrin 17b

Israel's Jews

Some 36% of the world's Jews live in Israel where they make up just over 80% of the population of about 6.5 million (2002). There has been a continuous established Jewish presence in the country since Joshua's conquest in 1273 BCE; even following the destruction of the Temple and the dispersal of the majority throughout the Diaspora, Jews maintained a continuous presence in the Land of Israel. Although during much of that time they were few in number, the Jewish population had started to grow significantly, well before the Holocaust and long before the establishment of the State of Israel in 1948. Following the creation of the Jewish state there was a large immigration of Jews from all over the world, who took advantage of Israel's Law of Return which guaranteed citizenship to all Jewish immigrants. Hence, Israeli society is very cosmopolitan and heterogeneous, with Jews of all backgrounds making up its population. They are drawn from all corners of the globe, with wide variation in ethnicity, religious adherence and practice and with a host of different mother tongues and social customs. There were Holocaust survivors from Europe, oriental Jews from eastern lands, Yemenite Jews, North African Jews and a myriad of others. These disparate groups have fused into a modern technologically advanced democratic state which is rarely out of the spotlight of world news. Curiously, religious practice as such, although always an emotive subject, is not a major feature of social and political life. The strictly religious orthodox represent a relatively small minority and those adhering to the strictly orthodox way of life tend to keep themselves isolated in their own communities and residential centres. Paradoxically however, because the system of proportional representation gives rise to the fact that most Israeli governments are coalitions, the various orthodox groups have tended to have a political influence disproportionate to their actual numbers.

British Jewry

History and background

There is some evidence that Jews first settled in the British Isles during the Roman occupation, possibly having been brought over as slaves following the destruction of the Temple by the Romans in 68 CE. Significant recorded Jewish settlement of Britain began with the Norman conquest in 1066 when merchants and scholars accompanied William the Conqueror. Jews settled in many cities round Britain, establishing small communities where they continued to live until they were expelled in 1290 during the reign of Edward I. Following their re-admission to England by Oliver Cromwell in 1656, the first settlers were mainly Sephardi Dutch merchants. For the next two centuries Sephardim were the major force in British Jewry and remained so until the second half of the nineteenth century when the balance changed and the Ashkenazim became the majority, following the rapid growth of the Jewish community, swelled by immigration. The main influx of Jews into London occurred during the latter part of the nineteenth century when large numbers of Ashkenazim arrived from Eastern Europe, having fled the pogroms, anti-Semitism and poverty. These immigrants were mainly impoverished craftsmen who settled close to their point of arrival, near the docks in London's East End. Although London always had the largest Jewish community, many smaller communities were being established throughout the British Isles, mainly in sea ports and in industrial towns.

At the turn of the twentieth century, London's Jewish population was centred around the East End, which was heavily populated with a poor but industrious community. As their material situation improved they gradually moved out of the East End to the then fashionable Hackney, Stamford Hill and Clapton areas. The next wave of movement was further north and east to London's new suburbs. During the 1930s and after the Second World War there was a further influx of European Jews, many of whom settled in the Hackney area. In the post-war years these groups have been added to by the arrival of some Sephardi groups, mainly from India, North Africa, Iran and Yemen. Today almost all groups of orthodox and Reform are represented to some extent in the wide spectrum of British Jewry. There has been a considerable rate of assimilation in Britain with large numbers being lost through intermarriage or merely as a result of individuals no longer wishing to identify themselves as being Jewish. However, in the last 25 years or so the main growth in British Jewry has been in the strictly orthodox and especially the Chassidic communities such as in the Stamford Hill area of north London where the birth rate is high and the assimilation rate negligible. Although the majority were of Central and Eastern European descent, most are now second or even third generation British by birth.

Away from London, Jewish communities are to be found in many provincial towns and cities in the UK, these consisting of various shades of orthodoxy or Reform, the strictly orthodox communities being now confined to just a few centres.

Jewish communities in Britain today

Whereas a century ago there were small Jewish communities in many provincial towns in all parts of Britain, besides the larger ones in the main urban centres, today most Jewish communities are based in the large urban areas, mainly the Greater London and Greater Manchester areas. There are smaller communities in other major cities including Leeds, Birmingham,

Newcastle, Liverpool and Glasgow, but in general the smaller provincial communities have shrunk rapidly in the last few decades. The largest communities today, both orthodox and Reform, are in the Redbridge/Ilford area on the London/Essex boundary, and the area of north-west London spreading out from Golders Green and Hendon to encompass Edgware, Stanmore and parts of Hertfordshire. Both north and south Manchester also have large communities. These areas have not only the main concentration of synagogues but also the other essentials of Jewish communal life including schools and kosher food outlets.

The main enclaves of the strictly orthodox in London are to be found in the Stamford Hill area of north Hackney and in the Golders Green and Hendon areas of Barnet, and in Manchester in the Broughton Park and Prestwich areas. There is also a small but important orthodox community in Gateshead in the north-east of England. The majority of orthodox Jews in the UK are Ashkenazim, but there is a significant and growing orthodox Sephardi element in most areas with orthodox communities. There are of course many Jews living away from the main centres of communal life, some associated with small local groups but many not associated or affiliated at all with any form of organised religion. Non-affiliated Jews are to be found almost anywhere. For most Jews affiliation to a Jewish movement or synagogue is less a matter of ideology and theology than a sense of community and belonging. For many, affiliation to a particular synagogue is related to belonging to that synagogue's burial society (*see* p 151), something which has always been seen as being important, particularly by British Jews. For those that do affiliate to specific communities or synagogues there is a wide range from the Progressive through to the orthodox, with various subdivisions.

Orthodox centres in the UK

Stamford Hill

The orthodox Jewish population of north-east London consists of several thousand families who live in the Stamford Hill area of Hackney and the South Tottenham area of Haringey, all within a mile of the main Stamford Hill road junction. The majority are Chassidim, and the Chassidic community is itself made up of a number of different groups of various sizes, each with their own synagogues, schools and colleges. The largest and best known groups are Satmar and Lubavitch (named after the East European towns where these groups originated), both of which are parts of international organisations with headquarters in New York. Other well known groups include Gur and Belz, also international organisations with headquarters in Israel. There are also many non-Chassidic orthodox Jews living in the same area consisting of both Ashkenazim and Sephardim. In Stamford Hill the non-Chassidic orthodox Ashkenazi groups consist of Misnagdim, who make up a shrinking proportion of the local orthodox population, and a growing number of Sephardi groups originating mainly from India, North Africa, Iran and Yemen.

North-west London

The orthodox Jewish community of north-west London which is based around the Golders Green and Hendon areas was founded when some families moved away from the Stamford Hill area in the 1930s, and expanded with the arrival of refugees from Europe before and after the Second World War. This is a large and growing orthodox community, of which Chassidim form a smaller proportion than they do in Stamford Hill, with Misnagdim making up the majority. In general, the Chassidic groups of north-west London are less insular and more outgoing than their Stamford Hill counterparts. There is also a significant and growing orthodox Sephardi community in north-west London. London's orthodox Sephardi community has now grown to the size where it has become viable for them to maintain their own strictly orthodox schools and *yeshivos* (talmudical college for young men).

Manchester and Gateshead

The orthodox Jewish and Chassidic communities in Manchester are centred around the Broughton Park and Prestwich areas and are a vibrant and growing centre of traditional authentic Judaism. There are now a number of well-established Chassidic groups, each with their own synagogues. There are also a growing number of schools, *yeshivos* (colleges) for young men and seminaries (providing higher education) for girls. In recent years there has been a tendency for orthodox young couples from London to settle in Manchester, where housing in the orthodox areas is less expensive and employment prospects are better. The Gateshead community is confined to a small area based around the local *yeshiva* and other educational institutions, for which this relatively small but intensely devout community is renowned throughout the orthodox Jewish world. In this entirely orthodox community, Chassidim and Sepharadim are a small minority.

Orthodoxy

British orthodoxy in the wider community is organised around various synagogal and community organisations, the largest of which is the United Synagogue, its religious head being the Chief Rabbi. Although the United Synagogue is led by fully orthodox and committed leaders and rabbis, not all members are totally committed to full strict traditional observance and many affiliated members are not particularly observant. Nevertheless this group is the largest and most representative group of orthodoxy in Britain today.

The Federation of Synagogues is broadly similar to the United Synagogue, with its own rabbinical court, *Kashrus* and other communal organisations. They have their own rabbinical leadership and do not come under the jurisdiction of the Chief Rabbi.

The largest very strictly orthodox movement in Britain is the Union of Orthodox Hebrew Congregations (often colloquially referred to as 'The Adass') who represent most of the strictly orthodox groups. It is a London-based organisation with closely associated synagogues in Manchester and Gateshead. They again have their own rabbinical council and court and do not recognise the jurisdiction of the Chief Rabbi. Even among this movement there is considerable variation in religious practice, customs, style of clothing and interaction with the wider community. There are some who dress in modern western attire and may only be distinguishable by their head covering, whereas at the other extreme are those Chassidic groups who dress in their traditional garb and speak Yiddish as their first language.

The best known and most conspicuous subgroup of orthodox Jews are the Chassidim. Following the destruction of their traditional way of life in the Holocaust, the remnants of the Chassidic movement settled in several centres around the world, notably in New York, Israel, Belgium and London, where they slowly began to recreate their traditional way of life, regrouping themselves around their various *rebbes* (spiritual leaders). Chassidic communities are deliberately very insular, keeping themselves to themselves and trying to be self sufficient (*see* p 48).

Reform

A significant minority of British Jews belong to non-orthodox synagogues. There are three main groups, the Reform, Liberal and Masorti, all of whom do not take literally the statement that God gave the entire *Torah* to the Jewish people at one moment on Mount Sinai, a belief central to all orthodox groups. Rather, they subscribe to the theory of progressive revelation, which they believe authorises rabbinic leaders to adapt Judaism to the norms and mores of the time. They believe that traditional practices and beliefs may be altered or jettisoned if considered to be anachronistic in a modern world. Orthodox Jews do not recognise these groups as upholding traditional Judaism, and do not recognise as valid their marriages, divorces, circumcisions or conversions.

The existing Reform movement in this country, which dates back to the nineteenth century, was given fresh impetus with the arrival in the 1930s of German refugees who re-established their communities in Britain, being led by well-known personalities from German Reform synagogues or temples. The largest non-orthodox group in Britain today is the Reform Synagogues of Great Britain which was founded in 1942 and whose slogan is 'Rooted in the past, responding to change'. They have a growing number of synagogues in London and in the provinces. Services are shorter than in orthodox synagogues and some parts of the services are read in English. References in the liturgy to the coming of the Messiah and the return to Zion (the Holy Land) have been reinterpreted. In contrast to orthodox practice, men and women sit together in the synagogue and women take an active part in the services. Women can be rabbis, something unheard of in orthodox practice. In the observance of the *Shabbos* (Sabbath) and the festivals many of the restrictions such as on travel, carrying and using electricity have been dropped and more emphasis is placed on the positive aspects of the festivals so that, for example, *matzos* are eaten on *Pesach*, but unlike the orthodox not exclusively so (*see* p 107). *Kashrus* (the kosher laws) is observed to a varying extent, often only on synagogue premises; as for the individual, observance is optional.

The Liberal movement was founded in Britain in 1902 and now also has synagogues throughout the country. It was founded in response to the feeling that the Reform movement had not gone far enough away from its traditional roots and therefore Liberal practices are even further from the orthodox tradition than those of the Reform. The Liberal view is that individuals can decide to observe Judaism as they choose. Synagogue services are similar to those of the Reform. Men and women sit together. Confirmation ceremonies are held for boys and girls at the age of 16, where they affirm their acceptance of their moral responsibilities. *Shabbos* and the festivals are observed with synagogue services but not with the strict observances and restrictions of the orthodox. The Liberal synagogues solemnise marriages but they accept civil divorce on its own. They do not believe in resurrection in the literal sense, one of the Thirteen Principles of Faith (*see* pp 11–12), and all references to it have been modified in the Liberal liturgy.

The Masorti movement is relatively new, having been founded in response to the view that the Reform had gone too far away from its traditional Jewish roots. The Assembly of Masorti Synagogues was founded in 1991, and aims to 'maintain the laws and practices of the past as far as possible', that is Judaism based on the orthodox style but without what they see as traditional doctrines that can no longer be accepted. Masorti belief is that God did not give the *Torah* at Mount Sinai but that Judaism has grown out of Jewish people's religious experiences, and that the *Torah* is made up of documents written at different times and places by a variety of authors. Jewish law (*Halochoh*) is of divine origin but has always evolved according to the needs of the times. Synagogue services follow the pattern of orthodox services, with a variety of practices in the different synagogues of the movement, such as mixed seating and women's participation in services. The observation of *Kashrus* is selective but is closer to the traditional orthodox practices than other Progressive groups. Masorti marriages and divorces, circumcisions and conversions are not recognised by orthodox rabbinical authorities.

Variation in religious practice amongst British Jews

There are Jews living in all parts of Britain, many of whom are non-practising, not affiliated to any synagogue or religious group and do not necessarily appear to be obviously Jewish. The orthodox tend to live in organised communities in the main metropolitan areas, with the so called ultra-orthodox living in tight-knit communities in a few localised areas. It is only healthcare professionals working near these areas who are likely to encounter large numbers of obviously Jewish patients, although it is likely that some will be seen in tertiary referral centres away from the large orthodox communities. Practices and observances vary considerably between different groups of Jews and even within those groups. It is important for healthcare professionals to recognise this variation before extrapolating from what they have seen in one patient and applying it to others. (*See* 'Variation in religious practice', p 17 for an outline of variations in practices amongst different groups of Jews and amongst Jews of various levels of observance, and Chapter 4 for details of orthodox practices). As always, when dealing with individual Jewish patients, it is best not to assume but to ask.

Socio-economic status of British Jewry

The socio-economic status of the Jewish community in Britain is broadly similar to the rest of the population. There is a myth, which continues to be perpetuated, that all Jews are wealthy, but this is far from the truth. There are indeed a number of prominent wealthy Jews but proportionately they are probably no more numerous relative to the population as a whole. The entire spectrum of financial status is to be seen in the Jewish community and in fact a large percentage remain at the lower end of the financial ladder. Jews are indeed well represented in the arts and sciences, possibly disproportionately so, and it is especially in these fields that so many have become famous. This is probably a result of the very high value that Jews generally have placed on education and attaining high academic results. Jewish schools, whatever their religious affiliation, seem to attain disproportionately good results time and again.

Socio-economically, the strictly orthodox Jewish population is very mixed and does not necessarily reflect the same characteristics as the non-Jewish population among whom they reside. All socio-economic groups are represented, and families from across the entire economic spectrum live side by side quite happily. Men may be engaged in many and varied fields and all occupations are represented within the community, from the professions through to unskilled manual work. Orthodox Jews are somewhat disadvantaged when seeking employment as for strict religious reasons they may not work on *Shabbos* (Sabbath, *see* p 99). This means that not only may they not work on Saturdays, but in the winter months they need to leave work early on Friday afternoons so as to be home before sunset. In previous decades there was a considerable amount of manufacturing industry based around north-east London and in the Manchester region, and many orthodox Jewish factory owners provided employment for other members of the community. This sector of industry has shrunk, as have the other traditional Jewish trades such as jewellery, clothing manufacture and wholesale merchandising. There are opportunities for part-time employment especially for women, for as the community has grown, so too has the number of schools and shops, where there is a constant demand for part-time workers. A growing number of strictly orthodox married men study in a *kollel* (an institute of advanced talmudic and rabbinical studies) for which they might receive a stipend.

Unemployment has taken its toll and in many families the main breadwinner may not be able to find employment, possibly due to lack of trained skills. Some unemployed orthodox men may spend much of the day in the synagogue engaged in private study or joining in the study groups at a *kollel* or attending lectures (*shiurim*). Pastimes and recreational activities rarely find a place in the daily routine.

There is a reluctance on the part of some orthodox Jews to attend non-Jewish training colleges or universities (in part at least on account of possible pressures to become involved in mixed student social activities and the menace of the current drug culture), but an increasing number of single-sex courses are available within the community, offering training in computer skills and business management amongst other subjects.

The cost of living for orthodox Jews is higher than for other groups, for a number of reasons. Orthodox Jewish families tend to be larger than average. Also kosher food prices are generally significantly higher than non-kosher equivalents (due to the additional costs of manufacture and supervision). Furthermore, almost all education from pre-school to adult is privately funded. Many families also contribute membership fees to the costs of running their synagogue, which may include a rabbi's salary and contributions to a burial society (*see* p 151). In addition, because of the need to live within walking distance of a synagogue (due to the restriction on travel on *Shabbos*), the cost of housing, whether rented or purchased, attracts a premium, so adding to the cost of living.

Poverty levels in the ultra-orthodox community are high, so that in the Stamford Hill area of north London, for example, over half of all families are in receipt of a means-tested benefit. There is reasonably good support within the community and less fortunate families may often be helped by others in better circumstances (*see* 'Care and support within the community', p 188). More affluent families may live surprisingly modestly and low income families may make the most of their resources, so that outwardly it may be quite hard to judge a family's economic status simply by looking at their appearance or standard of housing. The Jewish community enjoys a very rich and fulfilling communal life and this may serve to mask poverty as participation does not depend on financial status. Synagogal and communal activities are a great social leveller, particularly in the more orthodox and ultra-orthodox parts of the Jewish community.

Housing requirements relate to the need to be within walking distance of synagogues (as travel other than on foot is forbidden on *Shabbos*), as well as for access to the orthodox Jewish schools and food shops and the need for residential units for large families. There is a mixture of owner occupied and rented accommodation. Some areas with large orthodox Jewish communities now have their own housing associations. In the Stamford Hill area, with its high concentration of strictly orthodox Jews, more than half of all families live in privately rented accommodation and over a third of families live in seriously overcrowded homes.

Board of Deputies

The Board of Deputies, founded in 1760, is an umbrella organisation of some 330 elected deputies drawn from most British synagogues, synagogal bodies and communal organisations, other than from the strictly orthodox Union of Orthodox Hebrew Congregations. It describes itself as 'the elected, national representative body of the British Jewish community'. The Board protects, supports and defends the rights, interests, religious rights and customs of Jews and the Jewish community in the UK and promotes the development of the British Jewish community. It has participated in all developments affecting the political and civil rights of British Jewry. It conveys the views of the community to the government and other political bodies on policy and legislative matters which affect British Jewry and provides information about the Jewish community to the non-Jewish world. The Board examines legislative proposals which may affect Jews and ensures the political defence of the community. It also collects data and statistics on the British Jewish community and the data in the Appendix to this chapter is based largely (together with other sources) on their reports.

Summary

- Following the destruction of the second Temple in Jerusalem 2000 years ago Jews were dispersed to all corners of the globe.
- The two main divisions of Jews are *Ashkenazim* and *Sephardim* (approximating to those of European origin and those of North African, Middle Eastern and oriental origins respectively).
- There are about 300 000 Jews currently living in the UK; they descend mainly from late nineteenth-century Eastern European immigrants whose numbers were increased by refugees from Hitler in the mid-twentieth century.
- There is a wide range of religious observance amongst British Jewry; only a minority are strictly observant (orthodox), many are completely assimilated.
- Jews live in most parts of the UK but the majority are concentrated in the large conurbations especially Greater London and Greater Manchester; the main orthodox and ultra-orthodox centres are in north London and north Manchester.
- The strictly orthodox (ultra-orthodox) live in small but growing insular communities; their lifestyle is based on strict adherence to the details of Jewish law.

Further reading

Holman C (2001) *Orthodox Jewish Housing Needs in Stamford Hill.* Agudas Israel Housing Association, London.

Holman C and Holman N (2002) *Torah, Worship and Acts of Loving Kindness: baseline indicators for the charedi community in Stamford Hill*. Interlink Foundation, London.

Roth C (1942) *A History of the Jews in England*. Oxford University Press, Oxford.

Roth C (ed.) (1972) *Encyclopaedia Judaica*. Keter, Jerusalem. 16 vols (also single vol concise edn and junior edn) with yearbook and decennial updates.

Wein B (2001) *Faith and Fate – the story of the Jews in the twentieth century*. Shar Press, New York.

Appendix: demography and statistics of British Jewry[1]

By the end of the twentieth century the number of Jews in the UK had fallen below 300 000, from a peak of well over 400 000 in the decade after the Second World War. The downward trend continues. The decline is due to several factors, including assimilation (acculturation), emigration, and a declining average birth rate.

Approximately 70% of the Jewish population are affiliated to a synagogue, if only so as to belong to a burial society (*see* p 151). Of these, 61% affiliate to one of the mainstream orthodox synagogues, 27% to a Progressive (Reform or Liberal) synagogue, 10% to a strictly orthodox synagogue, and 2% to a Masorti synagogue.

Individual Jews are found all over Britain. However, because of the requirements of Jewish life, such as the availability of kosher food supplies, synagogues and educational facilities, Jews have tended to congregate in organised communities. In the latter part of the nineteenth century, there were small communities in many of the small towns in Britain, particularly around the ports and in industrial centres. The trend towards larger more centralised communities continued throughout the twentieth century, so that by its close, the main centres were in the largest conurbations with the smaller communities all but extinct.

The proportion of the Jewish population which now lives in the Greater London and south-east area has increased to some 70% of British Jews. This reflects a similar migration of the general population to the south east from other regions, a trend which continues. Approximate numbers in Greater London are: Barnet (50 000), Hackney (18 000), Redbridge (16 000), Harrow (14 000), south London (16 000); and outside Greater London are: the south Hertfordshire area (8000), north Kent and north Surrey (2500).

---

[1] Compiled from various sources including data supplied by the Board of Deputies, Agudas Israel Housing Association, Interlink Foundation, Surestart Project and others.

It has been estimated that there are some 80 cities or towns in the UK with identifiable Jewish populations, although about 50 of these have fewer than 300 Jews and several have as few as ten individuals. These range from places like Dundee, Newport and Torquay, each with a handful of Jews, to the largest centres, Greater London (195 000) and Greater Manchester (30 000). Away from these two largest Jewish centres, other Jewish communities include Leeds (c. 10 000), Glasgow (c. 5 500), Brighton and Hove area (c. 5000), Birmingham (under 4000) and then Liverpool, Southend and Bournemouth (with between 3–4000 each). There are smaller communities in Cardiff, Luton, Gateshead, Southport (with between 1–2000 each) and Hull, Newcastle-upon-Tyne, Nottingham and Edinburgh (these last three with less than 1000 each). There are about 8000 Jews in the rest of Great Britain living outside these main communities.

The elderly, as with the rest of the UK's population, represent a growing proportion of the community, but in the smaller provincial communities the elderly constitute a disproportionately large number because so many of the younger Jewish population have either moved to the larger centres, emigrated or no longer identify as Jews.

The strictly orthodox are to be found in the major urban centres, particularly in London and Manchester. It is difficult to get accurate data on the size of these communities and the following are approximate estimates for the main centres. London estimates are: Stamford Hill (20 000), Golders Green and Hendon 15–20 000; Manchester (9000); and Gateshead (2 500). There are some electoral wards in Hackney in north London where 18% of the population are orthodox Jews. Whilst the total numbers of the Jewish community in Britain are falling, the strictly orthodox sector, with its high birth rate (families with seven to nine children are common) continues to grow (in Stamford Hill the growth rate is estimated at 8% per annum, and 56% of the community are under the age of 16) and as such they represent a rapidly increasing proportion of the total Jewish community.

CHAPTER 4

The Jewish way of life

A description based on the orthodox tradition

A Jew starts his day starts by reciting the following immediately on awakening:

> *I thank You, eternal King for having compassionately returned my soul to me – Your faithfulness is abundant.*

He ends the day with the following prayer:

> *Into His hand I shall entrust my soul when I go to sleep – and I shall awaken . . . God is with me, I shall not fear.*

Daily Prayer Book

Introduction

In the previous chapter, I made reference to the wide variations in Jewish religious practice and observances. The orthodox or even ultra-orthodox represent one extreme of religious practice often described as fundamentalistic or less pejoratively as authentic Judaism. I feel it appropriate to devote a separate chapter to describing the orthodox lifestyle, because daily life within these communities is so very different to that of any other in Britain today.

Again, I must stress that variation in Jewish religious practice is very broad and most Jews in Britain and indeed throughout the world do not follow this lifestyle; it is only the minority of the most orthodox who adhere very closely to the way of life as described in this chapter. However it is fair to say that ultimately all Jewish religious practice, no matter how diluted, owes its origins to the fundamental practices adhered to by the orthodox, and most Jews, no matter how they interpret and practise their Judaism or no matter how secular or assimilated they may be, can ultimately trace their roots back to traditional orthodox origins.

Even amongst the orthodox there is considerable variation. There are Sephardi and Ashkenazi orthodox groups and communities, and subgroups of them. There are many orthodox Jews whose outward appearance is unobtrusive and differs little from others on the street and who integrate into the business and professional worlds. Of all the orthodox groups the most obviously recognisable are those among the Chassidim who are conspicuous because of their traditional clothing. Much of the description that follows in this chapter relates to their lifestyle. Other orthodox and less orthodox lifestyles can perhaps best be understood in terms of being variants of the description given, perhaps most fairly described as 'similar, but less so!'. When relating to individual Jews it is always best not to assume about their level of observance and practice but to ask and check with the person concerned.

Insularity (being different)

Chassidic communities deliberately try to insulate themselves from the secular world and its influences as much as possible. They maintain their traditional distinctive dress, they speak their own language, Yiddish, and they restrict contact with the outside world to the minimum necessary. They do not have televisions in their homes, many do not even listen to the radio and apart from newspapers specifically aimed at their own community most Chassidim do not read the national press. As a consequence they may be unaware of national healthcare campaigns such as immunisation drives or health promotion programmes in particular, and national or international news in general. They take the biblical ruling 'do not follow the customs of the nations' (Leviticus 18: 3) quite literally and deliberately try to be different from the secular society in which they reside.

Dress

The most obvious distinguishing feature of Chassidic Jews is their distinctive clothing. Most Chassidim still adhere to the traditional garb of Eastern Europe dating back to the eighteenth century. This is seen as being important, in that it singles out the Chassidic population and identifies them as a distinct entity and a separate community. There are some variations in the dress style of the different Chassidic groups, but the overriding factor is loyalty to the standards of the old, rejecting modernity in dress, as in many other spheres of life.

Traditionally, orthodox Jewish men will keep their heads covered at all times as a constant reminder that they are in the presence of God. Outdoors, they usually wear hats, under which they have a skullcap for indoor wear. The skullcap (*kappel* or *yarmulke*) is worn at all times and most men will only remove it for bathing. Some men may have a special *kappel* for wearing in bed, and they may want to keep it on when admitted to hospital. Adjusting a slipped head-covering for a sick patient would be appreciated, as this would enable a man to maintain his dignity. Many men grow sidelocks known as *payos*. Some Chassidic groups never trim their *payos*, whereas other groups may cut them when they grow beyond a certain length. *Payos* are left long and dangling by some groups, but others will tuck them away behind their ears or under their skullcaps or hats. Some groups do not cut the hair of boys before the third birthday. There is a prohibition in Jewish law against men shaving with a razor blade on the beard area. Almost all Chassidic men grow beards and most don't even trim them. There are many orthodox men who use electric shavers, which are permitted. Men wear a special garment called a *tallis koton* at all times. This is a four-cornered garment worn over or under the shirt with the *tzitzis* (tassels) on each corner, often seen dangling to the knees over the trousers. Some Chassidic men wear breeches instead of full length trousers.

Women tend to dress in a modest style. They do not expose much bare skin and even in summer will wear their sleeves and skirts long, their necklines high and their legs covered with stockings or tights. The emphasis is on modesty and adequate coverage rather than drabness, and many women dress relatively colourfully (but not too loudly) and most are neatly and elegantly turned out, rarely being seen out of doors in casual clothing. Most orthodox Jewish women do not wear trousers. According to Jewish law, married women must cover their hair at all times. The exact nature of the head-covering varies between different orthodox Jewish groups. Some women wear headscarves or hats, others wear wigs, yet others wigs and hats together. Many women will keep their own hair under their head-covering, sometimes at full length, while amongst some Chassidic groups all the hair may be shaved off. It is important to maintain a woman's dignity when in hospital or in a residential home, especially in situations where her head-covering might slip.

Female healthcare workers working closely within the orthodox Jewish community need to be sensitive to this dress code, especially if their work takes them into peoples' homes. Although visitors will not be expected to don Chassidic garb, they will be more easily accepted and be made more welcome if they wear long sleeves, skirts covering their knees and high necklines.

Boy or girl?

Gail was a newly appointed health visitor and was interested in learning about some of the different customs and the way of life of the many Chassidic families in her area. Her manager provided her with an induction training session, discussing various aspects of etiquette so as to prevent her 'putting her foot in it' too often! Everything seemed so strange. Even the children's names were different, but she resolved to learn to pronounce them if only to show her keenness! What really caught her out was when she asked a mother what her two year old girl was called, at the same time complimenting her on her beautiful golden locks. 'Oh she's actually a boy!' said the mother laughing. 'You see, we Chassidim have the custom not to cut our boys' hair until they are three. But don't be embarrassed – I'm so used to people getting it wrong. Those curls really are beautiful – in fact I'll miss them next month when he turns three!'

Language

Whereas most of the orthodox Jewish population do speak English, there are many Chassidic groups for whom English is a second language. An increasing number of the Chassidic community are going back to using Yiddish as a first language and some of the younger children may not be able to communicate in English until they learn it in school. Yiddish is a language of early medieval central European, Germanic origin and has been spoken by Eastern European Jews for many centuries. It is a very rich and expressive language and is not to be confused with Hebrew, the classical form of which is reserved by orthodox Jews for sacred purposes such as prayer and religious study. (Modern Hebrew by contrast is the everyday language of modern Israel and is hardly spoken by the Chassidic community.)

Healthcare workers may encounter language problems when dealing with the Chassidic community, especially with children or the very elderly. Such situations may occur when health visitors perform developmental assessments on young children or during audiological testing, or district nurses care for the elderly at home. A particular problem is speech therapy, especially as there are no Yiddish speaking speech therapists available in the relevant districts. Communication with reception and medical staff in doctors' surgeries or in hospitals may be a problem, and as with any other group, staff need to show extra patience. Even those who do speak English well may be unfamiliar with the names of parts of the body, as their knowledge of biological and anatomical terms might be poor.

Names and dates of birth

A problem commonly encountered by healthcare workers relates to patients' names and dates of birth. All orthodox Jews are given a Hebrew name. In addition, many Jews will also have a traditional English-type name on their birth certificates. These English names are sometimes direct equivalents of the Hebrew name, for example, *Yakov* and Jacob, *Dovid* and David or *Shloime* and Solomon, but some groups register an English name which may have no relationship at all to the Hebrew name. Yet others may only have a Hebrew name, and use this transliterated as their registered name on their birth certificates. It should be noted that personal names as recorded on birth certificates are known as first names, forenames or even registered names, but never Christian names!

Traditionally, boys are named at their *bris* (circumcision) ceremony on the eighth day of life. This may cause problems when the *bris* is delayed. When this delay is protracted, such as when the infant is unwell, a name might be allocated which is changed or added to when the *bris* does eventually take place. Girls are named within a few days of birth when the father attends a brief synagogue ceremony (*see* p 195 for more about naming girls). In Ashkenazi tradition children are only named after someone who is deceased, whereas in Sephardi circles children are frequently named for a living person.

Not only might healthcare workers encounter difficulties with the spelling or pronunciation of first names, but it is also not unusual to come across a Jewish patient who is so used to using his Hebrew name that he might not even remember his registered name. This may lead to misunderstandings when booking appointments and with the filing of patients' records. Since first names are often given in memory of deceased relatives, it is not unusual to find several cousins in an extended family sharing the same first name and surname when they have been called after a common grandparent, leading to obvious confusion! As with other patient groups it would be recommended to check dates of birth when booking appointments.

Many orthodox Jews use the Hebrew calendar in their day to day lives and therefore problems similar to the above may be encountered when asking patients their date of birth. The Hebrew calendar is based on the lunar year, as opposed to the solar year on which the civil calendar is based. This means that there is some fluctuation between dates in the two systems and dates such as those of birthdays and festivals may be out by a week or more in different years. The Hebrew calendar has an extra leap month every few years, so as to bring it back into alignment with the solar calendar. Conversion charts and computer programmes are readily available to convert Hebrew calendar dates.

Table 4.1: The Jewish calendar

Month	Number of days	Days of the month	Festivals
Autumn			
Tishri	30 days	1 & 2	*Rosh Hashona* (New Year)
		10	*Yom Kippur* (Day of Atonement)
		15–21	*Succos* (Tabernacles)
		22	*Shemini Atzeres* (festival appended to *Succos*)
		23	*Simchas Torah* (Rejoicing of the *Torah*)
Chesvan	29 or 30 days		
Winter			
Kislev	29 or 30 days	25	1st day of the eight days of *Chanukah*
Teves	29 days	10	Fast of 10th of Teves
Shevat	30 days	15	*Tu B'Shvat* (New Year for Trees)
Adar	29 (30 in a leap year)	13	Fast of Esther
		14	*Purim*
Adar II[1]	29 days	14	*Purim* in a leap year
Spring			
Nissan	30 days	15–22	*Pesach* (Passover)
Iyar	29 days	18	*Lag b'Omer* (33rd day of the period from 2nd day of *Pesach* to *Shavuos*)
Summer			
Sivan	30 days	6 & 7	*Shavuos* (Pentecost)
Tammuz	29 days	17	Fast of 17th Tammuz
Av	30 days	9	Fast of 9th Av
Elul	29 days		

[1] Adar II is a leap month added in seven times in a 19-year cycle, to allow for the solar calendar to catch up with the lunar calendar so as to ensure that *Pesach* is always in spring.

Addressing people

In strictly orthodox circles people tend to be addressed rather more formally than in the wider more modern society. Children rarely address adults by their first names almost always using more formal titles. 'Aunt' or 'Uncle' is often used to address older family friends, not necessarily literally. In many Chassidic families husband and wife might not call each other by their first names in front of the children, using the Yiddish 'Tattie' (Daddy) and 'Mummy' instead. As a general rule the best policy for non-Jewish health-care workers is to address adults using the standard English Mr, Mrs or Miss (or Rabbi, where appropriate) followed by the surname. Children are best addressed by their first names. (*See* 'Etiquette', p 58.)

The family and home

The family is seen as being central to the orthodox Jewish traditional way of life. Much as 'an Englishman's home is his castle', there are many Chassidic groups who feel uncomfortable at letting non-Jewish people into their homes, even if they are healthcare workers such as health visitors. Healthcare workers should not take this as a personal affront, nor should they be offended by this attitude. In many cases, advance notification, such as by telephone to arrange a visit at a mutually acceptable time or even at the healthcare worker's own place of work, may be advisable.

Each door (other than toilets and bathrooms) in an orthodox Jewish home or workplace will have a *mezuzoh* attached to the door post at shoulder height. This contains a small parchment scroll on which is written the *shema* (a passage from the Bible containing the fundamentals of Jewish beliefs, *see* p 7). Some people have the custom to touch or kiss these each time they walk through a doorway.

Because Jewish dietary laws (*see* Chapter 10) require meat and milk dishes to be kept apart, a healthcare worker given a cup of tea in an orthodox Jewish home may be asked not to put it down on a surface used for meat dishes.

Obligations: parents to children and children to parents

A father is obligated with respect to his son: to circumcise him; to redeem him (if he is a first born, *see* Pidyon ha'ben, p 196); to teach him *Torah*; to take a wife for him; to teach him a craft, and some say also to teach him to swim.

Talmud Kidushin 29a

There are two separate biblical commandments incumbent on a child with respect to his obligations to his parents. The first is in the Ten Commandments where it is written 'Honour your father and mother' (Exodus 20: 12). The second is stated in Leviticus (19: 3): 'Every man, you shall revere your mother and your father'.

> The Rabbis taught: What is proper 'reverence' for one's parents and what is proper 'honour'?
>
> 'Reverence' means that one may not stand in his father's (fixed) place, and that he may not sit in his (fixed) seat; he may not contradict his father's words and he may not offer an opinion (in a halachic debate to which his father is a party).
>
> 'Honour' means that one must give his father food and drink and dress and cover him, bring him in and take him out.
>
> Talmud Kidushin 31b

Thus honouring one's parents generally requires one to act in a positive manner to show respect whereas revering them means that one should not act in a way that denigrates their status.

> The Rabbis taught: there are three partners in the creation of a person; The Holy One Blessed be He; his father and his mother. When a person honours his father and his mother, The Holy One Blessed be He says: 'I consider it as if I had lived among them and they had honoured me'.
>
> Talmud Kidushin 30b

Synagogue (*shul*), prayer and study

In areas with large Jewish populations there will be many synagogues (*shuls*) providing for all the different subgroups found within the community. Some are housed in large, purpose-built buildings; others are in converted houses; whereas some are very small informal *shtibelech* (prayer rooms). Most of the large Chassidic groups have their own synagogues, which are often the focal point or base for that particular group.

Prayer is pivotal and essential to the orthodox Jewish way of life. Prayers are recited three times a day in Classical (biblical) Hebrew. Festivals and special holydays are marked by additional synagogue services.

The synagogue is much more than a place of worship. It is also a place of study and a meeting place; for many men it represents the pivot of their daily lives. Men spend a considerable amount of time in the synagogue, engaged in prayer and study.

Most orthodox Jewish men spend some time most days in the study of Jewish law, either on their own or in groups. Women spend far less time in the synagogue, many only attending occasionally on *Shabbos* or on *Yom-Tov* (festivals).

For the morning service, men don a *tallis* (a white prayer shawl with black stripes and *tzitzis* (tassels) on each of the four corners) and, other than on *Shabbos* and *Yom-Tov*, strap *tefillin* (leather boxes containing the *shema* (*see* p 7) and other scriptural verses) on the arm and forehead. It is extremely important to orthodox Jewish men not to omit putting on *tallis* and *tefillin* for even one day.

Whilst praying, men may make rhythmical swaying movements of the trunk and at certain points they will bow forward. Although some parts of the service are meant to be said standing and facing towards Jerusalem (approximately south easterly in the UK), an ill patient is permitted to pray whilst seated or lying in bed. An ill patient who cannot go to the synagogue would always try to make every effort to pray at home, or in hospital. Consideration should be given to Jewish hospital patients who request privacy in order to pray. This is particularly important in hospital wards, where there are incontinent patients, as it is forbidden to pray in such an environment. Similarly, orthodox Jewish patients may not be able to pray in mixed wards. Simple measures, such as pulling the bedside curtains to, may enable a patient to say his prayers. Inability to pray at the right time might result in considerable distress, and a little courtesy and forethought would always be appreciated and may contribute in very large measure to a patient's comfort in hospital. There are a few sections of prayer where interruption is strictly forbidden and the worshipper might appear to ignore someone who tries to interrupt him at such times. Nurses, doctors and other healthcare workers should not take offence at this.

Healthcare workers may find clients reluctant to book appointments if these coincide with prayer or study periods. Women may want to arrange their appointments around their husbands' prayer and study times so that their husbands would be free to baby sit.

Bar-mitzvah

In Jewish law a boy reaches the age of majority at the age of 13 when he becomes *Bar-mitzvah* (an adult required to keep the *mitzvos*, the religious laws). A girl becomes *Bas-mitzvah* at 12. From then on the child is regarded as a full adult for the purposes of Jewish law and religious practice including observances such as fasting on the fast days and, for boys, putting on *tefillin* daily. In contrast to some other Jewish groups, a *Bar-mitzvah* in the Chassidic community is a relatively low key affair, the occasion being marked by a celebratory meal for family and friends and a small synagogue ceremony, whereas for girls there is usually no public celebration.

Bar-mitzvah

Benjie was 12 when his parents brought him to see his GP complaining that he had a persistently hoarse voice. His *Bar-mitzvah* was still ten months away but they were worried that he would not be able to read from the *Torah* scroll in the synagogue or deliver his speech. He had just started lessons and his teacher was concerned that singing might strain or even damage his voice. He was referred to an ENT surgeon for visualisation of his vocal cords who found that there were nodules on both cords. Benjie had several sessions with a speech therapist who taught him how to avoid straining his voice. His *Bar-mitzvah* teacher accompanied him to one of the sessions. In the event, Benjie did himself, his parents and teacher proud! Follow-up laryngoscopy a year later showed that the nodules had fully resolved.

Education

Orthodox communities have their own schools, almost all of which are entirely funded by parents in conjunction with the wider community. All children go to kindergarten from the age of three and many start at play groups very much earlier. There are crèches for the infants of working mothers. The educational system carries pupils right through to full-time adult further (religious) education. The sexes are segregated right from the start of nursery school and most of the teaching is conducted in Yiddish. Hebrew reading is taught at quite a young age and the standard of literacy in Hebrew and Yiddish is extremely high. In fact, illiteracy due other than to illness or handicap is unknown in the orthodox Jewish community. In their teens, most young men go away from home to study in a *yeshiva* (full time college), where they study the *Talmud* and other aspects of Jewish life and Jewish law. After leaving school, many of the girls go on to full-time further education at seminaries where the courses consist mainly of Jewish studies, although some seminaries include vocational courses such as computer studies or teacher training. Some girls may go away from home for a year or so for these studies. On the whole the girls attain a somewhat higher level of secular education than the boys. All male adults will devote some time each day to religious study. There are a number of men who continue full-time study and research throughout their lives at institutes of higher religious study (*kollel*), of which there are a growing number.

Rabbis

The title rabbi (pl. *rabbonim*) literally means 'teacher'. In its most commonly used sense the title is applied to the spiritual leader of a community. Many large synagogues have a full-time rabbi. Smaller communities might have a rabbi on a part-time basis and yet others may have someone acting in that capacity on an honorary basis. The rabbi's role includes officiating in synagogue services, at weddings, attending circumcisions and other celebrations as well as officiating at funerals when necessary. In addition, most rabbis conduct *shiurim* (lectures or study sessions). Many rabbis will also rule and arbitrate on matters of Jewish law (*Halochoh*) and most are freely available for consultation even at short notice. A rabbi attached to a rabbinic court is given the title *dayan* (plural *dayanim*; judge). There are some experienced rabbis to whom people will turn for guidance and advice on all sorts of matters. Because Judaism places such emphasis on health, there are many rabbis who are very well informed about medical issues and the specialised aspects of Jewish law relating to them.

The qualities of leadership

When *Moishe Rabenu* (Moses Our Teacher), the greatest leader the Jews have ever had, described his role he said, '. . . and all the complex matters you shall bring to me and I will listen' (Deuteronomy 1:17). *Moishe*'s choice of words is most interesting, he does not say '. . . and I will solve them for you', or 'I will give you an answer' or some similar solution but 'I will listen'. The greatest form of support that a leader can give to someone with a complex problem is to listen. Here *Moishe* is telling us what qualities are required of a great leader, not necessarily to be able to give answers but to have the ability and patience to listen.

Heard from Rabbi J Dove in the name of his mentor
Rabbi Dr AJ Twerski

The great Chassidic leader, the *Rebbe* of Tulna, had spent a morning listening to a string of people asking him for advice. His secretary noted that he was drenched in sweat and looked exhausted. The secretary expressed his surprise; after all, the *Rebbe* had only been sitting still all morning, not obviously exerting himself, hardly physically demanding work. The *Rebbe* explained, 'When someone pours out his woes to me, the only way I can really understand his situation and empathise with him is for me to become him. I do this by imagining that I am getting into his clothes and feeling what it's actually like to be him; only then can I truly understand his predicament. When I have really understood what it is like to be him, I need to get back into my role of being a *Rebbe* and mentor, so I have to take off his clothes and put my own back on. Having given him my advice, the man has to consider it and understand it; but how do I know if he has really understood it? So I have to get back into his position to see my advice from his point of view ... By the end of the morning I have changed roles and clothes so often that I am well and truly exhausted!'

With thanks to Rabbi J Dove

There may be occasions when problems need discussion with a rabbi and a healthcare worker may need to liaise directly with a rabbi. Most rabbis will be happy to discuss problems over the phone and are generally easily accessible. A rabbi should be addressed simply as 'Rabbi' or as 'Rabbi Cohen' (or whatever his surname). A *dayan* would similarly be addressed as 'Dayan' or 'Dayan Cohen' (for example). The title 'Rabbi' is also often used as term of respect, such as to teachers or possibly to elderly learned members of the community.

The title '*Reb*' together with the first name (e.g. *Reb Duvid*) is often used by orthodox Jews as a term of respect and approximates to the use of 'Mister' in English. Non-Jewish people are best advised to stick to the English standard Mr/Mrs/Ms/Miss as in the general culture.

Etiquette

Although 'when in Rome do as the Romans do' is an important maxim in the British way of life, it is important for healthcare workers to understand that there are certain aspects of the Chassidic way of life which are of fundamental importance to members of that community and which many of them will not give up or change, even for the sake of politeness.

Physical contact between members of the opposite sex, except between parents and their children and between siblings, is strictly avoided. As a consequence there are a number of instances where this may be of relevance to healthcare workers. For example, many orthodox Jews will not shake hands with members of the opposite sex. This should not be taken as an act of rudeness but rather as an important aspect of orthodox Jewish cultural behaviour. Many orthodox Jewish patients might feel uncomfortable by the well-intentioned and common practice whereby a doctor or nurse places a hand on a patient to provide comfort and reassurance. Of course, where physical contact is necessary and unavoidable in strictly clinical situations there are no restrictions. For example, there would be no problems at all with a male obstetrician delivering a baby with all the physical (and even intimate) contact which that involves. However, a congratulatory pat on the arm or a reassuring hand on the shoulder following the delivery might make the mother feel rather uncomfortable. Because of the restriction on physical contact, some ultra-orthodox members of the community may not even pass objects directly to a member of the opposite sex, but will put them down first. This again should not cause offence in situations such as when reception staff hand prescriptions to patients or when giving change for the waiting room payphone. Many strictly orthodox patients might avoid direct eye contact, particularly prolonged eye contact, with members of the opposite sex. Healthcare workers used to working with the general population may find this quite disconcerting at first, but they must remember that this is a cultural behaviour and not intended in any way as an insult.

There is a Jewish law prohibiting being secluded with a member of the opposite sex, other than with very close immediate family, and there may be situations where this could cause problems. For example, a patient in hospital may not wish to be alone in a lift with an escorting nurse of the opposite sex when being moved from one department to another, and the patient may ask the nurse to wait until a third person comes along. A patient may ask a doctor or healthcare worker of the opposite sex to leave the door unlocked or even slightly open when being interviewed. These requests should not cause offence; they are important to the patient or client as religious requirements and are not in any way directed personally at the healthcare workers themselves.

Gender of carer

Rabbi Levin became housebound and aphasic following a cerebro-vascular accident at the age of 82. He needed help with dressing and personal care, and had a urinary catheter. His family noticed that he became agitated and distressed when attended to by the female district nurses but was much more relaxed when the male district nurse attended him. The availability of a male district nurse in the area which has many orthodox Jewish patients is greatly appreciated by all his carers.

Where possible, healthcare workers such as district nurses who visit patients or clients at home should ideally be of the same sex as their patients or clients, particularly in situations involving a great deal of physical contact such as the bathing of bed-bound patients or physiotherapy. (Orthodox Jews strictly prohibit mixed-sex swimming and bathing, and this may cause a problem where hydrotherapy is required, necessitating a therapist of the same sex, and together with other patients only of the same sex.) On the whole, most orthodox Jewish women will not mind seeing a male doctor, although if given the option they may prefer a female doctor particularly when a physical examination is required. Where the presenting problem is gynaecological in nature, they might feel more comfortable talking to a female doctor. Many orthodox Jewish men would not be happy to see a female doctor and might even refuse to see her, preferring to wait for a male doctor to become available.

Gender of doctor

Dr Hertz practised as a single-handed GP; most of his patients were orthodox Chassidic Jews. When he wanted to appoint an additional partner he sounded out his patients' views as to whether he should appoint a male or female partner. The response was unexpected and surprised him. As anticipated most men wanted another male GP. It was the women's response that was unexpected. It transpired that whereas many women welcomed the chance to have a female GP, a substantial number of women elected for another male doctor. The reason for this became clear when the women were questioned further. Of course, given the chance, they themselves would prefer a female doctor, but they didn't really mind consulting a man as they were used to it; however they couldn't envisage their husbands having to consult a female doctor, so they voted for another man!

In recent years, problems have arisen when orthodox Jewish patients have been admitted to mixed-sex hospital wards. Orthodox Jews may find this extremely uncomfortable or even distressing and indeed they may be reluctant to be admitted for this reason. This problem is even more marked in psychiatric units where patients are generally physically well and are encouraged to socialise and mix freely. Hospital managers must be sensitive to these feelings and should make provision for some degree of separate-sex accommodation where appropriate. The NHS Patient's Charter states that all patients can expect their 'privacy, dignity and cultural and religious beliefs to be respected'. In relation to hospital admission, the Charter also states 'If you prefer a single-sex ward, your wishes will be respected where possible'.

Because the sexes tend to be segregated in their daily lives, some orthodox or Chassidic Jews may feel uncomfortable if seated between members of the opposite sex in situations such as at meetings. Arranging the seating with men and women on opposite sides of the table (or room) would be appreciated.

Conclusion

As stated at the start of this chapter, the practices described here are those of the strictly orthodox and are not those of the majority of less strictly observant Jews likely to be encountered by most readers. Nevertheless, the practices described are the fundamentals of traditional Jewish practice on which all others are based but generally observed to a lesser extent. The warning given at the end of the first chapter concerning the extrapolation of practices seen in one group of Jews to others is particularly pertinent when seen in the light of what to many are seen as fundamentalist and extreme practices.

Summary

- The strictly orthodox lifestyle is based on adhering rigidly to the *Torah*, both biblical and rabbinic law, which encompasses every aspect of the orthodox Jew's life.
- The Chassidic lifestyle, through its traditional dress and language, deliberately aims at insularity and non-integration; being different is an intentional attempt 'not to be like other nations'.
- Life revolves around the family, keeping the *mitzvos* and studying *Torah*, observing the *Shabbos* and the festivals, and the synagogue, which is more than just a place of prayer, but also a place for study and a social centre where many strictly orthodox men spend much of their time.

- Strictly orthodox Jews will not compromise on their beliefs, religious practice or customs except in life-threatening circumstances.
- It is appreciated when healthcare professionals make an effort to observe the basics of etiquette and protocols when providing services to this community. Individual practices vary and it is always best to ask rather than assume.

Further reading

Aaronson A (2000) *The Foundation of Judaism* (2e). Targum/Feldheim, New York.

Blech B (1999) *The Complete Idiot's Guide to Jewish History and Culture*. Alpha Books, Indianapolis.

Blech B (1999) *The Complete Idiot's Guide to Understanding Judaism*. Alpha Books, Indianapolis.

Carmell A (1991) *Masterplan, Judaism: its program, meaning, goals*. Feldheim, Jerusalem/New York.

Cohn-Sherbok L and Cohn-Sherbok D (1998) *A Concise Encyclopaedia of Judaism*. Oneworld, Oxford.

Forta A (1995) *Judaism*. Heinemann, Oxford.

Ganzfried S (1961) *Kitzur Sulchan Aruch: code of Jewish law* (trans H Goldin). Hebrew Publishing Co, New York.

Hirsch SR (1962) *Horeb: a philosophy of Jewish laws and observances* (trans I Grunfeld). Soncino Press, New York.

Hirsch SR (1994) *The Nineteen Letters on Judaism*. Feldheim, Spring Valley.

Spitzer J (2002) *A Guide to the Orthodox Jewish Way of Life for Healthcare Professionals* (3e). J Spitzer, London.

Wein B (2002) *Living Jewish: values, practices and traditions*. Artscroll, New York.

Wouk H (1992) *This is My God – the Jewish way of life*. Souvenir Press, London.

CHAPTER 5

God the Healer

God is the Healer – doctors are his agents

*Heal us, O God – then we will be healed, save us – then we will be saved, for
You are our praise. Bring complete recovery for all our ailments, for You are
God, King, the faithful and compassionate Healer. Blessed are You, O God,
Who heals the sick of His people Israel.*

From the Prayer of Eighteen Blessings which devout Jews recite three
times daily

*Since a doctor is acting as God's agent, . . . the invalid is obliged to follow
the doctor's instructions, no more or less than any of the laws in the
Shulchon Oruch.*

Code of Jewish Law

*A person is required to attend to his own treatment just as he is obliged to
help someone else to be healed . . .*

Based on *Gesher Hachaim* 1: 1: 2 and Letters of *Chazon Ish* 1: 138

Introduction

Jews recognise that all healing is in the hands of God, who is referred to in
prayers and scripture variously as 'the Healer of all flesh', 'the Creator of
remedies' or 'the faithful Healer'.

However Jews recognise that even though ultimately healing comes
from God, this may be brought about through doctors acting as the agents
of God. Jews are required by *Halochoh* (Jewish law) to consult doctors when
ill. From the earliest times Jewish writings have always included medical
material and the *Talmud* itself contains a great deal of medical advice and
details of therapeutic herbs, potions and other cures.

Praying on behalf of the sick

The following is an extract from the Prayer of Eighteen Blessings which devout Jews recite three times daily.

Heal us, Hashem – then we will be healed, save us – then we will be saved, for You are our praise. Bring complete recovery for all our ailments, for You are God, King, the faithful and compassionate Healer. Blessed are You, Hashem, Who heals the sick of His people.

On occasions an individual might insert the following prayer for a close relative or friend who is ill.

May it be Your will, Hashem, my God, and the God of my forefathers, that You quickly send a complete recovery from heaven, spiritual healing and physical healing to the patient (here mention his/her name) *among all other invalids of Your people.*

The time when the *Torah* is read in the synagogue is especially auspicious for prayer on behalf of the sick and someone may wish to contribute to charity in the invalid's merit. When doing so he has the following supplication read out:

He Who blessed our forefathers Abraham, Isaac and Jacob, Moses and Aaron, David and Solomon, may He bless and heal the sick person (here mention patient's name) *because* (name of supplicant) *will contribute to charity on his/her behalf. In reward for this, may the Holy One, Blessed is He, be filled with compassion for him/her to restore his/her health to heal him/her, to strengthen him/her, and to revive him/her. May He send him/her speedily a complete recovery from heaven, among the other sick people of Israel, a recovery of the body and a recovery of the spirit, swiftly and soon. Let us respond: Amen.*

Healing through prayer

When the Israelites were punished with a plague of snakes (Numbers 21) and they pleaded with Moses to get rid of them, he prayed to God, who commanded him to make a copper snake and to erect it on a high pole. 'So it was that if a snake bit a man, he would stare up at the copper snake and he would live.' The rabbis ask, 'Can an inanimate, man-made copper snake cause death or give life?' Rather the purpose of the snake, they explain, was 'so that when the Israelites would look upwards towards the snake on the pole they would direct their hearts towards their Father in Heaven (and thus pray to Him), then they would be healed.'

Talmud Rosh Hashanah 29a

Prayer and healing

My Lord, my God, I cried out to You and You healed me. Lord, You saved me from the risk of death, You kept me alive.

Psalms 30: 3,4

The practice of medicine

The practice of medicine has always been highly regarded in Judaism and is considered as being a sacred vocation. Indeed many great and famous rabbis have also been physicians. The *Talmud* refers to several of the great sages variously as Rabbi so and so 'the Healer' or 'the Physician'. Perhaps the best known is Maimonides (1135–1204), who in Jewish learning is regarded by many as only second to Moses. He was one of the very greatest codifiers of Jewish law, whose works are still studied in great depth by Jewish scholars to this very day. He earned his living as a doctor in Cairo and was court physician to Saladin. He also wrote medical texts, some of which were regarded as standard works in the Arab medical world for many generations. To this day, medicine is still a popular career amongst Jews and they are well represented in most branches of the profession, although there are disproportionately fewer drawn from the orthodox, particularly the so-called ultra-orthodox extreme. This to some extent reflects their poorer secular educational standards and the strictly orthodox's reluctance to attend universities (*see* p 42) as well as the implications that modern technologically dependent medical practice has for practitioners who are strictly observant of the *Halochoh* (Jewish law), especially the *Shabbos* laws (*see* p 100).

The physician's prayer[1]

Classical Jewish literature is replete with physicians' prayers, some for daily recital, others to be said in times of need. Most are of medieval origin, of which several are ascribed to Maimonides, Rabbi Moishe ben Maimon, the great Rabbi and Physician (1135–1204). The following is a translated example of one such prayer to be recited daily before starting work.

> Supreme God in heaven!
> Before I begin my holy work, to heal the human beings whom Your hands formed, I pour out my entreaty before Your throne of glory, that You grant me the strength of spirit and great courage to do my work faithfully, and that the ambition to amass riches or goodness shall not blind my eyes from seeing rightly. Give me the merit to regard every suffering person who comes to ask my advice as a human being, without any distinction between rich and poor, friend and foe, good person and bad. When a person is in distress show me only the human being. If physicians with greater understanding than mine wish to teach me understanding give me the desire to learn from them, because there is no limit to the learning of medicine. But when fools insult me, I pray: let my love of the profession strengthen my spirit, without any regard for the advanced age of the scorners and their prestige. Let the truth alone be a lamp to my feet, for every yielding in my profession can lead to perdition or illness for a human being whom Your hands formed. I pray You compassionate and gracious Lord, strengthen and fortify me in body and soul, and implant an intact spirit within me.

[1] Although this prayer is often ascribed to Maimonides, Rabbi Moishe ben Maimon, the great Rabbi and Physician (1135–1204), it clearly dates from a later time and first appeared in print in 1783. The author is possibly the physician Dr Marcus Herz (Germany, 1847–1902) (Jakobovits I (1975) *Jewish Medical Ethics*, Bloch Publishing Company, New York).

Jewish law recognises a doctor's rights (and obligation) to practise; a principle which is derived from a biblical source. When the *Torah* talks about the requirement for an assailant to pay his victim damages, it states 'he shall cause him to be thoroughly healed' (Exodus 21: 18, 19), which is interpreted as referring to the victim's medical expenses which are to be included in the calculation of the compensation to be paid. It is from here, say the rabbis in their interpretation of the *Torah*, that we derive the source of the biblical licence giving doctors the right to practise. The rabbis extend this to make it a requirement for an invalid to seek and accept medical help, as well as it being an obligation on the physician to be required to practise his skills.

One who is trained as a physician is obliged to practise his skills so as to help restore people to health. The *Talmud* (Sanhedrin 73a) sees this as an interpretation of the obligation for anyone to return a lost object to its owner: 'you shall return it to him' (Deuteronomy 22:2). An invalid is seen as someone who has lost his good health. If a doctor is able to help restore his health he is required to do so, thereby returning that which has been lost.

Parable of the invalid and the farmer

It once happened that Rabbi Yishmael and Rabbi Akiva were walking through Jerusalem together with another person when they came upon an invalid who said to them 'My teachers! Tell me how can I be cured?' So they told him which herbs and potions he should take in order to be cured. The man accompanying them said to them, 'Who made him ill in the first place?' 'It was the Holy One Blessed be He' they replied. Said he to them, 'why do you meddle in matters that are none of your business? He made him ill and you advise on cure?!'

They asked to the questioner, 'What is your occupation?' He responded 'I'm a farmer, see, here is my scythe'. They said to him 'Who created the fields?' 'It was the Holy One Blessed be He', replied he. 'So why do you meddle in matters that are none of your business? He created the trees and fields, yet you eat his fruits?' they challenged. He replied 'were I not to plough, spread fertiliser and hoe the land nothing would grow'. So they said to him 'you are a fool, for have you not learned from your own work, for it is written: "As for man his days are like grass" (Psalms 103:15); just as the field if not ploughed or worked will not produce, so it is with the body; for the body is like the field, the fertiliser the medication and the farmer the physician.'

Midrash Shmuel 4

Similarly, a doctor is obligated to treat patients by virtue of the negative commandment, 'You shall not stand idly by the blood of your fellow man' (Leviticus 19:16), which is interpreted to mean that one who has the ability to help must do so, and that failure to act may be akin to manslaughter. Interestingly, the rabbis extend the meaning of the obligation not to stand by helplessly to include giving financial support to help save life if one is in a position to do so.

Rabbi Yossef Caro in his code of Jewish law, the *Shulchon Oruch* (Yoreh De'oh 336:1) states 'The *Torah* gave permission to the physician to heal; moreover, this is a religious precept and is included in the category of saving life; and if the physician withholds his services it is considered as shedding blood.'

The *Talmud* (Bova Kammah 46b) takes it as axiomatic that 'he who is in pain goes to a doctor'. The rabbis make it clear that one may not trust to providence and rely on miracles for cure but must do whatever is physically possible to maintain life and health including making full use of medical facilities: 'When in danger, never rely on miracles' (*Talmud* Kidushin 39b and Shabbos 32a).

Jewish law protects a doctor from being sued by his patients in the event of mishap, provided that he always acts within his level of training, competence and expertise and that he is licensed to practice by the relevant authorities in the place in which he practices. However, he must always exercise extreme skill and caution to avoid liability for negligence. If injury to the patient occurs following a genuine error by a fully qualified physician then he is held to be blameless; obviously he is always liable for intentionally caused harm, when acting negligently or when practising outside his own level of competence or training.

Complaints procedure

Miss Brucha Katz was upset with her GP, Dr Franks. She had telephoned to tell him that her elderly father had become acutely confused. When she phoned the next day to say he had not improved Dr Franks said that he would visit, but by the time he arrived later that day Mr Katz's condition had deteriorated and he had become severely unwell. Dr Franks arranged for his immediate admission to hospital where he subsequently died. Miss Katz felt that the GP should have visited earlier than he did and had he done so the outcome would have been different.

Because the patient and GP were Jewish, Miss Katz decided to make a formal complaint about what she felt was the doctor's negligence to the *Beis Din* (Jewish rabbinical court), requesting that they summons him to appear before the court to answer her charge of negligence. She felt that as all the parties were Jewish this was the appropriate way in which to seek justice. Having read the details of her complaint the clerk to the *Beis Din* felt that it would be inappropriate for the matter to be dealt with by a *Beis Din* as this was something which should be handled through the normal practice complaints procedure.

The doctor must be aware that he is but an agent or messenger (*shaliach* in Hebrew) of God, whose guidance and help he prays for and acknowledges each day. The patient asks God that the physician's treatment should be successful. Many Jews believe that effecting a cure for a specific illness is a matter of finding the right *shaliach* for them, for this particular illness, on this particular occasion; as the *Talmud* (Yerushalmi Nedorim 4: 2) puts it 'a person is not privileged to be healed through everyone'; hence they will sometimes go to a different doctor (or even several) for another opinion, in the hope that if the first was not the *shaliach* for them, the next doctor might be.

A tradition found mainly in Ashkenazi circles is the renaming of a patient (especially a relatively young one) facing a life-threatening illness. An additional name is given and the patient is referred to and called by his new name. This is done to 'confuse the Angel of Death'. Where it is believed that the patient may have been condemned to death by Divine decree, changing the name may help to avert that decree. Similarly the power of prayer, repentance and the giving of charity are seen as being able to change Divine decree and avert a patient's 'death sentence'. It is not uncommon to find relatives and friends sitting at a patient's bedside reciting prayers and *tehillim* (psalms).

Conclusion

Having accepted that there is a religious obligation to seek medical help and to be treated by conventional physical means, a Jew is obliged always to remember that God is the ultimate source of all healing: 'for I am the Lord your Healer' (Exodus).

Summary

- Although all healing is ultimately in God's hands, Judaism requires invalids to seek medical advice and help and be treated in conventional ways.
- Medicine has always been regarded by Jews as a valued and even sacred vocation; many of the greatest rabbis of the past were also physicians.
- Biblical law obliges a suitably qualified doctor to care for the sick and do his best for patients and, unless negligent, Jewish law protects him from liability.
- A doctor is God's agent (*shaliach*) and because 'a person is not privileged to be healed through everyone', Jewish patients may feel free to shop around for further opinions.

Further reading

Bleich JD (1981) *Judaism and Healing: halachic perspectives*. Ktav, New York.

Finkel AY (1995) *In My Flesh I See God; a treasury of rabbinic insight about human anatomy*. Aaronson, New Jersey.

Friedenwald H (1994) *The Jews and Medicine*. Johns Hopkins University Press, Baltimore.

Heynick F (2002) *Jews and Medicine: an epic saga*. Ktav, New York.

Isaacs RH (1998) *Judaism, Medicine and Healing*. Aronson, New Jersey.

Meier L (1991) *Jewish Values in Health and Medicine*. Lanham, New York/London.

Munk E (1963) *The World of Prayer*. Feldheim Publishers, New York.

Ozarowski JS (1998) *To Walk in God's Name: Jewish pastoral perspectives on illness and bereavement*. Aronson, New Jersey.

Preuss J (1994) *Julius Preuss' Biblical and Talmudic Medicine* (trans F Rosner). Aronson, New Jersey.

Rosner F (1977) *Medicine in the Bible and Talmud*. Ktav, New York.

Rosner F (1984) *Maimonides Medical Writings* (series of several volumes published from 1984). Maimonides Research Institute, Haifa.

Rosner F (1984) *Medicine in the Mishneh Torah of Maimonides*. Ktav, New York.

Rosner F (1995) *Maimonides' Introduction to His Commentary on the Mishnah*. Aronson, New Jersey.

Rosner F (2000) *Encyclopaedia of Medicine in the Bible and the Talmud*. Aronson, New Jersey.

Rosner F and Kottek SS (1993) *Moses Maimonides: physician scientist and philosopher*. Aronson, New Jersey.

Schur TG (1987) *Illness and Crisis, Coping the Jewish Way*. NSCY/Orthodox Union, New York.

Wouk H (2000) *The Will to Live On: this is our heritage*. HarperCollins, New York.

Appendix

Ben Sira[1]

Judaism's attitude to the doctor practising his art as well as the patient's responsibility to seek medical attention is described in the well known description by Ben Sira (about 300 BCE) who describes the physician as God's tool.

- Befriend the doctor before you need him, for God has given him his role.
  The doctor's wisdom comes from God, and from the King he gets his vocation.
  The doctor's knowledge makes him distinguished and he will stand upright before those in positions of power.
- God brings forth medicinal herbs from the earth, which the man of understanding should not neglect.
  Was not the water sweetened by a twig so that mankind would know of His power?
  He gave man insight so that He might be glorified through His mighty works.
  Through them the doctor relieves pain, and the pharmacist makes medicines.
  His work always continues and its benefits to mankind.
- My son, when you are ill, do not delay, pray to God that He may heal you;
  Turn away from evil and from showing favour to people and cleanse your heart from all sin;
  Offer a sweet-smelling offering, a generous donation according to your means.
  But also give the physician his place, do not let him leave, for you may need him as well.
  There are occasions when his actions are successful for he too will pray to God;
  That he may make the correct diagnosis and that his treatment be effective and bring about a cure.
- He who is defiant towards his physician, commits a sin before his Creator.

---

[1] Ben Sira (38: 1–15). My own translation (with help from MM Guttentag) from the original Hebrew Cairo Geneza Manuscript in Segal, *see* the Bibliography at the end of the book.

Biblical sources related to the practice of medicine

The *Torah* permits and indeed requires a doctor to practise his/her skills, effectively licensing the practice of medicine. Caring for the sick is regarded as a *mitzvah* (meaning both 'a divine commandment' and 'a good deed') so that when a doctor goes about his professional duties he is constantly performing *mitzvos*.

The following are some of the biblical sources (the Written Law) from which the rabbis (in the Oral Law) derive the principles of Jewish law relating to the practice of medicine.

The licence to practise medicine
The biblical source that licenses physicians to practise medicine and is interpreted as obliging a physician to exercise his skills where needed is: 'If men quarrel and one strikes the other . . . he shall provide for healing' (Exodus 21: 18, 19).

Here the *Torah* talks about the requirement for an assailant to pay his victim damages. It states 'he must provide for his healing', which is interpreted as referring to the cost of the victim's medical expenses which are to be included in the calculation of the compensation to be paid. It is from here, say the rabbis in their interpretation of the *Torah*, that we derive the source of the biblical licence giving doctors the right to practise. The rabbis extend this to make it a requirement for an invalid to seek medical help as well as it being an obligation on the physician to be required to practise his skills where needed.

The mitzvos *a doctor performs whilst looking after the sick*
There are five main *mitzvos* 'commandments' which a doctor performs by attending to a sick patient (three positive and two negative, *see* p 11). They are based on the following biblical references:

> . . . *you shall return it to him.*   Deuteronomy 22: 2

This is written in relation to returning a lost object to its owner. The rabbis interpret this verse to include the obligation to help restore an invalid's lost good health, obliging a surgeon to practise his skills, a physician to provide his expert advice and a wealthy person to supply funds in order to 'return that which has been lost', i.e. to help return him to full health.

> . . . *you may not ignore it.*   Deuteronomy 22: 3

This verse continues from the one discussed in the last paragraph and also relates to returning a lost article to its owner. This commandment prohibits someone from ignoring a lost article which he happens to come across; which, as previously, the rabbis interpret to include the loss of good health and helping to return a person's lost health. Thus a doctor who is in a position to help to restore lost health to a patient is required to do so and may not look away and ignore the patient's plight.

> *You shall not stand aside whilst your fellow's blood is being shed* (You should not stand idly by whilst someone's life is in danger).
>
> Leviticus 19: 16

One who has the ability to save someone's life, and does not do so, violates this prohibition. One is obliged to help to save one's fellow man's life. From this verse, say the rabbis, we learn that if, for example, one sees someone drowning one is obliged to jump in to save him (provided one has the appropriate skills and is unlikely to endanger oneself as well).

> *If your fellow becomes impoverished . . . you shall strengthen him . . . and let your brother live with you* (help him survive).   Leviticus 25: 35

Literally this refers to helping a poor person, obliging everyone to help others less fortunate and thereby survive in life. The rabbis extend this and interpret it to mean that one must do one's utmost to help one's fellow man to live, provided that one's own life is not put at significant risk – as the verse states: 'with you' not 'in place of you'. Thus doctors are required to help the less fortunate, that is the sick, as part of their obligation to act charitably. (This does not of course preclude doctors from charging for their services where appropriate!)

> *You shall love your neighbour as yourself.*   Leviticus 19: 18

This commandment, when applied to medical practitioners, obligates a doctor to care for patients, even in non-life-threatening situations. A truly dedicated doctor fulfils this commandment when caring devotedly and self-lessly for others.

Additional Torah *references to a doctor's obligation to treat the sick*
Other than the above five main sources there are a number of other biblical references to a doctor's obligation to treat the sick; these include:

> *However, your blood which belongs to your souls I will demand.*
>
> Genesis 9: 5

Man does not own his body – it belongs to God, and man is accountable to Him for how he uses or abuses the body, which is given to him as a receptacle for the soul. This includes the prohibition against committing suicide.

*You shall observe My decrees and My laws which man shall carry out and by
which he shall live – I am God.*   Leviticus 18: 5

From this juxtaposition of the command to observe God's decrees and laws
and the words 'and you shall live through them', the rabbis derive the principle that all restrictions of Jewish law are set aside where there is danger to
life – 'You shall live through them (i.e. the commandments) and not die
through them'.

Look after yourselves and guard your souls.   Deuteronomy 4: 9
You shall look after your souls carefully.   Deuteronomy 4: 15

These two exhortations to look after oneself encompass both the physical
and the spiritual; the physical by looking after one's body and physical health, and the spiritual by looking after one's soul and its spiritual
health.

You shall not place blood (cause injury or death) *in your house.*
                                                                    Deuteronomy 22: 8

Said in connection with building a parapet around one's roof to prevent
anyone falling off. One is required to ensure that his property does not
cause injury by adhering to basic safety precautions. Observing the basics
of safety and self preservation including health prevention is enshrined in
this commandment.

You shall not wantonly destroy.   Deuteronomy 20: 19

Although written in relation to destroying fruit trees, the rabbis interpreted
this to refer to any form of destruction active or passive of any living thing
including the human body which by extension includes preserving and
protecting life as much as possible.

*You shall not harden your heart or close your hand against your destitute
brother. Rather you shall open your hand to him; you shall lend him his
requirement, whatever he lacks.*   Deuteronomy 15: 7–8

Again this obligation, whilst incumbent on every Jew to help provide what
another less fortunate person lacks, when applied to doctors requires him
or her to help provide what the patient lacks, that is good health, and to
help the patient back on the road to full health, to the best of his/her ability.

You shall follow his ways.   Deuteronomy 28: 9

Finally, there is the exhortation for everyone to emulate God's qualities.
This, when applied to a physician, requires him/her to act in ways that

display kindness, care, compassion and all the positive qualities that would be expected of a skilled professional engaged in the art of healing the sick.

The obligation to study medicine

The *Talmud* makes it clear that the study of medicine has intrinsic value:

> Rav Hunah asked his son Rabbah, 'Why don't you go to the study sessions of Rav Chisda, who is such an astute teacher?' He replied, 'Why should I go to him, for when I do go to study with him, he teaches me mundane things, rather than *Torah*. For instance, he said to me 'one who enters the toilet should not strain too much, so as to avoid rectal prolapse (by stretching the muscles supporting the rectum)'. Rav Hunah replied to his son, 'Rav Chisda is dealing with matters concerning the lives and health of people, and you say that these are mundane matters? Definitely should you go and learn from him'.

> *Talmud* Shabbos 82a

The commentaries to this talmudic text explain that Rav Hunah's message to his son was not only that he should acquaint himself with medical facts, but that these were a part of *Torah* as well and as such he was obliged to study them.

On studying medicine

> Medical practice is an important introduction to intellectual and ethical pursuits, to the knowledge of God, and to achieving true success; thus will the physicians' study and ambition become one of the great occupations, unlike weaving or carpentry.

> Maimonides, The Eight Chapters
> (Introduction to his commentary on Avos 5)

Maimonides was of the opinion that the study of nature, science and mathematics was a prerequisite to the knowledge and love of God. The first four chapters of his magnum opus *Mishne Torah* (the Repetition or Summary of the *Torah*), his code of Jewish law, consists of a description of the structure of the world, explaining that 'When a person contemplates these matters and recognises all creations and creatures ... and sees God's wisdom in all that exists, his love for God grows' (Yesodey HaTorah 4: 12). Earlier he asks 'How can one learn to love and revere God?' The answer is 'through contemplation and study of His wonderful and magnificent works and creatures, and deducing from them His limitless and infinite wisdom, he will immediately love God' (Yesodey HaTorah 2: 2).

Maimonides was a prolific writer not only on Jewish law, Bible and philosophy but on science and medicine as well (*see* works listed under Rosner in the Bibliography). It is noteworthy that in *Mishne Torah* Maimonides' medical advice concentrates on preventive rather than curative medicine, through the maintenance of a sound body.

On practising medicine

The *Torah* has given a physician the licence to heal *(verapoh yerapeh*, Exodus 21: 19), it is a *mitzvah* (an obligation) and it is *pikuach nefesh* (life saving), and if he desists therefrom – he is a murderer.

Shulchon Oruch Yoreh De'oh 336: 1

CHAPTER 6

Jewish medical ethics in a nutshell

The answers to modern questions are to be found in ancient Jewish law

Keep my decrees and laws, since it is only by keeping them that a person can (truly) live – I am the Lord.

Leviticus 18: 5

Ben Bag-Bag said: 'Delve into it (the Torah) and then delve into it some more, for everything is to be found in it'.

Avos 5: 26

All wisdom and knowledge is contained in *Torah*, a scholar need only delve deeply into it to find the answers to all problems.

Introduction

It is a truism that there is no specific concept of ethics as such in Judaism; for all of Jewish teaching and practice is contained in the halachic codes and is enshrined in Jewish law. Thus, Judaism has the concept of Jewish medical law, rather than Jewish medical ethics; the difference between the two concepts is that the term 'ethics' implies a degree of subjectivity and acting according to one's conscience, whereas Judaism treats medical issues objectively in accordance with the principles of Jewish law (*Halochoh*).

Deciding on matters of Jewish law or ethics

When confronted by a medical problem or issue requiring a decision, the Jewish halachic (legal) position is based on a three-way discussion between a physician, or a patient, and a rabbinical authority who is conversant with the medical issues and is an expert in relevant areas of Jewish law. A decision will be based on Jewish legal principles combining all the vast resources of biblical and rabbinic law, as well as with the accumulated literature of *responsa* (written answers to questions of Jewish law, laying out the sources and logical basis on which a decision is made) written over many centuries. Even the most contemporary of problems will be decided on those principles, many of which can be found in the discussions recorded in the *Talmud*. Some rabbis have built up an expertise in medically related aspects of Jewish law and are well informed about modern medical advances and progress.

It is remarkable that modern topics such as doctors' liability and the licensing of physicians are discussed in talmudic literature. Rabbinic literature shows that psychological and social aspects of patient care were taken into consideration by talmudic and medieval authorities and are still valid today. Medical ethics is a discipline which asks questions to which the answers may be difficult for ethicists to formulate. *Halochoh* by contrast is dynamic and multifaceted. Through the centuries, rabbinic *responsa* have provided answers to medical problems, according to the contemporary state of medical knowledge. These *responsa* are always based on earlier decisions and ultimately find their source in talmudic literature. This decision-making process continues to this day. Any problem, whether relating to modern technological developments or rare diagnoses, would still be approached by halachic authorities in this way.

A wise physician

A person needs a wise physician to endeavour on his behalf. If he can prescribe a remedy for the body, good! If not, he should provide a remedy for his soul. (This is the sort of physician that the Holy One Blessed be He looks after both in this world and in the world to come.)

Zohar Deuteronomy 299a

An example

Jewish law relating to medical and ethical topics is a complex subject with a vast and rapidly growing literature and in recent years a great deal has been published in this field (*see* Further reading on pp 82–3 for some suggested titles in English). A detailed discussion of the principles involved is beyond the scope of this book.

Perhaps a brief summary of an area where contemporary secular views differ from those of Jewish law will give the reader some insight into this field. The balancing of the concepts of patient autonomy ('it's my body, I can decide what to do with it') on the one hand, with paternalism ('doctor knows best') on the other hand, whilst at the same time maintaining the principle of beneficence (doing what's best for the patient), provides such an example.[1]

In contemporary medical practice there has been a swing in attitudes to patients' involvement in decision making from the traditional paternalistic approach to that of patient autonomy. Today much of the medical world recognises autonomy as the major overriding factor in decision making. Judaism differs in its approach. The primary premise on which autonomy is based is not accepted by Judaism. The body, and the life within it, does not belong to the individual. Man was created by God in his image and life belongs to God, not man. Judaism puts absolute value on life as an entity in its own right. Life is God's gift to mankind. Man is given custody over his body during his lifetime and is required to look after it and care for it. A human does not own his body, nor does he have unrestricted licence to do with it as he may desire. (Judaism thus does not allow an individual to choose to disfigure his own body, so, for example, tattooing is forbidden.) Fundamental to Jewish belief is the concept that God granted man his own freewill. Man can choose how to lead and run his life and is able to make his own decisions. He is instructed to base those choices on the parameters set out by God in the *Torah* as interpreted by the rabbis (Jewish law or *Halochoh*) and run his life accordingly. This results in the constant conflict between the freewill of the individual and the constraints placed on him by Jewish law.

In the Jewish view a patient can be forced to accept treatment against his will so as to effect a cure for the body which does not belong to him and over which he does not have jurisdiction. This paternalistic attitude is balanced by the ruling in Jewish law that in a situation where a doctor feels that the

---

[1] Based on Flancbaum, with the author's permission, *see* Further reading at the end of this chapter.

patient's condition is such that there is no risk, or potential risk to life, but where the patient feels and believes that there is a risk, or even potential risk, then we follow the patient's view and proceed with the treatment even if this might involve a violation of Jewish law. (For as has been stressed elsewhere, in life-threatening situations where treatment would involve what would normally be a violation of Jewish law all prohibitions are set aside and treatment becomes not only permitted but encouraged.) The patient is thus given the same rights as the doctor to judge whether his life is in danger. The rabbis who interpret(ed) *Halochoh* were and are sensitive to patients' feelings and rights within the framework of their medical condition and the application of the principles of Jewish law.

The late Lord Jakobovits (1921–99), former Chief Rabbi of Great Britain, who was well known as a medical ethicist, summarised some of the halachic or Jewish ethical principles involved here as follows.[2]

1   It is a religious obligation to protect human life and health, incumbent upon a doctor as upon any other person in a position to do so.
2   A doctor is therefore never morally entitled to withhold or withdraw his services, whether or not a contractual relationship exists between him and his patient, unless a more competent doctor is available. A refusal to render medical aid where required is deemed as tantamount to shedding blood.
3   A patient has no right to refuse medical treatment deemed essential by competent medical opinion for the preservation of his/her life or health, and his/her consent need not be procured for such treatment.
4   In the discharge of the doctor's obligation to save life and limb, and in the absence of the patient's consent, the doctor may even be required to expose himself to the risk of legal claims for unauthorised assault and battery.
5   While the patient should always be informed of treatments and procedures to be applied, both as a matter of respecting rights and to secure co-operation, prior consent is required, and should be sought, only in cases of a) high risk treatments, b) doubtful or experimental cures, and c) differences of opinion among equally competent medical experts.
6   The onus of choosing between various alternative forms of medical treatment, or none at all, rests upon the doctor, and patients should never be expected to render what are purely medical decisions. However, in the instance of the availability of reasonable medical alternatives, patient choice is called for.

---

[2] Adapted from Flancbaum, with the author's permission, *see* Further reading at the end of this chapter.

There are many examples of discrepancies between the concepts of autonomy, paternalism and beneficence as represented by secular legal and ethical systems and as interpreted by *Halachoh*. These dilemmas can be resolved by consultation between medical experts and the rabbis who interpret and establish the *Halachoh* in each generation in a three-way relationship including the patient.

Another area where traditional Jewish views differ from currently accepted medical practice, and which relates to the discussion above about the differing views on medical paternalism and patient autonomy, is informing a patient about a terminal diagnosis. Whereas the contemporary medical view is to tell a patient everything about his illness, its diagnosis and prognosis, even where the outcome is definitely fatal, the Jewish view, in contrast, would be not to tell a patient about a terminal prognosis. This is discussed in Chapter 12 , *see* 'Terminal diagnosis and prognosis', p 145.

Conclusion

Individual Jewish patients and doctors must establish links with their own rabbis in order to discuss ethical problems that arise. Such a relationship, when executed properly, becomes symbiotic, with each party benefiting from the wisdom of the other. In recent years, with the rapid advance of the frontiers of medical knowledge and techniques, experience has shown that by establishing and maintaining a system based upon honest and open communication, commitment and trust amongst all of the parties, Judaism can effectively answer the most difficult dilemmas in the area of medical ethics. Solutions can be reached that are both logical and compassionate, affirming the Jewish tradition's respect for the dignity of the individual.

Summary

- All Jewish medical ethics are based on the principles of Jewish law, which is rather more objective than the implied subjectiveness of the term 'ethics'.
- There is a vast talmudic and post-talmudic literature covering almost every possible situation and even the most modern questions can be answered by an analysis of the basic principles involved in relation to existing case law.

- There are some instances where current medical practice is at variance with the principles of Jewish law.
- Practical ethical or halachic problems are best solved in discussion between the individual patient (or carers), healthcare professionals and rabbinic authorities.

Further reading

Abraham SA (1980) *Medical Halacha for Everyone: a comprehensive guide to Jewish medical law in sickness and health.* Feldheim, Jerusalem/New York.

Abraham SA (1990) *The Comprehensive Guide to Medical Halacha.* Feldheim, New York.

Abraham SA (2000/2002) *Nishmat Avraham: medical Halachah for doctors, nurses, health-care personnel and patients* (vols 1/2). Artscroll, New York.

Bleich JD (1977/1981/1989/1995) *Contemporary Halakhic Problems* (vols 1–4). Ktav, New York.

Bleich JD (1981) *Judaism and Healing: halachic perspectives.* Ktav, New York.

Bleich JD (1991) *Time of Death in Jewish Law.* Z Berman Publishing Co, New York.

Bleich JD (1998) *Bioethical Dilemmas: a Jewish perspective.* Ktav, New York.

Carmell A and Domb C (1988) *Challenge: Torah views on science and its problems.* Feldheim, Jerusalem/New York.

Dorff E (1998) *Matters of Life and Death.* Jewish Publication Society of Philadelphia, Philadelphia.

Flancbaum L (2001) *'... And You Shall Live By Them' – contemporary Jewish approaches to medical ethics.* Mirkov Publications, Pittsburgh.

Ganzfried S (1961) *Kitzur Sulchan Aruch: code of Jewish law* (trans H Goldin). Hebrew Publishing Co, New York.

Hirsch SR (1962) *Horeb: a philosophy of Jewish laws and observances* (trans I Grunfeld). Soncino Press, New York.

Isaacs RH (1998) *Judaism, Medicine and Healing.* Aronson, New Jersey.

Jakobovits I (1975) *Jewish Medical Ethics.* Bloch Publishing Company, New York.

Koenigsberg M (1997) *Halacha and Medicine Today: experts discuss the application of Halachah to contemporary medical practice.* Feldheim, New York.

Levin F (1987) *Halacha, Medical Science and Technology: perspectives on contemporary Halacha issues.* Maznaim, Jerusalem.

Meier L (1991) *Jewish Values in Health and Medicine.* Lanham, New York/London.

Preuss J (1994) *Julius Preuss' Biblical and Talmudic Medicine* (trans F Rosner). Aronson, New Jersey.

Rosner F (1991) *Modern Medicine and Jewish Ethics.* Ktav, New York.

Rosner F (1997) *Pioneers in Jewish Medical Ethics.* Aronson, New Jersey.

Rosner F (2000) *Encyclopaedia of Medicine in the Bible and the Talmud.* Aronson, New Jersey.

Rosner F (2001) *Biomedical Ethics and Jewish Law.* Ktav, New York.

Rosner F and Bleich JD (2000) *Jewish Bioethics*. Ktav, New York.

Rosner F and Tendler MD (1997) *Practical Medical Halacha*. Aronson, New Jersey.

Shulman NE (1998) *Jewish Answers to Medical Ethical Questions*. Aronson, New Jersey.

Sinclair DB (1989) *Tradition and the Biological Revolution: an application of Jewish law to the treatment of the critically ill*. Edinburgh University Press, Edinburgh.

Spero MH (1986) *Handbook of Psychotherapy and Jewish Ethics*. Feldheim, Jerusalem/New York.

Steinberg A (1980) *Jewish Medical Law*. Gefen Publishing, Jerusalem/California.

Weiner Y (1995) *Ye Shall Surely Heal: medical ethics from a halachic perspective*. Jerusalem Centre for Research, Jerusalem.

Zohar NJ (1997) *Alternatives in Jewish Bioethics*. State University of New York, New York.

CHAPTER 7

Healthcare values

Concern about illness; neglect of prevention

Take heed of yourself, and take care of your life.

Deuteronomy 4: 19

You shall look after your souls carefully.

Deuteronomy 4: 15

These biblical exhortations to look after oneself, explain the rabbis, encompass both the physical and the spiritual. The physical by looking after one's body and physical health, and the spiritual by looking after one's soul and its spiritual health.

A person should have the intention while eating, drinking, having intercourse, sleeping, awakening, moving and resting that he does so for the purpose of physical health. His intention in seeking physical health should be to prepare a healthy and strong receptacle for the soul, so as to be able to acquire wisdom and intellectual and emotional strengths to enable him to reach the goal of knowing God.

Shmone Perakim of Maimonides 5

Health

According to Jewish teaching a person's body belongs to God. The human body is regarded as a receptacle for the soul (*neshoma*) and the individual is obliged to care for and look after his/her body. Good health is regarded extremely highly and it is considered to be a religious obligation to seek medical help when illness presents. This is taken quite seriously by the orthodox Jewish community and they do avail themselves freely of medical facilities when unwell. Orthodox Jews regard illness as being the will of God, but nevertheless Judaism obliges them to avail themselves of medical facilities in order to achieve a cure, even at considerable physical and material cost. If, having tried everything, a patient is unfortunately not cured, then the outcome is likely to be stoically accepted as being God's will.

Although good health is so highly regarded, it is somewhat paradoxical that orthodox and Chassidic Jews are not particularly keen sportsmen and as a rule tend to lead rather sedentary lives, exercising very little, if at all. Obesity is relatively common and the morbidity from ischaemic heart disease is rather high. Health promotional activities are largely ignored. Similarly, dental health is comparatively neglected by the Chassidic community (but not by other orthodox Jewish groups) and their dental hygiene is rather poor. Dental caries is rampant especially amongst the children and the need for routine check-ups is largely ignored.

The use of medical facilities is generally based around traditional orthodox medicine and patients will consult their GPs, seek hospital referrals and generally make use of all the healthcare facilities that are available. Nevertheless it is not uncommon for patients to consult alternative or complementary practitioners. There may be occasions when following a consultation with a Gentile healthcare professional, an orthodox Jewish patient may consult an orthodox Jewish professional for a further opinion. This attitude is in some part due to the concept of finding the doctor or practitioner who is the right *shaliach* (God's agent, *see* p 69) for that specific patient with that specific problem. However there are, as stated previously, relatively few medical practitioners who come from the most orthodox groups (*see* p 65), and the few that there are, are becomingly increasingly overwhelmed (especially because of the rapid growth of the orthodox community) with requests from patients seeking the opinion of a doctor who shares their own values or from rabbis wanting to discuss issues involving an issue of Jewish law (*Halochoh*) with a doctor who has a working understanding of both the medical and halachic principles involved. In this context it is worth noting that strictly orthodox patients may paradoxically prefer to see a non-Jewish practitioner rather than a non-observant Jewish one, as they might feel (whether correctly or not) that the latter may not only be unsympathetic to their views but could possibly be antagonistic to them.

The *Rebbe*'s advice

Mrs Laufer, a member of the Belzer Chassidic sect, was diagnosed by her GP as having plantar fascitis. He injected the area with methylprednisolone and lidocaine and this produced good relief but after three months her pain returned. She was referred to an

orthopaedic surgeon who advised her that there were two management options, either further local injections or a surgical excision of
the calcaneal spur.

Mrs Laufer sent a message to the *Belzer Rebbe* at his headquarters
in Israel asking for his advice. He recommended that she consult
another orthopaedic surgeon for a further opinion. She then asked
Mr Berman, a member of her community who had some medical
expertise, to recommend an orthopaedic surgeon for another opinion.
When requesting a new referral letter, she explained to her puzzled
GP that she believed that the *Rebbe* always gave the right advice, 'we
have had many good experiences, the *Rebbe* might help direct me to a
surgeon who is the right *shaliach* for me'. She also explained that Mr
Berman, although a layman, had built up a good rapport with various
consultants due to his work with Jewish medical charities.

Because some orthodox and all Chassidic families do not have televisions
and many have no radios in their homes, and since most do not read the
national press, they may be unaware of national healthcare campaigns
such as immunisation drives or health promotion programmes. Important
health information or advice, such as might need to be provided during epidemics, may need to be publicised in the orthodox Jewish press in order to
reach the intended audience.

Attitudes to illness

Physical illness

Within the orthodox Jewish community it is not unusual for serious illness
to be kept secret and not mentioned or discussed, even with close family
and friends. Patients and their family may be reluctant to use words such
as 'cancer' and might substitute euphemisms, confounding clear communication. Contrary to current beliefs and practice in the healthcare professions, most orthodox Jews would not want an elderly relative to be told of a
terminal diagnosis. There are some who might go so far as to say that telling a relative could possibly be contrary to Jewish law, where one must
never give up hope (this topic is discussed in detail on p 145). A great deal
of tact and patience is required in the management of terminally ill patients
and their families (*see* p 147).

Hereditary illnesses (*see* Chapter 13, pp 157–73) or chronic diseases are frequently concealed and might not even be disclosed to a healthcare professional who is trying to obtain a medical history (especially if the patient does not see its relevance), unless specifically asked for.

The reluctance to discuss serious illness and the wish to conceal hereditary diseases are particularly evident in strictly orthodox and Chassidic families. There are several reasons for this including a belief that talking about serious illness encourages 'the evil eye' and may adversely affect the prognosis. This applies particularly to Chassidic Jews and to a lesser extent many Sephardim as well, who more than other Jewish groups believe in mystical and supernatural powers (*see* p 16). As mentioned above, another reason is that of possibly causing a sense of loss of hope and feelings of despair in the invalid and carers. Another important reason why illness might be concealed even from close family members is due to the perceived stigma to the individual or family when it comes to a *shidduch* (that is the term used to describe the arrangements made for a young couple to be introduced to each other with a view to marriage; *see* p 124). In this context it should be noted that it is not unusual for healthcare professionals to be consulted and asked about the state of health of a prospective party to a *shidduch*; needless to say practitioners who get involved in these matters are best advised to get written consent (from both parties) before disclosing any confidential information.

Psychiatric illness

Psychiatric illness carries a particularly powerful stigma and sufferers and their families might go to considerable lengths to keep it hidden. Denial is particularly powerful, which unfortunately may be to the detriment of the patient, delaying presentation and diagnosis. This can also lead to isolation of patients with mental health problems. It may be hard for patients and their carers to recognise and accept psychological problems, whether presenting problems in their own right or as components of other conditions. Frequently, patients or their relatives will hide behind a pragmatic medical model of illness, denying a psychiatric or psychological component, and may look for a purely medical cure. In the strictly ultra-orthodox community there is considerable opposition to forms of therapy including counselling, clinical psychology, psychotherapy or any form of treatment where the medium is essentially some form of 'talking therapy'. They are suspicious of the methods employed, which many feel involve techniques that are contrary to their beliefs. Many will go as far as to say that even if the therapist is an orthodox practising Jew him/herself this would make no difference, as the training received and the methods used are intrinsically un-Jewish and therefore suspect. They would rather seek the advice of a rabbi. Attitudes are changing slowly but with the anti-therapy groups having been quite vociferous it will take a long time to make any really acceptable differences. On the rare occasions where psychotherapeutic or counselling advice is sought the patient might be accompanied by a rabbi or close family confidant who may wish to stay in during the consultation as the patient's advocate or facilitator ('culture-broker', *see* Greenberg and Witztum in Further reading at the end of this chapter). Some parents of children with disabilities or learning difficulties may be reluctant to accept that there is no cure, thereby delaying the start of special educational help and other forms of treatment in their unrealistic hunt for the elusive 'nothing short of a total cure'. In addition, many orthodox Jewish patients who have led quite isolated lifestyles and who may not have mixed socially with non-Jews might find the environment of in-patient psychiatric hospitals very alien and intimidating. The significance of the stigma of mental illness is even more marked in relation to *shidduch* enquiries than that of physical illness. These factors can make the management of orthodox Jewish psychiatric patients particularly challenging for all concerned. (*See also* p 170 regarding clinical aspects of psychiatric illness.)

Rehabilitation and convalescence

Rehabilitation or convalescence following an illness will for many Jewish patients involve a return to religious life and practice, so that orthodox patients, especially men, will put great emphasis on getting back to the routine of going to the synagogue once or more each day for prayer and getting back to the regular routine of *Torah* study and *shiurim*. Even if an illness is incurable an observant patient will benefit tremendously from being able to get back to these routines, which will often provide a tremendous psychological boost.

Hygiene

Hygiene is central to the orthodox Jewish way of life and many religious activities may only be performed in a clean state. Even if their hands are physically clean, orthodox Jews will wash their hands in a ritual manner and recite a special *brochoh* (blessing) on waking up after sleep, after going to the toilet and before meals (especially when bread is served). The washing is mostly done by pouring water over the hands from a cup. Some

people will also wash their hands before praying. When bed-bound, orthodox Jews may request a bowl and cup to wash their hands before eating,
praying or after using a bed pan, even if their hands appear to be completely clean.

Many men will attend the *mikveh* (ritual bath house) on a regular (even
daily) basis for ritual immersion. Bathing in the *mikveh* pool is done purely
for ritual purposes, and is usually preceded by a shower or bath.

Cleanliness is a *mitzvah*

The Midrash says that when Hillel the Elder took leave of his disciples, they asked him, 'Rabbi, where are you going?' He replied,
'I am going to perform a *mitzvah*'.[1] 'What *mitzvah*?' they en-
quired. 'I am going to bathe in the bathhouse', he replied. 'Is that
considered a *mitzvah*?' they asked. 'Indeed it is', he answered.
'Look at the fellow who is in charge of the statues of the emperor
in the theatres and circuses, he cleans and shines them every
day. I am created in the image of God, as it says "God made man
in his own image" (Genesis 9: 6); surely I should be meticulous
about my cleanliness'.

Midrash Vayikra Rabbah 34

[1] *Mitzvah*, a meritorious act or good deed.

***Brochoh*: acknowledging God's beneficence**

Every activity in a Jew's daily life has a spiritual dimension and Jews
recognise and acknowledge God's beneficence by saying a *brochoh*
(blessing/benediction) before or after most activities.

On saying *brochos* before eating

Preparing for a pleasure doubles the enjoyment. This advantage
has someone who says a *brochoh* with sincerity, devotion, concentration and understanding (the single Hebrew word *Kavonoh*
encompasses all these meanings).

Rabbi Yehuda HaLevi (1075–1141) in *Kuzari* 3: 17

Bodily functions

Even the mundane activity of eliminating the body's waste has its own *brochoh*. The *brochoh* acknowledges God's creation of the human body with its precise balance of anatomical design and physiological function, as well as the intricate design of all the various internal organs and their interface with the external world, and recognises the way in which the physical body fuses with the spiritual soul to form a human being.

On coming out of the toilet and having washed one's hands thoroughly the following is recited:

> Blessed are You, O God, our God, King of the universe, Who fashioned man with wisdom and created within him many openings and many cavities. It is obvious and known before Your Throne of Glory that if but one of them were to be ruptured or but one of them were to be blocked it would be impossible to survive and to stand before You. Blessed are You, O God, Who heals all flesh and acts wondrously.

On taking medication

On taking a medication or undergoing treatment one says: 'May it be Your will that this action shall be curative for me'.

On recovering from sickness

On recovering from an illness one says: 'Blessed are You who heals the sick'.

Whether it's good or bad news, God is blessed

The *Talmud* explains that just as one is required to bless God for the good, so one is obliged to bless Him for the bad, so that when one hears bad tidings he shall say the *brochoh*:

> 'Blessed are You the true judge'.

Summary

- A person's physical body belongs to God and must be carefully looked after and maintained.
- When ill, Jews are required to ensure the best medical treatment to get better; but paradoxically preventive medicine including sports is much neglected by the strictly orthodox.
- The ultra-orthodox may not have direct access to the health information provided for the general population; special provision might need to be made.
- Illness, both physical but especially psychiatric, might be kept secret from members of the family and wider community. Psychiatric illness and mental health problems still carry considerable stigma.

Further reading

Abbott S (2002) *Health Visiting and the Orthodox Jewish Community*. City University, London.

Abraham SA (1980) *Medical Halacha for Everyone: a comprehensive guide to Jewish medical law in sickness and health*. Feldheim, Jerusalem/New York.

Abraham SA (2000/2002), *Nishmat Avraham: medical halachah for doctors, nurses, health-care personnel and patients* (vols 1/2). Artscroll, New York.

Aiken L (1996) *Why Me, God?: a Jewish guide for coping with suffering*. Aronson, New Jersey.

Amsel A (1969) *Judaism and Psychology*. Feldheim, New York.

Amsel A (1976) *Rational Irrational Man*. Feldheim, Jerusalem/New York.

Cohen J (2002) *The Bedside Companion for Jewish Patients*. Genisa, Stanmore.

Fuller JHS and Toon PD (1988) *Medical Practice in a Multicultural Society*. Heinemann, Oxford.

Greenberg D and Witztum E (2001) *Sanity and Sanctity – mental health work among the ultra-orthodox of Jerusalem*. Yale University Press, New Haven.

Heynick F (2002) *Jews and Medicine: an epic saga*. Ktav, New York.

Isaacs RH (1998) *Judaism, Medicine and Healing*. Aronson, New Jersey.

Lamb N (1969) *The Jewish Way in Death and Mourning*. Jonathan David Publishers, New York.

Meier L (1991) *Jewish Values in Health and Medicine*. Lanham, New York/London.

Qreshi B (1989) *Transcultural Medicine*. Kluwer, London.

Rabinowitz A (1999) *Judaism and Psychology; meeting points*. Aronson, New Jersey.

Spero MH (1980) *Judaism and Psychology: halachic perspectives*. Ketav, New York.

Spero MH (1986) *Handbook of Psychotherapy and Jewish Ethics*. Feldheim, Jerusalem/New York.

Spitzer J (2002) *A Guide to the Orthodox Jewish Way of Life for Healthcare Professionals* (3e). J Spitzer, London.

Wein B (2002) *Living Jewish: values, practices and traditions*. Artscroll, New York.

PART 2

The Jewish patient

CHAPTER 8

An introduction to Judaism and medical treatment

The body, loaned to man by God, must be cared for

When in danger, one must not rely on miracles.

Based on *Talmud* Shabbos 32a and Kidushin 39b

An invalid is obliged to seek medical help, and one who does not, concerning him it is written, 'However, of your blood which belongs to your souls I will demand an account' (Genesis 9: 5).

Man does not own his body – it belongs to God and man is accountable to Him for how he uses or abuses the body which is given to him as a receptacle for the soul. This includes the prohibition against neglecting illness or even committing suicide.

Based on *Talmud* Bova Kama 91b

Virtually all forms of required medical treatment are permitted and indeed encouraged in Jewish law (*Halochoh*). So, for instance, there are no restrictions or prohibitions on blood transfusions, or on the injection or other parenteral methods of administration of non-kosher products such as insulin of porcine or bovine origin.

There are, however, areas where Jewish law does have specific guidelines regarding medico-legal and ethical matters. Examples include organ transplants, timing the moment of death, abortion, treatments that have not been adequately evaluated or the use of potentially life-threatening forms of medical treatment. Fertility treatment, contraception and organ donation are other examples of areas where there are specific Jewish guidelines based on the principles of *Halochoh*. There are some rabbis who are well informed on modern medical developments and have built up an expertise on issues at the interface between medical problems and Jewish law.

Specific difficult situations which give rise to the most frequently encountered problems are the areas of *Kashrus* (Jewish dietary laws), for example whether a Jewish patient may be given non-kosher foods or medications, and the area of *Shabbos* observance, for instance whether certain treatment may be given to a Jewish patient on *Shabbos* or *Yom-Tov* (festivals).

The overriding principle of *Halochoh* is that all treatments are permitted and are indeed required if deemed necessary to save life (*pikuach nefesh* – the saving or preserving of life). Where a patient's life is in actual, immediate danger or may possibly be in danger and where there is no time or it is impractical to consult a rabbi for advice, then all treatments to save the patient's life should be undertaken immediately without delay. Judaism considers one who refuses to administer life saving treatments as little short of being a murderer; and one who delays by asking for rabbinical guidance in a potentially life-threatening situation, a *chossid shoteh* (a righteous fool).

The righteous fool

One who rejects the services of a doctor relying purely on God's help is like the famished man who refuses to eat his bread hoping instead that God will deliver him from the illness called hunger.

Maimonides, *Sefer Hakezoroh* 47

Summary

- Judaism has a long tradition of respect for medicine and its practitioners.
- There is no conflict between Jewish belief and most mainstream medical practices.
- The preservation of healthy life is accorded top priority in Jewish law through the overriding principle of *pikuach nefesh* (the saving or preserving of life) which takes precedence over almost all other aspects of Jewish law, so that almost all laws (e.g. fasting, *Shabbos*

restrictions or circumcision) are set aside where there may be risk to life.

- The use of medical interventions is seen not only as desirable but as a religious obligation.

Further reading

Abraham SA (1980) *Medical Halacha for Everyone: a comprehensive guide to Jewish medical law in sickness and health*. Feldheim, Jerusalem/New York.

Abraham SA (1990) *The Comprehensive Guide to Medical Halacha*. Feldheim, New York.

Abraham SA (2000/2002) *Nishmat Avraham: medical halachah for doctors, nurses, health-care personnel and patients* (vols 1/2). Artscroll, New York.

Bleich JD (1977/1981/1989/1995) *Contemporary Halakhic Problems* (vols 1–4). Ktav, New York.

Bleich JD (1981) *Judaism and Healing: halachic perspectives*. Ktav, New York.

Ganzfried S (1961) *Kitzur Sulchan Aruch: code of Jewish law* (trans H Goldin). Hebrew Publishing Co, New York.

Isaacs RH (1998) *Judaism, Medicine and Healing*. Aronson, New Jersey.

Koenigsberg M (1997) *Halacha and Medicine Today: experts discuss the application of Halachah to contemporary medical practice*. Feldheim, New York.

Levin F (1987) *Halacha, Medical Science and Technology: perspectives on contemporary Halacha issues*. Maznaim, Jerusalem.

Preuss J (1994) *Julius Preuss' Biblical and Talmudic Medicine* (trans F Rosner). Aronson, New Jersey.

Rosner F (2000) *Encyclopaedia of Medicine in the Bible and the Talmud*. Aronson, New Jersey.

Rosner F and Tendler MD (1997) *Practical Medical Halacha*. Aronson, New Jersey.

Steinberg A (1980) *Jewish Medical Law*. Gefen Publishing, Jerusalem/California.

CHAPTER 9

Caring for Jewish patients on the *Shabbos*, festivals and fast days

Jewish life revolves around the cycle of the calendar: weekly, monthly and annually

Remember the Shabbos day to keep it Holy − six days you may labour and do all your work but the seventh day it is Shabbos to the Lord your God, you may do no work . . .

Exodus 31:16

And Moses declared God's festivals to the Children of Israel.

Leviticus 23:44

On the tenth day of the seventh month it shall be a holy day for you (i.e. Yom Kippur) and you shall fast and not do any work.

Numbers 29:7

Shabbos (the Sabbath)

Introduction

So fundamental to Judaism is the observance of *Shabbos*[1] that it is ranked as the fourth of the Ten Commandments: 'Remember the *Shabbos* to keep it

---

[1] I have used the Hebrew word *Shabbos* throughout instead of the English Sabbath, as the latter doesn't truly capture the unique essence and nuance that the word *Shabbos* conveys to the practising Jew.

Holy'. The *Shabbos* is the central pivot around which the rest of the week revolves and it is one of the most cherished cornerstones of Judaism. From the very beginning of the establishment of Judaism, the *Shabbos* has been set aside as a special day different from the rest of the week. It is a day of rest and freedom from the outside world, a time of worship and study. *Shabbos* is truly a family day, with family meals at which everyone joins in the singing of hymns and when discussion of biblical texts or religious topics is a regular feature.

The degree to which *Shabbos* is observed varies markedly between different Jewish groups. The strictly orthodox observe the minutiae of the laws relating to *Shabbos* (as described below) meticulously and very rigidly. Others may hardly keep any of the *Shabbos* laws, and some may be selective as to which aspects of the *Shabbos* they choose to observe; for instance, there are many who, whilst lighting the special *Shabbos* candles and possibly having a traditional family Friday night at home, will not observe any of the many restrictions on performing *melocha* (that is creative work and activities, as defined by Jewish law, that are prohibited on *Shabbos*, described in detail later) and will otherwise conduct themselves as on any other day. In order to give a full understanding of the issues involved in caring for Jewish patients on *Shabbos*, I shall give a description of *Shabbos* as observed by orthodox Jews. Others may keep few or possibly none of the *Shabbos* laws. Of course, as always, it is best not to assume what an individual's level of observance might be; it is best to ask the patients themselves when appropriate.

Shabbos observances

Shabbos begins on Friday evening at sundown and ends on Saturday night after nightfall. There is thus considerable seasonal variation, with *Shabbos* in London commencing as early as 3.30 p.m. in midwinter but as late as 9 p.m. in midsummer. The termination of *Shabbos* after nightfall similarly varies between about 5 p.m. and 11 p.m. in London. Times in other locations vary with the latitude and of course seasonal variation must also allow for time changes between summer and winter. There may also be some slight variation in these times between different Jewish groups, due to differences in calculation.

Shabbos begins with the lighting of candles in the home, usually by the women, when the men go to the synagogue for the Friday night service. Even when in hospital a Jewish patient may want to light candles if it is safe to do so, otherwise another member of the family will light them at home on behalf of the patient. Candle lighting and the Friday evening service is followed by the traditional family meal which commences with *kiddush* (sanctification), a special blessing said over a cup of wine or grape juice. At the meal traditional foods such as *gefilte* (chopped) fish, chicken soup, kugel (potato or pasta puddings) and other delicacies are eaten, which in Chassidic circles reflect the Eastern European origin of the community. Sephardi groups have their own traditional dishes reflecting their own varied origins.

Shabbos morning begins with a synagogue service, which is usually attended by the whole family, except for mothers with young children at home, who do not attend. This is followed by a family meal at midday. The men will attend the synagogue again towards the end of the day, where they will meet to study and pray together or to hear a lecture by the rabbi. In some synagogues they will have a small communal meal towards dusk.

Shabbos ends after nightfall with *havdolah*, a short family ceremony, recited over a cup of wine or grape juice. A plaited candle is lit and a spice box is passed around so that all present can catch a whiff of the contents.

The traditional ceremonies, candle lighting and prayers are very important to many Jews, especially the orthodox, and a patient in hospital or in a residential home should be afforded every possibility to be able to perform them as far as possible. Friends or relatives may come in to assist ill or debilitated patients perform these ceremonies. Elderly, confused or demented patients may find comfort in the *Shabbos* traditions and may become disorientated if they are omitted.

During *Shabbos,* orthodox Jews do no *melocha* (that is creative work as defined by Jewish law) nor engage in workaday activities. This includes writing, using the telephone, travelling by car or public transport, switching lights on or off, or using any electrical equipment. They do not handle or even touch money on *Shabbos*. Cooking is also forbidden and all food served on *Shabbos* must be prepared beforehand. Cooked food is kept hot on a hot plate or in an oven from before *Shabbos*.

The prohibition on performing *melocha* is extremely strict and is a concept which is very difficult for non-Jews to understand. The extreme lengths to which orthodox Jews will go to avoid transgressing the *Shabbos* laws should not be derided, no matter how irrational the laws may seem. Wherever possible orthodox Jewish patients will try to avoid having to be in hospital on *Shabbos,* but obviously on many occasions it will be unavoidable. When in hospital on *Shabbos,* Jewish patients may need help with doing things that are forbidden by Jewish law, such as switching lights on or off, or using a lift when using the stairs would not be possible. Even tearing toilet tissue on *Shabbos* is a *melocha*, therefore orthodox Jewish patients will need to bring loose-leaf toilet tissue with them into hospital, if this is not provided. Turning a hot water tap on or off is similarly forbidden and staff may be asked to help run a bath. It may be permitted for the staff in hospital to heat a kosher meal for a patient but not for their relatives or carers. In a residential home where the residents are essentially well, the same rules apply as in a private home and all preparations must be completed before *Shabbos*; thus healthy Jewish residents may not have a meal that has been heated up or cooked on *Shabbos* by a non-Jewish member of staff.

Because carrying items into the street is a *melocha*, patients who are admitted to hospital on *Shabbos*, for example a woman in labour, would not be able to carry their personal effects to or from an ambulance and may well ask the ambulance driver to do this for them, even though the husband is in attendance. This should not cause offence, as it is not intended to demean, but is a necessity because of the strict *Shabbos* laws. Patients discharged from hospital on *Shabbos* day may wish to wait in the building until after nightfall before leaving for home. Similarly, because of the restriction on using motorised transport on *Shabbos*, visitors to hospitalised patients may have had to walk a great distance and might want to stay (after visiting hours) until the end of *Shabbos*, before taking transport home. Some flexibility with the visiting times on Friday afternoons and Saturdays would be appreciated. According to Jewish law, one may not ask another Jew, even a non-observant one, to do a *melocha* on *Shabbos*. Where not essential to the patient's immediate medical care, strictly orthodox patients might not directly ask a non-Jew to do a *melocha* specifically for them, but may hint indirectly. So for instance, if a light has been left on they may indirectly hint that they would like it turned off, such as by saying something to the effect of 'on *Shabbos* strictly orthodox Jews are not allowed to turn lights off', hoping that the message would be understood. Every courtesy should be extended to patients who are very strict about not transgressing the *Shabbos* laws and who may become distressed if not assisted or if forced to break these strict laws, even if the laws may appear to the uninitiated to be irrational or nonsensical.

Writing is a *melocha* and orthodox Jewish patients would normally be unable to sign consent forms on *Shabbos* or *Yom-Tov* unless there is an immediate threat to life. Hospitals in areas with orthodox Jewish patients might come to an arrangement whereby they accept verbal consent (possibly permitting a third party such as the surgeon or ward sister to sign on the patient's behalf) or agree to the patient or next of kin signing retrospectively after the end of *Shabbos*.

Recently, an organisation called *Ezer Umarpeh* (Help and Healing) have established facilities at hospitals in areas serving Jewish communities, in order that relatives, parents and carers might have food, hot drinks and religious requisites available if they need to stay with a patient at the hospital over *Shabbos*; this is especially useful if the patient is actually admitted on *Shabbos*.

Shabbos and life-threatening illness

When, on *Shabbos*, someone's life is in danger it is a *mitzvah* (an absolute requirement) to transgress the *Shabbos* on his behalf; he who acts quickly is praiseworthy; he who asks (and thereby delays life-saving treatment) is a murderer.

Shulchon Oruch Orech Chaim 328: 2

In emergency life-threatening situations, the *Shabbos* laws are set aside and in many cases there may need to be consultation between patients, their families, rabbis and healthcare workers.

Although all *Shabbos* restrictions are set aside where there is any risk to life, most orthodox Jews would wish to try to avoid being in hospital over *Shabbos* or *Yom-Tov* if at all possible. They may therefore be reluctant to schedule non-urgent routine admissions if it would mean being in hospital over *Shabbos* or *Yom-Tov*. Even where this is unavoidable they may be reluctant to undergo non-essential investigations such as blood tests or X-ray examinations on these days. Some orthodox Jewish patients may be reluctant to take non-essential medications on *Shabbos* and when prescribed medication on a long-term basis, they are likely to enquire about the advisability of missing out one day's treatment each week. The application of creams and ointments directly onto the skin on *Shabbos* may present some problems and, where essential, may have to be performed either by a non-Jewish assistant or by indirect application such as via a gauze swab.

Shabbos 1

The Kadouries had waited for 18 months for Natan (aged seven) to be admitted for much needed adenoidectomy and insertion of grommets. The admission letter finally came; surgery was planned for Friday afternoon on 12 January. Being winter, *Shabbos* started at about 4 p.m. They rang their GP asking if he could arrange an alternative admission day, date or time.

Shabbos 2

Sharon was barely aware of her Jewish identity when she started medical school. During the course of her studies she underwent a religious awakening with increasing commitment to religious observance. By the time she qualified, she had started to observe *Shabbos*. She realised that she would not be able to do house jobs that included working on Friday nights or Saturday. Initially, when approached, the dean of the medical school was rather unsympathetic but following a discussion with a local Jewish colleague he was able to appreciate the issues involved. Sharon was paired off with another graduate who wanted to job share and who was happy to let Sharon have *Shabbos* off in exchange for her covering other unsocial hours.

Yom-Tov (festivals)

Introduction

There are several major religious festivals during the course of the Jewish calendar year. As described in relation to the Jewish calendar (p 52), the exact dates of the festivals on the civil (Gregorian) calendar vary from year to year, within a range of about three weeks or so. As with *Shabbos*, these festivals commence before sunset on the preceding day and conclude after nightfall at the end of the festival. On *Yom-Tov*, as on *Shabbos*, most *melocha* is forbidden (with some technical differences). Most of the festivals are in paired days, which in effect is like having two days of *Shabbos* one after the other. (When the festivals fall close to a weekend, then together with *Shabbos* there could be three days in a row when most *melocha* is prohibited.)

Each of the festivals has its own special significance, rituals and customs. There are also special foods associated with the different festivals. Hospital patients or elderly residents in residential homes will derive great comfort from being able to observe and participate in the various rituals and traditions as much as possible.

As with *Shabbos*, the level of observance of the various festivals and their associated rituals varies amongst different Jewish groups. Even those groups who do not keep all the strict restrictions regarding work and *melocha* might still observe some of the customs which mark each festival's special identity. This is especially true of the High Holydays of *Rosh Hashona*

(New Year) and *Yom Kippur* (the Day of Atonement) when even those who are estranged from mainstream Judaism might possibly attend a synagogue service. Again in this section, as with *Shabbos*, I shall describe the festivals and their observance mainly from the orthodox perspective.

Rosh Hashona (New Year)

This generally falls during September. In marked contrast to the civil New Year, it is a relatively solemn occasion. It lasts for two days, which are largely spent in synagogue worship, praying for Divine blessing for the year ahead. One of the special features of *Rosh Hashona* is the blowing of the *shofar* (ceremonial ram's horn) during the synagogue service. Hospital patients or those in residential homes would probably wish to hear the *shofar* being blown. *Rosh Hashona* together with *Yom Kippur* are often referred to as the High Holydays (*Yomim Noraim*, literally, 'days of awe') indicating the solemnity of these days and the time of year in general. Stress levels may be raised and medical consultation rates increased. Many Chassidic men will travel, often abroad, seeking spiritual uplift by praying together with their *rebbe* at this time of the year.

Yom Kippur (the Day of Atonement)

This, the most solemn and holy day in the Jewish calendar, falls ten days after *Rosh Hashona*. It is marked by a 25 hour fast observed by all adults (girls over 12 and boys over 13). The entire day is spent in synagogue worship. The fast of *Yom Kippur* is regarded as being so important and central to Judaism that many Jews who may not otherwise be religiously observant will fast and possibly attend the synagogue sometime during *Yom Kippur*. Fasting is extremely important, but exemptions are available to those too ill or frail to be able to do so. Exemptions would normally only be given in discussion with a rabbi, who may first wish to confer with the patient's medical attendants. Exemptions are often only partial and may involve eating small amounts of food or liquids at specified intervals. The taking of medication may be permitted. Essential medication will always be permitted, but some patients might only agree to take them following discussion with the doctor or rabbi or possibly even both. Elderly patients or those with chronic illnesses, such as diabetics, who have been advised not to fast, may understandably be upset at not being able to fulfil what is a very important aspect of their Judaism, possibly for the first time in their adult lives. It may be necessary for a rabbinical adviser to explain and counsel them to help them come to terms with and to accept this ruling. The rabbi may wish to discuss with the doctors the risks involved. Most patients' drug regimens can be easily adjusted to accommodate the 25 hour fast. Care needs to be taken with insulin dependent diabetics, most of whom can fast if they adjust their insulin dosage to the eating and fasting pattern. Of course there will be those who will be unable to fast and should this present any risk to life, Jewish law would completely forbid fasting. In practice even those diabetics required to eat can do so by partaking of small volumes of food at intervals throughout the day in such a way that technically, in the eyes of Jewish law, may be considered as them nevertheless having fasted. As a rough guide this involves drinking no more than 30 ml of liquid or eating up to 30 g of solids at more than nine-minute intervals. In these circumstances the exact volumes, frequency and nature of the foods ingested may have to be computed and discussed in consultation with a rabbi and physician familiar with the patient, his specific needs and the details of Jewish law.

Yom Kippur

Hannah is an 87 year old resident at an orthodox Jewish nursing home. She is mentally fully alert, but her physical condition is such that her GP told her that in his opinion she should not fast on *Yom Kippur*. Her initial reaction was one of great shock, for fasting on *Yom Kippur* was something that has been central to her Judaism since the age of 12. It was only after a discussion between Hannah, her GP and the home's rabbinical chaplain that Hannah accepted the decision.

Yom Kippur and life-threatening illness

In relation to an invalid (or a woman within seven days of childbirth) fasting on *Yom Kippur*:

> If a doctor (even a non-Jewish one) says that if he/she doesn't eat it might be that their condition might deteriorate we follow the doctor's advice and give them to eat ... It goes without saying that this applies where there is any danger to life; but this also applies even if there is no danger at this point in time but if not

> given to eat now his or her condition might deteriorate later . . .
> Even if the invalid says I don't need to eat, we listen to the doctor
> . . . If the invalid says I need to eat or drink, even if a whole host of
> doctors say he could fast and that fasting will do him no harm,
> we listen to the patient . . . Where one doctor says he should eat
> and another says he can fast we give him to eat . . . For, when it
> comes to matters of food and drink, 'a person is the best judge of
> his own condition' (based on Proverbs 14: 10).
>
> Based on the Laws of *Yom Kippur* in the Code of Jewish Law

Succos (Tabernacles)

The *Succos* (Tabernacles) festival also falls in the autumn, five days after *Yom Kippur*, and is a joyous *Yom-Tov*. During this week-long festival, meals are eaten in a *succah*. A *succah* is a temporary hut-like structure which has an open ceiling covered with leaves and branches. Many orthodox men also sleep in the *succah*. A palm branch (*lulov*) and citron fruit (*esrog*) are waved and shaken ceremonially during synagogue worship. Ill patients are generally excused from eating in a *succah* but they may have a *lulov* brought to them so as to enable them to perform that ceremony. On the first two and last two days *melochoh* (work) is forbidden (similar to on *Shabbos*), but the interim days (*Chol Hamoed*), although still part of the festival, are less restrictive and are often spent as a time of family holiday and outings. On these interim days, orthodox and Chassidic patients continue to wear their festive *Shabbos* clothes throughout the day, possibly even when going to the surgery or visiting hospitals.

Pesach (Passover)

This festival falls in the spring (and often coincides with Easter) and commemorates the Jews' exodus from Egypt. Like *Succos*, it is also a week-long festival with *Chol Hamoed* between the first two and last two days. The most significant feature of this festival is the very strict prohibition on the eating of *chometz* foods. *Chometz* is food which is made of, or which contains in any form, any leaven or risen flour. *Matzoh* (unleavened crackers) are eaten instead of bread during the week of *Pesach*. On the first two nights of *Pesach*, families gather together for the *seder* ceremony, during which the story of the exodus from Egypt is read and discussed and at which a festive meal is served. The *seder* ritual includes not only the eating of *matzoh* but also the ceremonial drinking of four cups of wine and the eating of *morror* (bitter herbs).

The prohibition on eating (and possessing) *chometz* on *Pesach* is extremely strict and orthodox Jews will go to great lengths to ensure that there is no trace of *chometz* in their possession during the week of *Pesach*. The house is cleaned from top to bottom and a ritual search is made on the eve of *Pesach* to remove all traces of *chometz* from the home and Jewish owned workplaces. A separate set of kitchen utensils is used for *Pesach* and the normally strict dietary laws take on an added dimension. This may present problems relating to medicines which contain wheat starch or its derivatives, as these are *chometz*. Patients may enquire about suitable substitutes to use during the week of *Pesach*. The laws prohibiting *chometz* and their use in medicines are complex and medical staff may be contacted by rabbis to discuss individual patients' requirements over *Pesach*. Practices vary between Jews of different traditions and some groups additionally restrict the use of foodstuffs containing pulses (podded vegetables) including maize. However even those who do not use pulses or maize would generally allow them to be taken in medications for invalids. Maize starch is a common constituent of many tablets, and infant formulas often contain a soya bean base. Each year, shortly before *Pesach*, the *Beis Din* (rabbinic administrative organisation) produces a list containing details of medications and other preparations suitable for *Pesach* which is published in the Jewish press and in *Hakohol* in the weeks before *Pesach* (*see* Bibliography). This is one time when it may be necessary to prescribe medications by brand name rather than generically. Patients may request a fresh supply of medication for *Pesach* use, in case their regular supply has become 'contaminated' such as when medication has been taken at mealtimes or the containers placed on the breakfast table.

Pesach

In early April Mrs Feiner visited her GP complaining of persistent tiredness, insomnia and restlessness. Physical examination revealed no abnormalities and all investigations were normal. When reviewed some weeks later her symptoms had almost gone and she felt much better. When she re-presented the following spring complaining of almost identical symptoms, her GP recalled reading an article about stress-related symptoms occurring in Jewish housewives around the *Pesach* festival. *Pesach* preparations involved Mrs Feiner in a considerable amount of work and this, together with the strained relations between her and her mother-in-law (who always arrived for her annual *Pesach* visit a week before the festival 'so as to help'), easily accounted for the annual recurrence of her symptoms. Referral to a Jewish counsellor, who understood the pressures herself, resulted in helping Mrs Feiner to plan and prioritise her *Pesach* preparations in an efficient way and a diplomatic suggestion via her husband resulted in a rearrangement of the mother-in-law's stay to have her arriving only just the day before *Pesach* but staying for the week afterwards instead. Next spring her GP monitored her closely and she coped much better.

***Pesach* and life-threatening illness**

A patient who has been warned by the physician not to eat *matzoh* or *morror* (bitter herbs) or wine on the *seder* night, as this may endanger his life, but who nevertheless insists on doing so, has not only not performed a *mitzvah*, but is actually guilty of a serious offence.

Shulchon Oruch Orech Chaim

Shavuos (Pentecost)

Shavuos (Pentecost) is a two-day festival which falls six weeks after the end of *Pesach* (in the early summer). It commemorates the giving of the Ten Commandments on Mount Sinai and the time when Moses received the *Torah*, the sacred book on which all the teachings of Judaism are based.

Other festivals

The Jewish calendar also has some minor festivals on which normal workaday activities are permitted, although most orthodox Jews might try and take the day, or part of it, off work so as to be with their families, for what are essentially family occasions.

Chanukah

This festival (the Festival of Lights) falls in December and lasts for a week. It celebrates the victory of the Jews over the occupation of the Holy Land,

during the second Temple period, by Hellenistic forces whose culture threa-
tened to extinguish Judaism. *Chanukah* commemorates both the victory
over the occupying Greek army and the subsequent rededication of the
Temple with the miraculous re-lighting of the *menorah* (the seven branched
olive oil burning candelabrum which has become a well-recognised symbol
of Judaism). Each evening at dusk, there is a lighting ceremony when a
Chanukah menorah also known as a *chanukiya* (an eight branched candelabrum containing either olive oil with wicks or candles) is lit. On the first
evening a single light is lit and this increases nightly until eight are lit
on the last night. This is generally a happy family occasion, accompanied
by the eating of traditional sweetmeats (such as doughnuts and fried pan-
cakes) which are made with oily ingredients reflecting the celebration of
the lighting of the *menorah*.

Purim

This is a one-day festival which falls in the spring. It is a happy and joyous
occasion celebrating the miraculous thwarting of a plot to destroy the
Jewish people at the time of Queen Esther during the period of the exile in
Persia following the destruction of the first Temple. There are synagogue
services during which the story of *Purim* is read, as well as celebratory
meals. *Purim* is a time to relax, let one's hair down and party! *Purim* is possibly the one occasion where one might encounter an orthodox Jew in a
less than sober state! Children (and some adults) dress up in fancy dress.
Gifts of food are exchanged between family and friends and everyone has a
great time.

Fast days

Apart from *Yom Kippur* there are several other fasts. The most important of
these is *Tisha B'av* (the ninth day of the month of Av) which falls in midsummer and commemorates the destruction of both Temples in Jerusalem. It is
a 25 hour fast and it is normally observed almost as strictly as *Yom Kippur*,
except that *melocha* (work) is permitted. The rules on exemption from fasting are similar (but somewhat more lenient) to those of *Yom Kippur*. It is a
solemn day, on which people are supposed to dwell on the serious calami-
ties that befell the Jewish people at the time of the destruction of the Temples, as well as the many tragedies that have befallen the Jewish people over
the millennia ever since. Because it is a day of public mourning people

follow the traditional customs of mourning (*see* p 152). They do not wear leather footwear, do not greet each other and until midday only sit on low chairs or on the ground as a sign of mourning.

There are four other (minor) fast days during which eating is forbidden, but only during the hours of daylight. The rules for exemptions on these fast days are rather more lenient, especially for ill patients and pregnant or nursing women.

On fasting

He who fasts and is able to tolerate the fast is called holy; but if not able, being neither healthy nor strong, then he would be called a sinner.

Shulchon Oruch Orech Chaim 571

Clinical workload and the Jewish calendar

Practitioners working in areas with sizeable Jewish populations may find that they have a seasonal variation in their workload corresponding to significant dates in the Jewish calendar. The main pressure is felt around the times of the major festivals particularly around September time when a number of the festivals occur within the space of just over three weeks, and in spring when *Pesach* is celebrated. Because *melocha* is prohibited on *Yom-Tov* as well as *Shabbos* there may be several days in a row when patients will not attend for routine consultations, causing a rush beforehand and a build up afterwards. When Easter and *Pesach* coincide, Bank Holiday closures may compound these workload pressures, with some practices having to make special arrangements for additional opening hours.

In addition, because the festivals are family occasions, there is often a great deal of travel around the festival times, with an associated increase in anxiety levels and consultation rates. *Pesach* particularly is a time when large extended families get together and there is a clear association with an increase in relationship and psycho-social problems. *Pesach* preparations involve a great deal of physical work leading to an increase in consultation for physical and psychological exhaustion. Jewish colleges of further education (*yeshivos* and seminaries) have their main holidays to coincide with the major festivals, again leading to an increased consultation rate. These factors can cause quite a disruption to appointment systems and general practices with a high proportion of Jewish patients, particularly orthodox ones, will need to anticipate this consultation pattern to accommodate patients' needs and service provision.

Because *Shabbos* starts before sunset on Friday and continues until after dark on Saturday, *Shabbos* observant patients will not make appointments for Friday afternoons especially in the winter months, leading to an increase in general practice consultations on Friday mornings and an excess of late night out-of-hours calls on summer Saturday nights. Where patients receive hospital out-patient appointments for Friday afternoon, they may request being referred to an alternative clinic, which may be difficult in an area where the only clinic in a particular speciality is held on Friday afternoons. Similarly, patients may not want to be admitted for day-case surgery or investigations on winter Fridays when they would have to travel home after *Shabbos* has commenced. Obviously the same applies for non-emergency admissions on Saturday.

Conclusion

Shabbos and the various festivals, and the restrictions and rituals associated with them, are central to the Jewish way of life. For those who adhere strictly to these observances, they are of major importance, and they will not be put aside lightly. Even if it is hard for healthcare professionals to understand what might seem to be strange or illogical rules and restrictions, patients' beliefs and practices should be respected and accommodated as far as possible.

Summary

- Observance of *Shabbos* (the Sabbath) is one of the fundamentals of Jewish belief; the strictly orthodox observe its laws meticulously.
- *Shabbos* and the festivals run from sunset until nightfall the next day.
- The *Shabbos* laws are quite complex and difficult to understand logically but the details are important to observant Jews.
- All restrictions are set aside where there is real risk to life.
- The *Yom Kippur* fast is an important part of Jewish practice and, even when permitted to, invalids might be reluctant to eat.
- In areas with large Jewish populations, workload might vary with the Jewish calendar.

- The observance of *Shabbos*, the festivals and associated rituals are important to the well-being and comfort of patients in hospitals and residential homes.

Shabbos (Sabbath) in a nutshell

Salient features
- Pivotal point and highlight of the Jewish week.
- A day of rest both physical and spiritual.
- A family day with family meals and traditional dishes.
- *Shabbos* lasts from sunset on Friday to after nightfall on Saturday.
- Starts with candle lighting and ends with *havdolah* ceremonies.
- The day is spent in prayer, study and rest.
- Synagogue services on Friday evening and Saturday morning and afternoon.
- There are restrictions on the type of *melocha* (activities) that one may do on *Shabbos*.
- These prohibitions are strictly observed by the orthodox.
- *Shabbos* restrictions may only be set aside in life-threatening circumstances.

Some examples of activities restricted on *Shabbos*
- Travel by motorised vehicle.
- Carrying objects in an open public place (e.g. street).
- Using a lift.
- Switching on or off a light (including opening a fridge with an automatic light).
- Tearing paper.
- Writing.
- Using a telephone.
- Cooking.
- Turning a hot water tap on or off.
- Handling money.
- Using any electrical equipment (unless started before *Shabbos*, when it may continue to be used, e.g. lights, heating).

Further reading

Cohen SB (1992) *The Shabbos Kitchen*. Artscroll, New York.
Ganzfried S (1961) *Kitzur Sulchan Aruch: code of Jewish law* (trans H Goldin). Hebrew Publishing Co, New York.

Grunfeld I (1986) *The Shabbos: a guide to its understanding and observance*. Feldheim, Jerusalem/New York.

Hakohol. The annual magazine of The Union of Orthodox Hebrew Congregations (140 Stamford Hill, London N16 6QT) published before Passover and containing a list of kosher/non-kosher medication and preparations suitable for Passover.

Hirsch SR (1962) *Horeb: a philosophy of Jewish laws and observances* (trans I Grunfeld). Soncino Press, New York.

Katz M (1982) *Menucha v'Simcha: a guide to the basic laws of Shabbos and Yom Tov*. Feldheim, New York.

Pick E (1975) *Guide to Shabbos Observance*. Targum Press, Southfield, MI.

Rosner F and Tendler MD (1997) *Practical Medical Halacha*. Aronson, New Jersey.

Wagschal S (1993) *Care of Children on Shabbos and Festivals*. Feldheim, New York.

Wagschal S (1993) *The Practical Guide to Childbirth on Shabbos and Yom Tov*. Feldheim, New York.

CHAPTER 10

Kashrus (the dietary laws) and the Jewish patient

The *Torah* requires a Jew to think before eating

For not by bread alone does man live rather through the word of God does man live.

Deuteronomy 8: 3

A *Kashrus*-observing Jew is brought face-to-face with his belief in the Almighty every time he lifts his fork to his mouth or puts a box of cereal in his shopping cart. To achieve that complete sense of connectedness to the Holy, an extra set of dishes seems a small price to pay.[1]

Introduction

One of the best known characteristics of Judaism is the observance of a kosher diet. The word kosher means 'fit (to eat)' and food that is forbidden is commonly known as *treifah* (literally the word means 'torn'; it originally referred to animals killed other than in the kosher manner; it is now used colloquially to refer to any food that is not kosher.) As with all aspects of Jewish religious laws there is a wide spectrum in observance of *Kashrus* (the kosher rules), with those at one extreme adhering rigorously to the minutiae of the rules, whereas those at the other extreme may dispense with and disregard all of the restrictions. In between, there are those who

---

[1] *See* Robinson in the Bibliography at the end of the book.

are selective in their observances, perhaps keeping what they consider to be the spirit of *Kashrus* without becoming what they feel to be fanatically obsessed with what to them seem to be irrelevant details. There is a large group of Jews who keep the rudiments of *Kashrus* in their own kitchens at home, but might eat in non-kosher (possibly vegetarian) restaurants when eating out.

There are a number of practical implications of the kosher laws relating to the care of Jewish patients. These are addressed in this chapter, which opens with an outline of the essential laws of the kosher diet (*Kashrus*) and thus will provide healthcare professionals caring for patients who observe these laws details of where these may impinge on patient care.

The kosher dietary laws

Orthodox Jews adhere strictly to a kosher diet, that is a diet which complies with all the details of the Jewish dietary laws. Strictly orthodox Jews regard observing *Kashrus* (the kosher laws) as being an extremely important fundamental of Jewish practice and they will observe *Kashrus* with great meticulousness. *Kashrus* observance is considered to be a form of holiness and self-discipline.

Briefly, the main and most basic rules of *Kashrus* can be summarised as follows.

- Only certain species of animal or fowl are permitted. These must be slaughtered and prepared in a very specific way before they can be eaten. Before it can be cooked, meat must be soaked and salted in a precise way, to remove as much blood as possible. Therefore, not only must these products be purchased in a kosher shop, but to be acceptable they must also be prepared and cooked in an entirely kosher kitchen.
- Kosher food may only be prepared or processed with utensils which have never previously been used for *treifah* (non-kosher) foodstuffs. Preparing or even just re-heating in *treifah* cookware may render kosher food *treifah*.
- Meat and dairy produce, or foods containing them, must not be prepared, cooked or eaten together. They must also be kept completely apart in the kitchen, to the extent that separate utensils are required to be used for meat and dairy dishes. A strictly kosher kitchen will have two of everything – two sets of pots and pans, crockery, cutlery and kitchen utensils, and if possible two sinks and draining boards, one to be used for meat foods and the other for dairy foods. If space is at a

premium, the housewife will cover the work surfaces when changing from preparing meat to meals containing dairy products and vice versa. Meat and dairy dishes are not served at the same meal, and after eating a meat meal, a minimum period of three hours must elapse before dairy food may be taken (many people wait for up to six hours before consuming dairy products after a meat meal). Invalids may be given rabbinical dispensation to reduce this time interval. In general the interval after which meat foods can be consumed following dairy foods is very much shorter, the exact time depending on individual custom or tradition.

- Foods such as fish, fruit or vegetables, which contain nothing of meat nor dairy origin, are known as *parev* (neutral). These foods can be consumed with either a meat or dairy meal provided, of course, that they have not previously been cooked together with meat or dairy foods when they take on the characteristics of whatever they were cooked with, so that, for example, potatoes cooked with butter would be regarded as a dairy food and could not be eaten with a meal containing meat.

- All fruits and vegetables are kosher, but it is strictly forbidden to eat insects, no matter how tiny, dead or alive. Many people will be very particular to ensure that fruits and vegetables are completely free of infestation. Certain green products, such as brussel sprouts, are generally avoided, as it is extremely difficult to ensure that they are absolutely free of infestation.

- As with meat, only certain species of fish may be eaten. Seafood such as eels, crabs and shellfish are *treifah*. Fish is usually only purchased from a kosher fishmonger but where this is not possible fish may be bought anywhere as long as the species is clearly recognisable.

- Only the milk of kosher species of animal may be consumed. Milk used by orthodox Jews is milked and bottled under the supervision of a *Kashrus* authority. Orthodox Jews will usually not drink unsupervised milk. However invalids may be given rabbinical dispensation to drink unsupervised milk. The rennet used in the manufacture of cheese must itself be kosher.

- The ingredients of all drinks and beverages must also be kosher. This does not present much problem for tea or coffee (although the rules for milk apply as above). Most soft or fruit drinks and most alcoholic drinks are permitted. However, wine and grape juice and their derivatives are an exception and may only be drunk if produced under the supervision of a *Kashrus* authority and usually only if the seal containing the *hechsher* (*see* next section) is intact.

- All mineral products and chemicals derived from them are kosher.

- Some commonly used food or drink additives, particularly colourings, stabilisers and emulsifiers, may be derived from non-kosher sources and would thus be forbidden.

Kosher food products

The observance of the laws of *Kashrus* is extremely important and there are a number of rabbinical authorities who supervise the manufacture of kosher foodstuffs and who grant licences to butchers, restaurants and food manufacturers. Such a licence is called a *hechsher* and is normally printed on the wrapping or the packaging of supervised foods. It is often present in the form of a small inconspicuous logo, identifying the particular rabbinical authority granting the licence.

Many orthodox groups will only eat manufactured foods that have a *hechsher*, whilst some less meticulous individuals may eat certain unsupervised products, but which are known never to contain non-kosher ingredients. Yet other groups will be highly specific and will only use products given a *hechsher* by a certain rabbinical authority and will not use products supervised by other authorities. These variations and preferences may confuse healthcare workers, particularly those working with hospital in-patients where certain foods may be acceptable to one patient, yet not to another. These variations should be respected as they may be quite important to the individual, who may have difficulty in explaining his particular preferences.

Healthcare professionals should understand how important and fundamental the observance of *Kashrus* is to many Jewish individuals, particularly those of the orthodox community. Many orthodox Jews may not even accept a cup of tea prepared in a non-kosher kitchen and no offence should be taken when this is refused; or similarly, no offence is intended when a child is stopped by a parent from accepting a sweet that might be offered, say, by a nurse after an injection has been given. (A supply of kosher (sugar-free) sweets clearly labelled with a *hechsher*, obtainable from most kosher food shops, might be appreciated!)

Kashrus and health

The nutritional state of the orthodox Jewish community is generally very good. In many areas, kosher 'meals on wheels' are available for the elderly or infirm and can be arranged through the local Social Services department. For hospital in-patients, strictly kosher meals are available through the Hospital Kosher Meals Service. These meals are supplied to the hospital in pre-packed double sealed containers and are kept frozen in the hospital kitchen freezers. When requested by an orthodox Jewish patient, the meal is defrosted and reheated in an oven or microwave whilst still in the double sealed container. The meal is then delivered to the patient with the wrapping and seals intact; this is important as a strictly kosher observant patient might not eat a meal that has been unwrapped, however slightly.

Generally speaking, all food or dietary additives or indeed anything intended to be swallowed, when supplied for healthy individuals, must contain only kosher ingredients (for example milk formula and vitamin supplements for healthy babies).

When possible, medication should not contain any non-kosher ingredients. It is not commonly realised that many medicines contain ingredients that are not kosher and in many circumstances these may present problems for members of the orthodox Jewish community.

The following problem ingredients may be encountered, as they or their derivatives are present in a large range of medication.

- **Glycerine.** A sweet-tasting liquid added to many medications (especially children's medicines) to make them palatable. It may be derived from animal (usually non-kosher) or vegetable (usually kosher) sources. Patients might request a doctor to prescribe a product where the source is known to be of vegetable origin, for example Medinol® instead of Calpol®, when a children's paracetamol suspension is required.
- **Lactose.** A sweet-tasting sugar derived from milk as a by-product of the cheese making process, which is present in a wide range of tablets as a bulking agent. It is also used to make chewable and suckable tablets more palatable. Because it is a milk derivative, it presents problems with respect to the laws of milk and meat and also with respect to the requirements for the supervision of milk (*see* pp 116–17).
- **Gelatine.** A tasteless substance used in the manufacture of many capsules and sometimes used in powder form in tablets. It is usually of animal origin (although synthetic sources do exist).

In addition, the *Pesach* (Passover) festival presents other problems relating to medicines. During the week of *Pesach*, Jews are strictly forbidden to eat any leavened foods (that is, food containing flour that has risen). Medicines containing wheat starch or any of its derivatives will present problems prior to and during the week of *Pesach*, as discussed in more detail previously (*see* p 107).

The laws governing products derived from non-kosher substances are complex, but there are many situations where medications containing these ingredients might be permitted. Individual patients may wish to discuss specific cases with a rabbinical authority before using certain medications.

In general, the laws of *Kashrus* apply only to foods or substances that are ingested by mouth. Parenteral drugs (injectable or rectal preparations) are usually acceptable whatever their origin, so for example insulin of pork or beef origin would be totally acceptable. There are no restrictions on the parenteral use of blood products and blood transfusions (and donation) are unreservedly permitted. Hospitals in areas with orthodox Jewish patients are becoming increasingly aware of the need to keep stocks of kosher medicines.

A very high proportion of infants are breast fed, but where a formula substitute is required, this should be one known to contain no non-kosher ingredients. There are now several baby milk formulas available made under supervision and which have a *hechsher* symbol.

Jewish law makes it clear that in life-threatening situations, the laws of *Kashrus* (and *Shabbos* and indeed most other laws) are set aside. Except in the most critical circumstances this should only be done with rabbinical guidance.

Conclusion

Observing *Kashrus* is central to the practice of Judaism and every consideration must be given to those patients to whom these laws are important, to help them observe them even when unwell.

Kosher medication

When Miriam was admitted to hospital following a febrile convulsion, her parents asked whether the hospital stocked brands of paracetamol and ibuprofen that were known not to contain non-kosher ingredients. The pharmacist consulted the latest list of kosher medication and was quickly able to reassure them that the brands supplied by the hospital pharmacy were indeed suitable.

Summary ·

- An important fundamental of Judaism is that all food that is eaten must be kosher, that is in accordance with the Jewish dietary laws.
- Only certain species of animal, fowl and fish are permitted and these must be slaughtered and prepared in a specific way.

- Dairy and meat products may never be cooked or eaten together.
- Kosher food must be cooked in utensils used exclusively for kosher food.
- Oral medications must be kosher.
- The kosher laws may be set aside where there is serious risk to life.

The essentials of *Kashrus* (kosher laws)

- Only certain species of animal or fowl are kosher (permitted); these must be slaughtered and prepared in a very specific way.
- Kosher food may only be prepared or processed with utensils used exclusively for kosher food.
- Meat (or poultry) products and dairy produce, or foods containing them, must not be prepared, cooked or eaten together.
- Only certain species of fish may be eaten.
- Only the milk of kosher species is permitted.
- All fruits and vegetables are kosher (but not the insects in or on them).
- All mineral products and chemicals derived from them are kosher.
- The individual ingredients of all foods, including additives such as colourings, stabilisers and emulsifiers, must also be kosher.
- Certain products may only be eaten if manufactured under supervision.

Further reading

Adler A and Spiro MD (1986) *Medicines and Kashrus: a practical guide to the Kashrus of medicines*. Gateshead. Published privately. Regular updates published in *Hakohol*, see below.

Cohen SB (1992) *The Shabbos Kitchen*. Artscroll, New York.

Forst B (1993) *The Laws of Kashrus: a comprehensive exposition of their underlying concepts and applications*. Artscroll, New York.

Ganzfried S (1961) *Kitzur Sulchan Aruch: code of Jewish law* (trans H Goldin). Hebrew Publishing Co, New York.

Grunfeld I (1989) *The Jewish Dietary Laws*. Soncino Press, London, Jerusalem & New York.

Hakohol. The annual magazine of The Union of Orthodox Hebrew Congregations (140 Stamford Hill, London N16 6QT) published before Passover and containing a list of kosher/non-kosher medication and preparations suitable for Passover.

Hirsch SR (1962) *Horeb: a philosophy of Jewish laws and observances* (trans I Grunfeld). Soncino Press, New York.

Wagschal S (1997) *The Practical Guide to Kashruth*. Feldheim, New York.

CHAPTER 11

Women's health

Marriage, sex and related topics

God said, 'It is not good for man to be alone; I will create a mate for him . . .
Therefore a man shall leave his father and mother and be united with his wife
and they shall become one flesh'.

Genesis 2: 18, 24

God blessed them and said to them, 'be fertile and become many and fill the
world'.

Genesis 1: 28

Introduction

In this area, more than in any other, a sensitive approach is required in
trying to understand problems from the Jewish patients' perspective. Traditional Jewish practices, ideas, attitudes and concepts are in very many
cases so different from contemporary understanding and mores that those
caring for Jewish patients, particularly orthodox ones, may have considerable difficulty appreciating concepts that they may find conflicting with
their own values and training.

As ever, there is a very wide spectrum of religious practice and observance and many of the laws and customs described in this chapter will not
be observed by all Jews. Nevertheless, I shall describe orthodox practice,
which will give the reader a picture of observances at one end of the spectrum. He/she will then be able to extrapolate from these descriptions
models for other Jews whose observances may be limited to some or few of
the practices described here.

Marriage

The strictly orthodox lifestyle does not encourage unmarried people to mix with members of the opposite sex. In Chassidic and many orthodox communities the sexes are segregated from an early age; even nursery schools are single sex. Chassidic couples tend to marry at a relatively young age, the girls at about 18 and the boys at 20 or so. Other orthodox groups also marry young but perhaps a few years later. Marriages are not arranged as such, but couples are usually brought together through arranged introductions (a *shidduch* arranged by a *shadchan*). The decision of whether to marry is entirely up to the young couple themselves; indeed Jewish law does not permit marriages between unwilling parties. According to Jewish law, both parties must be Jewish in order to marry.

In other less restrictive Jewish groups, couples might meet and date in a much more open and conventional way. All orthodox groups only recognise marriages where both parties are Jewish and consider marriages between Jewish and non-Jewish couples as being a major disaster, bringing considerable shame upon the family. 'Marrying out', as it is known, is seen by some as being the ultimate rejection of all that Judaism stands for, and as an irreversible break in the long chain of Jewish tradition going back to the times of Moses. Because Jewishness is transferred through the mother (*see* p 12) children born of a union between a Jewess and a non-Jew would still be regarded by Jewish law as being fully Jewish. On the other hand, where only the father is Jewish the child would not be considered Jewish. Some progressive groups by contrast, whilst not necessarily condoning it, have a much more relaxed and lenient approach to mixed marriages. Liberals regard a child of a mixed marriage as being Jewish if the parents bring it up as a Jew, dispensing with any formal conversion. They may convert the non-Jewish spouse to Judaism for the purposes of marriage and might similarly convert any offspring. Orthodox rabbinic courts will generally not convert someone to Judaism specifically for the reason of marriage, and reject the Reform practice of arranging conversions for this purpose, recognising neither the conversion nor the marriage.

Although Jewish law does allow for divorce, the divorce rate is still comparatively low in most Jewish groups, particularly in orthodox circles, and most marriages appear happy. The low divorce rate is possibly due, in some part at least, to the fact that Judaism revolves so strongly around a family culture and couples will often attempt to work out their problems and differences possibly over a period of time often with the support of counsellors, family and rabbis, rather than opt for an early break-up. Children are brought up in an atmosphere where they see a commitment to marriage and family relationships, and this sense of commitment is still passed on from generation to generation. Domestic violence involving physical or psychological abuse (or child abuse) is rarely encountered within the orthodox Jewish community. Where problems do arise within a marriage, couples are quite likely to seek help and advice from a rabbi or close relative and there are good facilities within the Jewish community, including the orthodox community, for marriage guidance (and other) counselling.

Traditionally the wedding ceremony takes place out of doors, a practice still observed by many Jews, especially the strictly orthodox. Indoor weddings especially in synagogues have now become the norm in most other Jewish groups. Married women wear wedding rings, most men do not. Orthodox Jewish women start to cover their hair from the time of the wedding. In addition to wearing the traditional *bekeshe* (shiny long black jacket), Chassidic men start to wear the *shtreimel* (round fur hat) on *Shabbos* and festivals only after they are married.

Although young couples may get considerable social support from their extended families, they are nevertheless encouraged to live independent lives so that even where a young couple live quite close to their parents (as many do) they would have their own accommodation.

Sexual relations

Sexual matters are regarded as a very private matter and would not be discussed freely. Sexual intercourse within marriage is viewed as a positive, joyous and pleasurable act for its own sake, not just for procreation. In Jewish law a husband is obliged to ensure that his wife enjoys sexual fulfilment, and Judaism is probably unique in giving priority to the woman's sexual needs over the man's; a man has conjugal responsibilities towards his wife, whereas she has conjugal rights. Thus Jewish law forbids a man to force himself on his wife, whereas the woman is encouraged to initiate sexual intimacy.

Mutual love and respect of husband and wife

The mutual love and admiration of husband and wife for each other are beautifully depicted by Maimonides as follows:

> The Sages have ordained that a man should honour his wife more than his own self, and love her as himself; that if he has money, he should increase his generosity to her according to his wealth; that he should not cast undue fear upon her; and that his discourse with her should be gentle – that he should be prone neither to melancholy nor to anger.

They have likewise ordained that the wife should honour her husband exceedingly and hold him in awe, that she should arrange all her affairs according to his instructions, and that he should be in her eyes as if he were a prince or a king; while she behaves according to his heart's desire, and keeps away from anything that is hateful to him. This is the way of the daughters and sons of Israel who are holy and pure in their mating, and in these ways will their life together be seemly and praiseworthy.

Maimonides, *Mishne Torah*, Book of Women's Matters, Marriage
15: 19, 20

Most orthodox Jewish schools do not provide sex education, but prior to marriage, individual guidance is given on a private one-to-one basis by an experienced marriage tutor of the same sex. Where appropriate, and only then, healthcare workers should approach the subject cautiously and in a respectful manner. Unsolicited advice, such as on contraception, given by health visitors and midwives, may result in alienation of clients or patients. Tact is required to give clients or patients the opportunity to discuss these subjects where appropriate. The names of parts of the body are likely to be unfamiliar to many of those brought up in a strictly orthodox environment.

Intercourse is forbidden during menstruation or any uterine bleeding (*niddah*) and for seven days thereafter. Seven days after bleeding has ceased, the woman goes to the *mikveh* (ritual bath), following which intercourse is again permitted. If possible, routine gynaecological procedures should be deferred until the next period or just after bleeding has ceased. It is not uncommon for an orthodox Jewish woman to consult a doctor or nurse in order to determine the source of vaginal blood loss, so as to ascertain whether the bleeding is uterine in origin (*niddah*) or whether it is due to local irritation such as from thrush (and therefore not *niddah*). Following any gynaecological examination, women may enquire whether there has been any contact bleeding, even if only a small amount. During the time when a woman is *niddah*, all forms of physical contact between husband and wife are forbidden. Couples will not hand objects directly to each other, but they will put things down for the other to pick up. As previously mentioned, some Chassidic people will never directly hand an object to any member of the opposite sex. During the time that the wife is *niddah* they will also sleep in separate beds.

The women's immersion in the *mikveh* is performed for ritual, not for hygiene purposes. Indeed she must be completely clean beforehand, and therefore immersion in the *mikveh* is preceded by a wash and soak in a bath. In order for the immersion to be valid, it is essential that all parts of the body come into direct contact with the *mikveh* water. Wound dressings, skin sutures, some prostheses or even temporary dental fillings may invalidate the immersion by preventing the water coming into contact with the whole body, forming a *chatzitzah* (a barrier or intervening substance). Patients may request that non-essential minor surgery or dental treatment is arranged so as not to interfere with the timing of their visit to the *mikveh*, and where possible this request should be accommodated. The technical rules of what constitutes a *chatzitzah* are quite complex and occasionally a rabbi might need to be consulted for a ruling. He in turn may wish to discuss this with the doctor before reaching a decision.

Orthodox Jews are very strict in their observance of these laws (known as the Laws of Family Purity) and although they may seem hard for non-Jews to understand, respect and consideration will be greatly appreciated. There may be occasions when a couple might consult a rabbi about these intimate matters and he in turn may wish to discuss them with the couple's medical practitioner. Less orthodox couples may be less rigorous in observing the *niddah* laws, some being selective as to the degree of detail they observe. It is sensible not to make assumptions as to the level of observance of a particular Jewish couple, especially as some groups who are not too meticulous about keeping other aspects of Judaism may be quite particular about observing various aspects of these laws. This is particularly true of some Sephardi groups.

The *niddah* laws have some implications for patient management in a number of clinical areas. Women may occasionally request medication (such as norethisterone) in order to defer their periods, particularly at holiday times, either so as to ensure that they do not have a period whilst on holiday, or if they are travelling to places where they do not have access to a *mikveh*. Similarly, doctors may be requested to arrange menstrual manipulation for a bride before her wedding. Orthodox Jewish menopausal women requesting treatment for climacteric symptoms may be reluctant to take any form of hormone replacement therapy (HRT) which would necessitate re-commencement of menstruation.

There may be occasions where a women has some vaginal blood loss, possibly even only a small amount of spotting or light intramenstrual bleeding, and she may consult her doctor requesting an examination to ascertain the source of the bleeding, wanting to know if it is uterine in origin or if it could be attributed to another cause such as vaginal thrush or cervical ectropion. Although this distinction may be of little clinical significance it may be important for the patient to know so as to ascertain whether the bleeding constitutes *niddah* bleeding or not; not knowing can cause considerable distress and strain. Sometimes there may be a degree of urgency in finding an answer, perhaps where the blood stain or spotting is found close to the time of her immersion in the *mikveh*. Practitioners practising in areas where there are a significant number of women who observe the *niddah* laws may find that they are requested to deal with these questions at short notice, especially where a woman has been asked by her rabbi to get an answer. Occasionally a woman may present with mid-cycle spotting associated with the oestrogen dip that occurs prior to ovulation, which although of little clinical significance can be quite problematic for an orthodox Jewish woman as it can prevent her having intercourse and could be a cause for infertility. A small dose of oestrogen supplement given for a few days before the spotting is anticipated can prevent the spotting without suppressing ovulation. Similarly, for a woman with a short cycle who ovulates before she has been to the *mikveh*, a short course of oestrogen given early in the cycle, at a dose sufficient to delay ovulation, but without suppressing it, can be used. Pre-menstrual staining due to luteal phase insufficiency can be treated with progesterone supplement. There are further clinical implications of the *niddah* laws which are of relevance to childbirth and infertility treatment; these are discussed in the relevant sections below. Some rabbis have built up an expertise and are well informed on gynaecological matters and there may be occasions when a couple might consult such an expert when confronted with a specific problem. Perhaps one of Judaism's most striking paradoxes is the dual requirement for women to be meticulously modest in dress and disposition, and yet simultaneously open and specific when approaching a rabbi or doctor with an intimate question about their menstrual cycle, irregular bleeding and other issues relating to the Laws of Family Purity.

Spotting

Dalia's baby was some ten weeks old when she consulted her GP because of persistent vaginal bleeding, requesting a referral for a gynaecological opinion. The GP took a detailed history and realised that what Dalia was describing was the small amounts of staining found when she examined herself to see if all cervical bleeding had ceased following the birth so that she could attend the *mikveh* (ritual bath) and resume marital intimacy with her husband. Each time she inspected the cloth she used for self examination she found a tiny stain of fresh blood on it. Her rabbi had advised that she consult her GP 'to be checked out'. Visualisation of the cervix using a speculum showed some cervical ectropion, which her GP explained caused contact bleeding, but which was of no pathological significance. However, because it was clearly causing Dalia problems, the GP treated the ectropion by painting the cervix with topical silver nitrate and within a few days the bleeding had stopped.

Extramarital sex and sexual variation

Orthodox Jews are strictly monogamous, and extramarital (including premarital) sexual relations are absolutely forbidden. Homosexuality, bestiality, incest and masturbation (by males) are regarded as sins transgressing biblical prohibitions. Homosexual relationships are forbidden, but this negative attitude is nevertheless tempered with considerable compassion towards homosexuals and unless openly practising they are generally fully accepted in the community. Where homosexual relationships do occur, especially within the orthodox community, they will usually be conducted with utmost secrecy. Recent studies suggesting that homosexuality may be genetically determined do not affect the underlying biblical prohibition. Although masturbation (other than when required for medical reasons) is forbidden as it involves 'wantonly destroying seed', intercourse between a married couple is permitted (except where the wife is *niddah*, *see* p 126) even where conception is not possible (e.g. where the couple is infertile, post-menopausal or where contraception is used).

Extreme sensitivity and assurance of confidentiality is required when dealing with issues of sexuality and sexual variation in orthodox Jewish individuals. Less orthodox groups have a more liberal approach to homosexuality and sexual relationships outside marriage in general, but all Jewish groups believe that a stable family is the basis for nurturing children and enabling a family to continue the Jewish tradition and line. Sexually transmitted diseases (although not unheard of) are relatively rare amongst orthodox patients, as is HIV infection and AIDS.

Contraception

The family is central to the Jewish way of life and many orthodox Jewish families are quite large. Marriage is almost universal and having a family and bringing up children is considered to be extremely important. Within the orthodox Jewish communities a married couple are encouraged to 'be fruitful and multiply' (Genesis 9: 7) except where there is a good reason not to. Large families are seen as God's blessing and the elderly will look at their (often very large) extended family with many children, grandchildren and great grandchildren with a great sense of pride and fulfilment. Nevertheless, Judaism's attitude to contraception is somewhat more liberal than that of some other religions.

Many couples might choose to space their families by relying on the relative contraceptive effect of breast feeding which, although not by any means a reliable or predictable form of contraception, may reduce relative fertility for some months in some women by suppressing ovulation.

A couple might consider using contraception where, for example, a woman's physical or mental health might be compromised by a (further) pregnancy. Many couples will only use contraception if they have received approval from a rabbi and often, after an initial medical consultation, a woman may go away to consult her husband who will possibly want to discuss it with a rabbi first. Occasionally, a rabbi, particularly amongst the Chassidic groups, might request a discussion with the couple's medical adviser as to the indications for contraception and at times may even request a written note to that effect, before giving consent for contraceptive use.

Where contraception is used, there is a hierarchy as to which methods are the most acceptable. Methods which interfere with the normal mechanism of intercourse, particularly if it involves 'destruction of seed', are strictly forbidden. According to Jewish law the oral contraceptive pill is the method of first choice. Where the pill is unsuitable or contraindicated then the IUCD or diaphragm may be acceptable. Condoms are not acceptable in Jewish law. Diaphragms, because they are worn entirely internally by the women, are not seen as interfering with the mechanism of intercourse or as destroying seed, even if used with spermicides, whereas condoms are exactly the opposite, placing a barrier between the penis and vagina as well as catching the semen ('destroying seed') and are therefore proscribed. Vasectomy is strictly forbidden, whereas tubal ligation may occasionally be permitted, for instance where a pregnancy would be life threatening. In addition to using the natural relative (but somewhat unreliable) contraceptive effect of breast feeding to space families, some couples may practise the rhythm or other natural methods of family planning, but most rabbinical opinions would prefer the pill where contraception is indicated. Contraceptive injections, although acceptable as an alternative to the oral contraceptive pill, do have the disadvantage of causing irregular and unpredictable uterine bleeding which may cause *niddah* problems. (The same is true of the newer progesterone impregnated IUCDs and, to a much lesser extent, the progesterone-only pill.) Where the combined pill is used some women might bi-cycle or even tri-cycle pill packs, that is they take two or three packs of the combined pill continuously, without the usual seven-day break after the first or second pack. This reduces the frequency of withdrawal bleeds, making her *niddah* less frequently. Individual women can work out how long they can continue without a break before getting breakthrough spotting, and then tailor their pill use accordingly.

How urgent?

Mrs Talia Braun was diagnosed as having scoliosis at the age of 17 and (non-urgent) surgery for spinal fusion was advised. However she married at 19 and had several pregnancies in close succession. The scoliosis was slowly progressive and she was followed up intermittently by the orthopaedic consultant, who whenever he saw her was unable to request an X-ray as she was either pregnant or possibly pregnant. She then presented at the age of 30, six weeks after the birth of her latest baby, asking her GP to arrange a review X-ray of her spine and an urgent referral for spinal surgery. She had decided to take the oral contraceptive pill to delay a further pregnancy pending the surgery, but was only prepared to take it for as short a time as possible. Her GP explained that she would probably have to wait her turn on the consultant's waiting list but that he would mention her own feelings of urgency in his referral letter to the consultant. Furthermore, he advised her that although the oral contraceptive pill might be her first choice of contraceptive method, being the most acceptable from the halachic point of view, it might not be the best if she was contemplating major surgery. Following discussion with her rabbi, she had an IUCD fitted.

Termination of pregnancy: abortion

Jewish law regards a foetus as being part of the mother's body and it is not regarded as an independent being until the onset of labour. Judaism nevertheless regards all life as being of infinite value and abortions are generally prohibited. However in rare circumstances abortions may be permitted, such as when the mother's life would be endangered by continuing the pregnancy, as in Jewish law the health of the mother takes precedence over that of the unborn foetus. It is unlikely that abortion would be permitted by orthodox rabbinical authorities for reasons of foetal abnormality alone. Women might want to consult a rabbi for a ruling before contemplating a termination. The mother's current and future physical and, importantly, her mental health are taken into account when making a decision. Where a termination is permitted, ideally the procedure should be carried out as early as possible in pregnancy.

Childbirth

There are a number of specific issues surrounding pregnancy and child-birth which may affect Jewish couples. Orthodox families may be large; eight or more children are not uncommon and birth is considered a natural process. Couples might ask for full details of any investigations or procedures advised, such as induction of labour or caesarean section, and may want a detailed explanation of the indications and alternative options. Because abortions are generally forbidden, other than for reasons of danger to the mother's life, women may be reluctant to undergo certain screening tests and procedures where the only practical outcome would be the offer of a termination of the pregnancy (e.g. tests for Down's syndrome). Obviously, where there is the possibility of useful, practical therapeutic intervention then screening tests would be encouraged (e.g. screening for hydronephrosis). When offering screening tests the indications and the practical outcome possibilities should be discussed with the woman who may want to discuss it with her husband, her GP or even her rabbi before reaching a decision.

Because of the relatively large size of families, women may be reluctant to undergo caesarean sections unless absolutely clinically indicated, as this often limits the number of subsequent pregnancies. Of course where there is any question of risk to the mother's or infant's life, caesarean section would be accepted without question (*see also pidyon ha'ben*, p 196). Induction of labour for other than sound clinical indications involving risk to the mother or infant may be a questionable issue for some orthodox Jewish women. This is because some orthodox Jewish and especially some Chassidic groups have strong feeling about babies arriving at the most auspicious time that has been predetermined for them; induction might be seen as interfering with this. Where possible, elective procedures should be timed to avoid *Shabbos* or *Yom-Tov*.

Induction of labour

When Devorah had gone two weeks past her due date, the consultant obstetrician advised her to come in for an induction of labour on the following Monday morning. Devorah and her husband Yoel belonged to the strictly orthodox Chassidic community, who believe that babies are best born naturally at the time that providence has preordained to be the most auspicious for them. Yoel consulted his *rebbe* as to whether Devorah should be induced. The *rebbe* asked him to find out what the exact clinical indications were, before giving his advice.

A women is considered to be a *niddah* (*see* previous sections) from the onset of established labour, throughout labour and during the postnatal period until she goes to the *mikveh* seven days after all uterine blood loss (lochia) has ceased. This has a number of practical implications. Physical contact between husband and wife is forbidden, so that during labour he is unable to hold her hand or rub her back. Some husbands may wish to remain in the delivery room whereas others might want to sit nearby, possibly reciting *tehillim* (psalms). Some husbands will remain until the second stage but will then leave the room for the actual delivery. Many women find it easier to have a female relative or friend with them during labour. There is a voluntary Jewish women's organisation, Labour Support, which provides labour supporters (doulas), who will, if needed, stay with orthodox Jewish women throughout labour. They have been trained in the techniques of breathing and pain relieving methods and are very supportive. Some hospitals also have orthodox Jewish maternity liaison workers. Because of *niddah* restrictions on physical contact between a couple, they might not display the expected usual intimacy straight after a birth. Observers unused to this must be aware that this is not a reflection of the couple's relationship, but is a religious constraint.

Childbirth

The midwife who attended the birth of Shifra and Meir Heller's fifth baby rang the couple's GP saying that she was concerned about the couple's relationship which she felt was dysfunctional. She had noted that following the birth, Meir did not display any of the usual signs of affection that she normally saw after a birth; he did not hug or kiss his wife, but seemed rather distant. The midwife felt that his behaviour was suggestive of serious marital strife or possibly even psychiatric problems. She was concerned about the couple's ability to care for the newborn baby. The GP, who knew them well, explained that they were a caring, loving couple and that the midwife need have no concerns about their ability to look after the new baby; they were strictly orthodox Jews who observed the *niddah* laws meticulously and therefore were not allowed any direct physical contact for some weeks following the delivery.

As with all restrictions in Jewish law, those discussed above in relation to obstetric care are set aside wherever there is any risk to maternal, foetal or infant life. A woman who goes into labour on *Shabbos* may call the labour ward, telephone for an ambulance, travel by car and do anything necessary for her safety and that of her baby. She should of course have prepared as much as possible before *Shabbos* and, where possible, acts normally forbidden on *Shabbos* should be minimised or done by a non-Jew, but not if that would cause undue delay or increase any element of risk.

Puerperium

Mrs Bernard phoned her GP requesting a visit as her three week old baby had been crying incessantly for days. She was asked to bring the baby to the surgery but refused saying that as she had not yet been to the synagogue, traditionally the first place visited after a birth (so as to offer a thanksgiving prayer), she could not go out to the surgery. The doctor (herself a Jewish mother of three) pointed out that in fact, whereas she was right in that going out for relatively frivolous purposes took second place to the synagogue visit, it was perfectly permissible and in fact her obligation to take the baby out to seek medical advice.

There are a number of different support groups providing services to Jewish women during pregnancy, labour and in the puerperium. These include ante-natal classes, birth supporters (doulas, as mentioned previously) and support with meals and home help in the postpartum weeks. Strictly orthodox women might feel uncomfortable in general ante-natal classes where they might be concerned about modesty, discussing intimate physical details and watching videos of labour and birth, especially with men present. They (and their husbands) might also feel uncomfortable doing exercises whilst other women's partners are present. Since touch between husband and wife is forbidden during labour they may not want to practise massage or birthing positions that involve the husband physically supporting his wife. A leaflet is available for distribution to Jewish women at ante-natal clinics with useful information specific to their needs (*see* Rottenberg and Spitzer (2001) in Further reading list). The amount of support for mothers within the Jewish community is at a level far beyond the expectations of most mothers in the general population. Health visitors might find that advice offered on topics such as breast feeding and basic childcare is superfluous as many mothers have considerably more experience than the health visitors themselves, and that the support offered by the mother's own family, friends or voluntary organisations is heeded in preference to that given by the health visitor. (*See also* 'Care and support within the community', p 188.)

Beis Brucha

A facility that merits separate mention, because it is relatively unique, is *Beis Brucha*, the orthodox Jewish Mother and Baby Home in north London (a similar facility is planned for Manchester). This is a facility where mothers can stay together with their new babies after discharge from hospital following birth. It gives the mother the opportunity of having some time out with her new baby before returning to the hurly-burly of life at home. There are full time, experienced and trained nursery staff on duty 24 hours a day, and mothers can opt to have their babies in their room with them or looked after in the nursery. Visiting is strictly limited so as to ensure peace and quiet for the mothers. Mothers tend to stay on average for about a week to ten days.

Miscarriage, stillbirth and neonatal death

An unborn foetus is not regarded in Jewish law as an independent being until the onset of labour, nevertheless Judaism believes that all life is sacred and must be treated with dignity and respect. A very early miscarriage (of less than 40 days gestation) is generally not regarded as a miscarriage, rather as a late period, and the products of the conception may be disposed of routinely. A later miscarriage or stillbirth is regarded as being the loss of a pregnancy and if lost at a time when the products are recognisable they should be disposed of in a dignified way, preferably through the services of a burial society (*chevra kadisha, see* p 151). Having a miscarriage before a first normal birth has some relevance in Jewish law, particularly in relation to the ceremony of *pidyon ha'ben* (redemption of the firstborn) (*see* p 196). There are no official mourning rituals such as *shiva* following a miscarriage or stillbirth. Independent life begins with birth but full long-term viable status only starts 30 days after birth, the difference being that where a baby dies within the first 30 days not all of the mourning rituals apply (*see* p 152); burial is arranged through the burial society.

Breast feeding

Unless there is a compelling reason not to, almost all orthodox Jewish women breast feed their babies. However, they will only do so in private and never in a public place. Even at home they will not feed openly (especially in mixed company), unless discreetly draped. Breast feeding might be continued for rather longer than is usual in the UK, commonly for well over a year and occasionally even past the second birthday. Sometimes, as discussed above, this may in part be with the hope of suppressing ovulation so as to try to space the family. Prolonged breast feeding brings with it the risk of vitamin deficiency in the infant and supplements should be advised. If a breast pump needs to be used on *Shabbos*, strictly observant mothers may prefer to use a mechanical one rather than an electric one and whilst still in hospital they may ask for assistance in switching on an electrical pump. Occasionally, at home, some women may use time switches to turn on breast pumps at prearranged intervals.

Breast feeding

Although breast feeding is the accepted norm amongst the orthodox Jewish population it is done discreetly even at home, and never in public. When visiting the doctor's surgery Mr and Mrs Goldenfarb (very strict *Chassidim*) walk into the waiting room where Ms Pamela Jones is sitting and prominently breast feeding her baby – he is visibly shocked and embarrassed, and his wife complains to the receptionist, about this 'inappropriate and indecent behaviour'.

Infertility

Because so much of the Jewish way of life revolves around the family and because having children is so central to the Jewish way of life, infertility may be a source of great distress. Jewish couples may go to extraordinary lengths to obtain help with infertility problems, even where medical opinion might regard them as hopeless cases. It is important for healthcare workers in this area to be sensitive to these feelings when counselling such couples. Because larger than average families are the norm, orthodox Jewish couples may request help for secondary infertility and this needs sensitive handling by infertility workers, especially where resources are limited and secondary infertility is not regarded as an important problem. Furthermore, because in many strictly orthodox circles couples do not use contraception, especially before starting a family, they may perceive themselves as being under pressure from family and peers if they have not become pregnant within a year or so of marriage, unlike others where deferring starting a family for career or other purposes is the acceptable norm. The strictly orthodox might be further disadvantaged because, as they do not read magazines or the press, they may not know what facilities are available or where to start seeking help, and because of the stigma and pain of infertility they may be unwilling even to ask.

Infertile couples may wish to adopt or foster a child or two and indeed adoption and fostering are considered to be a great *mitzvah* (meritorious act or good deed) (*see* 'Adoption and fostering', p 196).

Infertility 1

David and Ruth had been married for eight years and were on an IVF programme. They were advised to attend the regional infertility unit for an ultrasound scan and possible egg collection on a Saturday morning. This was unacceptable to them because as orthodox Jews it would have meant violating the *Shabbos* laws. The initial response from the consultant was one of anger as she felt that they were being awkward and uncooperative and were abusing valuable facilities. However after some discussion and explanation, the injections were timed so as to delay ovulation until the following Monday. Their twins were born 38 weeks later!

Infertility 2

Sheindy Lawrence was becoming increasingly depressed; the youngest of her three children was now almost eight. Her siblings and friends all had many more children and they always seemed to be pregnant. She went to see her GP for advice on why she was not falling pregnant. Her GP was not particularly sympathetic and was reluctant to even arrange for basic blood tests. She explained to Sheindy that secondary infertility was not a priority for NHS funding and that she should be happy with the children she already had. Sheindy's depression deepened and she eventually consulted another GP privately who arranged for some basic investigations which resulted in a diagnosis of PCOS (polycystic ovarian syndrome). Sheindy conceived on her second cycle of clomiphene. As the pregnancy progressed her depression lifted!

Infertility investigations, treatments and *in-vitro* fertilisation (IVF)

Investigation of infertility and its treatment, producing semen samples or testicular biopsy may be complicated by some aspects of Jewish law such as the laws of *niddah, Shabbos* and *Yom-Tov.* No matter how distressing their infertility, a couple may not be willing to set aside or transgress such fundamental principles of Jewish law. Where possible, these issues should be handled sensitively and efforts made to accommodate the couple's needs and feelings. For example, where a couple are involved in an IVF programme, it may be necessary to time treatment cycles to take account of these important aspects of an orthodox Jewish couple's life. It may be necessary to liaise closely with a rabbi who has a special interest in this area. Where gamete donors are involved the halachic principles underlying what is and what is not acceptable become quite complex necessitating the involvement of rabbinical experts in infertility management. Determining exact parentage (according to the halachic rules) in children is absolutely vital in Judaism, for unless parentage is known, individuals may not get married because of the possibility, no matter how remote, of unwitting sibling consanguinity (incest).

Obtaining semen samples for analysis may be problematical for some strictly observant couples. Jewish law strictly forbids masturbation, as this is seen as 'wantonly destroying seed'. Orthodox couples may wish to defer this stage of the diagnostic process until all other investigations have been performed, and many may not proceed without rabbinical advice. Many halachic authorities feel that the prohibition on masturbation is waived in this situation, because the act would not be considered as 'wantonly destroying seed' as the purpose in this situation is exactly the opposite. Some authorities require that the semen is produced through normal intercourse using a special condom without any spermicide (some authorities insist on there being a tiny perforation in the condom allowing, theoretically at least, for the passage of sperm).

Artificial insemination by the husband is permitted by most halachic authorities, and most permit obtaining the sample by masturbation by using a special condom as discussed above. Similarly most halachic authorities permit sperm banking in cases of anticipated infertility (such as prior to undergoing chemotherapy) but only for a married man. Donor insemination is altogether different, and few rabbinic authorities permit it as technically at least it could be construed as adultery. Where it is permitted most halachic authorities would specify that the donor must be non-Jewish, so as to further reduce the risk of consanguinity. In such a situation the child would still be Jewish, as Judaism is determined matrilineally. Ovum donation is very much more problematic and few orthodox authorities permit it. Where a birth does result from ovum donation, halachic ruling might require the resulting child to undergo formal conversion, in order to be considered Jewish. Here again, where done, it would be preferable for the ovum to come from a non-Jewish donor.

Testicular biopsy also presents its own halachic problems, as there is a biblical prohibition in interfering in any way with the integrity of the structure of any of the seminal pathways from the testis to the urethral meatus (Deuteronomy 23: 1). Aspiration of the seminal tubercles or vas deferens to obtain sperm for IVF involving puncture of the transport system could also be problematic and orthodox couples might wish to consult a rabbinical authority before undergoing investigations or treatment involving these procedures.

Most forms of IVF using the husband's sperm are halachically permitted. Where a couple decide to undergo IVF treatment they may, especially if particularly orthodox, wish to do so in close liaison with a rabbinical authority. One area where halachic guidance may be required is where a couple undergoing treatment might want it to be timed to fit in with the *niddah* laws, so that ovulation, insemination or fertilisation and reimplantation take place after the wife's visit to the *mikveh*. Another requirement might be for there to be a *shomer* (an independent Jewish supervisor) constantly present in the IVF laboratory whenever the couple's biological material is being handled and for it to be sealed by the *shomer* whenever it is put into storage and then for the seal to be reopened only in the *shomer*'s presence. Laboratories might be reluctant to accept this restriction, but with diplomatic negotiation it is usually possible. The fate of unimplanted surplus fresh or frozen fertilised eggs does not present any halachic problem, for according to Jewish law, they are not considered to be embryos and may be destroyed. Surrogacy can involve using the wife's or a donor's ovum and most orthodox rabbinic authorities forbid both. If surrogacy were permitted, then for the reasons discussed previously, the surrogate should be a non-Jewish woman. Where a child has been born through a surrogate pregnancy, then in most instances, orthodox rabbinic authorities would not consider the resulting child to be Jewish and would give the child the option of being formally converted at the age of *Bar-mitzvah* (boy at age 13) or *Bas-mitzvah* (girl at age 12).

IVF

When Shuli and Ben were referred to a well known IVF centre, their rabbi advised them that he could only approve treatment if a *shomer* (independent Jewish supervisor) could be present in the laboratory at all times that their biological material was being handled and that when it was put into storage the *shomer* would have to seal the containers himself. Removal from storage could only be done in the *shomer*'s presence. The consultant in charge was extremely offended and angry; he took the requirement for a *shomer* to be a slur on his professional integrity, a personal insult as well as undermining the laboratory's reputation. Some years later when interviewed by the press, following a well publicised mix-up at an IVF clinic, the same eminent consultant was reported to have said 'that no system is infallible and that errors could, albeit rarely, happen even in the best of clinics'.

Cervical smears

Statistically it has been shown that Jewish women, particularly those from the orthodox and Chassidic communities are amongst the lowest risk groups for cervical cancer in the world. The low incidence is thought to be due to a combination of factors including the low number of partners, the fact that males are circumcised and also possibly due to the prohibition on intercourse during and immediately after menstruation. One could argue that the low incidence is all the more reason to encourage screening because as the risk is so low, the clinical index of suspicion is consequently reduced and a case would be more likely to go undetected.

Because intercourse is forbidden following vaginal bleeding, women may be reluctant to have cervical smears, for although in most cases taking a smear does not cause any bleeding, there may occasionally be a small amount of contact bleeding from the cervix. In order to avoid any problems caused by the possibility of bleeding started by taking a smear, orthodox Jewish women may time a smear to coincide with the end of a menstrual period or just before the anticipated onset of the next period. Similarly, routine smears on pregnant women are best left to the postnatal examination or before intercourse has been resumed. Flexibility and understanding will help to encourage high uptake rates for cervical screening programmes.

Conclusion

These topics and the Laws of Family Purity tend to be amongst the hardest aspects of Jewish religious practice for non-Jewish healthcare professionals to understand. They highlight what is one of Judaism's most remarkable paradoxes; sexual matters are extremly private and are not discussed openly and there is the requirement for women to be modest in dress and disposition, yet simultaneously they have to be open and specific when approaching a doctor or rabbi with an intimate question about their menstrual cycle, irregular bleeding and similar issues. For those patients who observe these laws, an understanding, uncritical attitude will be greatly appreciated and go a long way to foster a trusting professional relationship.

Summary

- Judaism has a positive attitude to sexual matters but only within a married relationship.
- Jewish teaching is that women are entitled to sexual satisfaction from their husbands, and this forms part of the marriage contract.
- In strictly orthodox Chassidic circles there is little contact between the sexes outside the family; introductions are arranged between potential marriage partners; Jewish law requires both partners to freely consent to marriage.
- Sexual relations are forbidden during menstruation and during any uterine bleeding (*niddah*) and for some days thereafter until the woman has immersed in a *mikveh*.
- Contraception may be permitted for reasons of a woman's health; not all methods are acceptable.
- Although the *niddah* rules may seem outdated and hard to understand, to observant Jews they are of fundamental importance and should be respected as such.
- Jewish life is very family centred and infertility can be socially isolating; for observant couples infertility treatment needs to be within the bounds and practicalities of Jewish law.

Further reading

Abbott S (2002) *Health Visiting and the Orthodox Jewish Community*. City University, London.

Feldman D (1974) *Marital Relations, Birth Control and Abortion in Jewish Law* (3e). New York University Press, New York.

Feldman DM (1995) *Birth Control in Jewish Law*. University of London Press, London.

Feldman E and Wolowelsky JB (1997) *Jewish Law and the New Reproductive Technologies*. Ktav, New Jersey.

Ganzfried S (1961) *Kitzur Sulchan Aruch: code of Jewish law* (trans H Goldin). Hebrew Publishing Co, New York.

Grazi RV (1994) *Be Fruitful and Multiply: fertility therapy and the Jewish tradition*. Genesis Jerusalem Press, Jerusalem.

Rottenberg G and Spitzer L (2001) *Maternity Issues and Halcha*. Norwood Children & Family Services, London.

Schott J and Henley A (1996) *Culture, Religion and Childbearing in a Multicultural Society: a handbook for health professionals*. Butterworth-Heinemann, Oxford.

Sinclair DB (1989) *Tradition and the Biological Revolution: an application of Jewish law to the treatment of the critically ill*. Edinburgh University Press, Edinburgh.

Spitzer J (1996) *The Surgery of Bris Milah (Jewish Religious Circumcision)*. Initiation Society, London.

Spitzer J (2002) *A Guide to the Orthodox Jewish Way of Life for Healthcare Professionals* (3e). J Spitzer, London.

Wagschal S (1993) *The Practical Guide to Childbirth on Shabbos and Yom Tov*. Feldheim, New York.

Webster YD (1997) *The Halachos of Pregnancy and Childbirth*. CIS Publishers, Lakewood.

CHAPTER 12

Caring for Jewish patients at the end of life

Preparing for the world to come

I kill and I make alive, if I wound, I will heal; there is none who can escape from My power.

Deuteronomy 32: 39

An extract from the prayer to be recited by someone who is close to death:

I acknowledge before you God, . . . that my recovery and death are in Your hand, may it be Your will that You heal me completely, but if I die may my death be an atonement for me . . .

God gave, and God has taken away – Blessed be the name of God.

Job 1: 21

Rabbi Yakov said, 'This world is like the entrance lobby to the next world; prepare yourself well in the entrance lobby so that you may enter the palace'.

Mishne Avos 4: 21

Introduction

The end of life is for many people a time when religious feelings come to the fore, even in those whose lives have been devoid of any religious content. Jews are no exception and, for some, death and its aftermath may be one of those rare occasions which can bring them and their families into contact with religious practices and ritual. Healthcare professionals dealing with terminally ill or dying patients or those confronted by sudden death may feel uncomfortable when confronted with attitudes and practices with which they are unfamiliar, particularly if faced with distressed relatives as well. Trying to do 'the right thing' or at least trying not to do 'the wrong thing' can be stressful and embarrassing. Hopefully this chapter will help to inform and advise about these sensitive issues.

The cycle of life

He (Rabbi Elazar HaKapper) used to say:

> The newborn will die; the dead will be born again: the living will be judged ... against your will you were created; against your will you were born; against your will you live; against your will you die; and against your will you will be destined to give an account before King of kings, the Holy One Blessed be He.

> *Mishne* Avos 4: 29

> A generation goes and a generation comes, but the earth endures forever. The sun rises and the sun sets; then it rushes to its place and from there it rises again.

> Ecclesiastes 1: 4, 5

The value of life

Jews consider all human life to be sacred and all human life is considered to be of equal and infinite value. Concepts of the value of life or even the relative value of life, or the relative value of one human life over another, are totally alien to the Jewish way of thinking. Because of the belief that all life is of infinite value, it follows that even the smallest part of any life is still of infinite value – because a small part of infinity is still infinity. To those Jews who really believe that all life is of equal value, the life of a child born with multiple handicaps is no less valuable than that of a venerable sage or a young breadwinner. The elderly, no matter how weak, sick or demented, are afforded great respect both from close family and the wider community and are often cared for lovingly at considerable material and emotional cost.

Jewish belief is that all individuals have as much right to life as any other. Comments from doctors or nurses which make value judgements about patients' relative quality of life will be vehemently rejected and contested. Orthodox Jews will go to extreme lengths to preserve and prolong life. Jewish families may lavish every level of care on a severely handicapped child or the moribund victim of a stroke, often at great personal or financial cost. This is one area where close liaison between patients, their families, their GPs and local consultants (as well as their rabbinic advisers) is absolutely vital and can be most productive.

Intensive care

Even when extremely ill and on the intensive or coronary care ward, Jewish patients (especially the orthodox) or their relatives or carers may go to considerable lengths to fulfil their religious obligations. For example the kosher food regulations and the *Shabbos* and *Yom-Tov* laws will continue to be observed as much as is possible within the intensive care environment. Male patients will want to continue to put on their *tefillin* daily, even if they need help to do so. A female patient will want to keep her hair covered and even an unconscious patient should be afforded the dignity of having her hair covered at all times. Relatives of orthodox Jewish patients may wish to stay with them constantly and may arrange a 24 hours a day bedside rota, especially if there is the possibility that the patient may succumb to the illness. At this time prayer both by the patient, if possible, and by relatives and carers may become of extreme importance. Consideration should be given to providing an environment suited to prayer, such as by ensuring that the patient is decently covered (even if only with an hospital gown) and that catheter drainage bags and suchlike are covered over, where possible. The invalid or relatives may wish to recite *tehillim* (psalms), possibly as part of an around-the-clock bedside vigil.

Terminal diagnosis and prognosis

An important area where traditional Jewish views differ from currently accepted medical practice relates to informing a patient about a terminal diagnosis. Whereas the contemporary medical view is to tell a patient everything about his/her illness, its diagnosis and prognosis, even where the outcome is definitely fatal, the Jewish view, in contrast, would discourage telling a patient about a terminal diagnosis. This is related to the differing views about medical paternalism and patient autonomy (*see* p 79). Even though Judaism always encourages telling the truth and condemns falsehood, it is permitted to be sparing with the truth and modify it in order to prevent emotional distress and to encourage hope. Patients are entitled to be kept informed about the basics of their illness and treatment and to be given a chance to put their affairs in order and make essential plans for their families and other responsibilities. However they should not be given information which might lead them to despair or to give up. They must always be provided with hope even in the worst scenario. Judaism recognises that despair and depression can cause serious setback to the patient, adding anguish and fear to his/her suffering and thereby hastening death, and it is forbidden to do anything that might hasten death. Similarly, Judaism believes that as long as there is life, there is hope. There is always room for prayer, repentance and charity, which it is believed can influence and avert God's decree, either by the patient, relatives or anyone acting on his behalf. A prayer central to the High Holyday service states 'Repentance, prayer and charity can avert the evil decree' (High Holyday prayer book). Another rabbinical maxim states: 'Even if a sharp sword rests upon a person's neck he should not refrain from praying for mercy, as it is stated (in connection with Job's tribulations) "Although He kills me, I will pray to Him" (Job 13: 15)' (*Talmud* Berochos 10a); even at death's door one should hope for rescue and salvation. Medical practitioners might find it hard to accept these views, which may contrast markedly with their own, and they may find it helpful to discuss these matters with the patient's or family's rabbinic adviser.

Averting the evil decree

Repentance, prayer and the giving of charity may avert the evil decree.

(High Holyday service)

It once happened that a woman came to Binyomin The Righteous who was the treasurer of a charitable fund and said to him 'Rabbi give me some alms so that I may live'. He replied 'I regret to say but alas the coffers are empty'. She said, 'my Rabbi, if you don't give me something, I and my four sons will die'. So he gave her money from his own pocket.

Some time later Binyomin The Righteous became ill and was in bed suffering in pain. The angels said to the Holy One Blessed be He, 'Master of the Universe, You said: if someone saves a single soul it is as though he has saved a world full of people; how much more so Binyomin The Righteous who saved the lives of a widow and her four sons and who is now suffering and ill in bed'. Immediately their plea for mercy was answered and the decree against him was rescinded and he lived for another twenty-two years.

Avos d'Rebbi Nosson 3: 10

Palliative or terminal care

Because, as discussed above, all human life is considered to be sacred and of infinite value, many Jews, especially the orthodox, will often feel that any life whatsoever is worth preserving. Staff working on wards caring for the very old, those with terminal illness, or the very young with major handicaps must constantly bear these values in mind when dealing with Jewish patients (even though these may neither coincide with their own views or values, nor with accepted hospital policy). Even in situations where life expectancy is short, families may request measures to prolong life for just a little longer (such as the putting up of a fluid drip in a patient who is in a coma, so that he does not die of dehydration). Liaison with the local community rabbi, the Jewish hospital chaplain or the visitation committee may be of value to the patient, his/her family and hospital staff.

Any form of assisted death or euthanasia is anathema and utterly abhorrent to Jews, as well as being a very serious offence in Jewish law. Nothing whatsoever may be done to hasten death. Because of the adverse publicity that this issue has engendered, relatives of elderly patients in hospital may be concerned that their loved ones might, in the worst extreme, be actively helped to die, or just allowed to die if only by treatment being passively withheld. These fears may not be expressed openly but might be hinted at by those attending the bedside of the elderly or dying, and manifested by the patient not being left unattended even for a short time. In some instances, Jewish law makes a distinction between the provision of the basic necessities of life, such as water, food and air (needed to sustain life) and the giving of active heroic treatments (so as to prolong life). There may be situations where Jewish law might see the provision of the latter as being unnecessary, whereas the provision of the former, to which all humans are entitled, is almost always required.

Sensitivity is required when discussing resuscitation plans and policies. Decisions on matters relating to the end of life, such as the turning off of life support equipment, should always involve relatives and carers who will quite probably want to involve a rabbi in these major decisions; no two cases are alike.

(Not) for resuscitation?

Dr Lewis, an orthodox Jewish GP, was awoken at four in the morning
when a patient of his rang him with the following urgent question.
His elderly mother-in-law, an orthodox Jewess and also a patient
registered with Dr Lewis, had been rushed by ambulance to hospital
with severe respiratory failure. She was now in the Accident and
Emergency department's resuscitation room, and the registrar had
asked him whether or not he would want his mother-in-law to be
resuscitated should she suffer a cardiac arrest. He has turned to his
Jewish GP for guidance as to what was the right thing to do.

Death

A patient who is dying may wish to recite the *shema* (the declaration of faith
in God; *see* p 7) and possibly also *viddui* (the death bed confession).
If he is unable to say these himself they may be said by someone else on his
behalf. Arrangements can be made through the local community rabbi, the
chevra kadisha (burial society; *see* p 151), Jewish hospital chaplains or
through the visitation committee for someone to attend. Where a death is
anticipated, it is considered to be a great honour for the departing soul if a
quorum of ten Jewish men (a *minyan*) is present at or around the moment of
death. Even in hospital, the family may request that a *minyan* be present
and where possible every effort should be made to try and help, such as by
providing a side room. The *minyan* may well include members of the *chevra
kadisha* who normally try to be in attendance at an anticipated death. If a
Jewish patient dies suddenly or before a rabbi or the *chevra kadisha* can
attend and where they are unlikely to arrive shortly, then the eyes should
be closed and the body laid flat with hands open, arms parallel and close to
the body, and the legs stretched out. Nothing further should be done other
than cleaning the orifices only as far as is required to preserve human dignity, and the body should be covered in a white sheet. If possible the body
should not be left unattended.

In Jewish law, a dead body is accorded great respect. Jewish law forbids
mutilation of the human body, hence post-mortem examinations are not
allowed unless a coroner insists on one and relatives may go to great
lengths to avoid one being performed. In the rare instances where the coroner insists on a post-mortem examination, the autopsy should be carried

out as soon as possible after death so as not to delay the funeral and be as partial or limited as necessary. Pieces of tissue removed for histological examination should be returned for burial if at all possible. In some areas, coroners may be prepared to accept non-invasive alternatives to an autopsy, such as an MRI scan, if this gives sufficient information. This would, of course, be much more acceptable under Jewish law.

Although organ donation after death is theoretically permissible, the criteria for the confirmation of death in Jewish law are such that by the time they became available, organs would no longer be suitable for use. Jews may receive organs and bone marrow as well as blood transfusions. Donation from live donors of blood, bone marrow and live donor organs, such as kidneys, is considered to be a great *mitzvah* and an act of considerable *chessed*.

Post-mortem examination

Mr Raymond, although in his eighties, had always been sprightly and had rarely had cause to consult his GP. One morning he suddenly collapsed towards the end of morning service in the synagogue. Hatzolah (the emergency first aid volunteers, *see* p 193) and an ambulance were called and cardiopulmonary resuscitation was commenced almost at once. When his condition had stabilised sufficiently he was transferred to hospital, but sadly died later that day. As he was an orthodox Jew his family were most reluctant to permit a post-mortem examination. Following discussion with the *chevra kadisha* (*see* p 151) the coroner agreed that she would accept the findings of a MRI scan,[1] for which the family gladly paid. The scan showed cardiac ischaemia, and the coroner issued a death certificate accordingly. The funeral took place later the same day.

[1] *See* Bisset *et al.* in the Bibliography at the end of the book.

Miscarriage, stillbirth and neonatal death

As discussed in the previous chapter (*see* p 131), an unborn foetus is not regarded in Jewish law as an independent being until the onset of labour and the products of a very early miscarriage (of less than 40 days' gestation) may be disposed of routinely. Products of a later miscarriage or stillbirth, if lost at a time when the products are recognisable, should be disposed of in a dignified way, preferably through the services of a *chevra kadisha* (burial society, *see* p 151); the products of conception should be wrapped in a white sheet pending the arrival of the *chevra kadisha*. There are no official mourning rituals such as *shiva* following a miscarriage or stillbirth. Independent life begins with birth but full long-term viable status only starts 30 days afterwards, the difference being that where a baby dies within the first 30 days, not all of the mourning rituals apply (*see* p 152); burial is arranged through the *chevra kadisha*. A male child who dies before he has been circumcised is circumcised (without any ceremony) prior to burial. Because of the lack of rituals following a miscarriage, stillbirth or early neonatal death, parents might not have the usual supports, generally associated with a Jewish death, around them at this time, which might add to some parents' distress.

Funerals

It is considered a great honour for the departed to be buried as soon as possible after death, and a funeral would normally take place within hours of death. Delaying a funeral for more than a few hours or overnight (other than when a death occurs late on a Friday afternoon or on a *Shabbos*, when funerals may not take place) is considered to be disrespectful to the departed. Doctors may come under pressure from relatives to issue death certificates soon after a death, so as to enable burial to proceed with minimal delay. This might necessitate the issue of a certificate at unsocial hours; however, a doctor's co-operation might mean a great deal to grieving relatives. In areas with large Jewish communities, the registrar for deaths may make arrangements to be available on Sundays and Bank Holidays, to ensure that funerals can take place without delay.

Death certification

Mr Leader, who had advanced gastric carcinoma, was sent into hospital by his GP following a large haematemesis. He died six days later in the early hours of Easter Sunday. As the duty medical staff had not seen him alive they were unable to issue a death certificate. The family were told that they would not be able to get a death certificate until the team who had been caring for him returned after Easter

Monday. The family wanted the funeral to take place as soon as possible. The GP was approached to issue a death certificate and as he
had recently seen the patient and was clear as to the cause of death
he was able to do so. The registrar of deaths issued the full death certificate and the authorisation for burial form on Sunday morning and
the funeral took place late on Easter Sunday morning.

According to Jewish tradition, a body should not be left alone or unattended from the time of death until the funeral. Relatives of the deceased
or members of the *chevra kadisha* (burial society, *see* below) will arrange a
rota to 'guard' or 'watch' a body (known as *shemirah*). Where possible,
hospitals and mortuaries should allow someone to be in close proximity to
the body at all times, whether by sitting in the same room on a ward, or
outside the door of the cold room in the mortuary.

The body is prepared for burial by members of the *chevra kadisha*, men
attending male bodies and women female bodies. The body is washed
and dressed in a simple cotton shroud and placed in a simple coffin. Men
are buried wearing a *tallis* (*see* p 55). Jewish funerals tend to be relatively modest occasions, with basic, unadorned wooden coffins and a short,
simple service. In the orthodox tradition there are no flowers and the burial
is only attended by men. Cremation is not allowed by orthodox Jews but is
becoming increasingly popular amongst Reform and Liberal Jews.

Many Jews and almost all orthodox Jews are paid up members of a *chevra
kadisha*, an organisation which often consists of volunteers although some
of the larger burial societies do have some paid officials. The *chevra kadisha*
make all the arrangements for the final rites for the dead and for burial.
They tend to work anonymously and modestly and because the financial
arrangements have on the whole been pre-arranged, the bereaved families
need not feel under any obligation to them. Sometimes bodies are trans-
ported to Israel for burial there; in these cases too, the arrangements and
details will be handled by the *chevra kadisha*. Even when transporting a
body to Israel delay is avoided and a body might well be on its way within
very few hours of death.

When an orthodox Jewish patient dies in hospital when no relatives are
present, the body should be touched as little as is possible. Relatives should
be informed and they will make arrangements with the *chevra kadisha* for
the handling and removal of the body. Tubes and dressings which were in
situ at the time of death should be left in place and only be removed by
members of the *chevra kadisha*. Where there are no relatives, the ward staff
should contact the *chevra kadisha* directly, whatever the time of day or

night. Where appropriate, details of how to contact the society should be recorded in the patient's notes.

Amputated limbs should be given to members of the *chevra kadisha* for dignified burial. Similarly, they will arrange to collect stillbirths and the products of miscarriages (where large enough to be identifiable) which according to Jewish law should be buried.

Mourning

Following the funeral, the departed's immediate family (first degree relatives only: spouse, parents, siblings and children) begin a period of mourning called *shiva* (from the Hebrew word for seven, i.e. seven days or a week), which in orthodox groups lasts for a week. Some Reform groups have shortened the *shiva* period, some to as little as one day. During the *shiva* time, mourners do not go to work or leave the house, but stay at home, sit on low chairs as a symbol of mourning and receive condolence visits from family and friends. Daily prayer services are held at the *shiva* house. *Shiva* and mourning rituals are suspended over *Shabbos* and festivals. During the *shiva* first degree close relatives have a symbolic tear made in their outer clothing as a gesture of mourning. Shaving and haircuts are forbidden. The *shiva* has a comforting effect, especially when mourners and visitors talk about the departed, and this can greatly help the grieving process. In many communities visitors may provide comfort and support by bringing gifts of food and neighbours might organise a rota to provide meals, which helps lift the burden of cooking from the bereaved family. Following the *shiva*, there is an extended period of mourning during which time the special *kaddish* prayers are recited daily by the sons (or where there are no sons, the husband, father or brother) of the deceased in the synagogue and the mourners do not attend joyous communal festivities. Children of the deceased continue this period of mourning for 12 months, but for other relatives it lasts for only 30 days. The anniversary of a death (*yahrzeit*) is similarly marked by the saying of *kaddish* in the synagogue and the lighting of a candle at home which burns for 24 hours. Some have the custom to fast on the day of the anniversary, except if it falls on *Shabbos* or *Yom-Tov*; others may hold a small memorial meal. On the major festivals and High Holydays prayers are said in the synagogue for the souls of the departed and charitable pledges are made in their memories. In this country the convention is that a tombstone is erected towards the end of the first year after the death and there is often a ceremony at the graveside to mark the occasion, to which friends and relatives are invited and at which a rabbi officiates and says some words of comfort and inspiration in the departed's memory.

Suicide

Suicide is considered to be a serious sin equal to murder, for as discussed previously a person's life is not his own to do with as he pleases. Similarly life is in God's hands and it is not for man to determine when it should end. A suicide victim is shunned in Jewish law and is not permitted to be buried in the main cemetery, but rather at the edge or even outside it. There is no *shiva* or other mourning rites. However in practice, Judaism is extremely compassionate to most suicide victims and their families, taking the approach that anyone who commits suicide must have suffered, if only temporarily, from some psychiatric aberration, so that at the time of the act they were not in control of their full faculties and therefore not responsible for a deliberate act of self destruction. This attitude then absolves the subject from responsibility for his actions and thus permits him full burial rights and other mourning rituals. Because of the stigma of suicide and the lenient attitude to it following death, considerable efforts are made, particularly in the more orthodox circles, to disguise the true cause of death, and a suicide will never be referred to as such. Great tact might be required of healthcare professionals involved with the family in the aftermath to provide caring sympathetic support without making direct reference to the mode of death, unless of course the bereaved specifically want to do so. In such situations it is best to use one's professional skills and be led by the patient or client as appropriate. Where an inquest is held, requests might be made for it to be held in another area and for the details to be kept out of the press, if at all possible.

Conclusion

The period around the end of life is a particularly emotive one and can bring religious feelings to the fore. Jewish patients' and their families' views about the value of life and the need to prolong it may conflict with and vary from those of healthcare professionals, and sensitive handling is required especially at such difficult times. Jews have their own practices and rituals associated with this time and should where possible be allowed to follow them especially in environments away from home such as hospitals, residential homes or hospices. Many Jews belong to a burial society whose members would be happy to provide guidance.

Summary

- Judaism considers all human life to be sacred and Jews will go to great lengths to preserve and prolong life.
- Patients should be helped to be able to continue to perform their religious rituals and practices as far as possible and for as long as possible even in an intensive care environment.
- There are some areas where some Jewish attitudes may be in conflict with current medical practice, particularly relating to telling a patient of a terminal prognosis.
- Many Jews are paid up members of a burial society, which takes care of all arrangements following a death, including laying out of the body and all details of the funeral preparations.
- It is considered to be an honour to the departed for burial to take place as soon as possible after death (even within a few hours) and doctors may be asked to issue documentation at unsocial hours.
- Many Jews will observe the mourning rituals of *shiva*, which can help the grieving and bereavement processes.

Further reading

Aiken L (1996) *Why Me, God?: a Jewish guide for coping with suffering*. Aronson, New Jersey.

Bleich JD (1991) *Time of Death in Jewish Law*. Z Berman Publishing Co, New York.

Cohen J (2002) *The Bedside Companion for Jewish Patients*. Genisa, Stanmore.

Dorff E (1998) *Matters of Life and Death*. Jewish Publication Society of Philadelphia, Philadelphia.

Ganzfried S (1961) *Kitzur Sulchan Aruch: code of Jewish law* (trans H Goldin). Hebrew Publishing Co, New York.

Lamb N (1969) *The Jewish Way in Death and Mourning*. Jonathan David Publishers, New York.

Munk E (1963) *The World of Prayer*. Feldheim Publishers, New York.

Ozarowski JS (1998) *To Walk in God's Name: Jewish pastoral perspectives on illness and bereavement*. Aronson, New Jersey.

Robinson G (2000) *Essential Judaism – a complete guide to beliefs, customs and rituals*. Pocket Books, New York.

Schur TG (1987) *Illness and Crisis, Coping the Jewish Way*. NSCY/Orthodox Union, New York.

Sinclair DB (1989) *Tradition and the Biological Revolution: an application of Jewish law to the treatment of the critically ill*. Edinburgh University Press, Edinburgh.

Spitzer J (2002) *A Guide to the Orthodox Jewish Way of Life for Healthcare Professionals* (3e). J Spitzer, London.
Swirsky M (1996) *At the Threshold: Jewish mediations on death.* Aronson, New Jersey.
Wein B (2002) *Living Jewish: values, practices and traditions,* Artscroll, New York.
Wouk H (2000) *The Will to Live On: this is our heritage.* HarperCollins, New York.

Jewish genetic diseases

Judaism – the unbroken chain linking Jews of today directly to the Patriarchs

Three parties combine to form a human being, the father, the mother and the Divine Spirit (God).

Talmud Kidushin 30b

No man without a woman; no woman without a man; and neither together without the Almighty.

Midrash Bereshis Raba 8:9

God created man in His image, in the image of God He created him, male and female He created them.

Genesis 1:27

Introduction

There are a number of diseases which are found more frequently in Jews than in non-Jews, and more frequently in one or other particular group of Jews than in others. Many have a clearly defined genetic basis, of which probably the best known is Tay-Sachs disease. However for other conditions, such as Crohn's disease, there is clustering in families and genetic susceptibility, but no clear genetic pattern. Many of these 'Jewish' diseases are extremely rare and beyond the scope of this book, and only the best known, those of clinical importance and those for which screening tests are available will be described. Whether there is any selective advantage to the various Jewish gene mutations is a matter of some debate; none has ever been proved conclusively. It does however seem curious as to why so many of these conditions are caused by specifically similar gene mutations for sphingolipid disorders (metachromatic leukodystrophy, Niemann-Pick disease, Gaucher's disease, Canavan disease) and indeed why specific Tay-Sachs variants are common within descendants of the Jewish community of Eastern Europe. The genetic basis for the concentration of these diseases, which in the main are autosomal recessive, is based on the genetic principles of gene drift, founder effect, endogamy and relatively high rates of consanguinity.

Autosomal recessive inheritance

Most of the genetic diseases that are found in excess in Jewish patients are transmitted in an autosomal recessive way. This means that both parents must carry the gene for a child to be affected. With respect to most of the diseases mentioned in this chapter, carriers (heterozygotes) themselves are completely normal, perfectly fit and healthy and would not know that they are carriers; there is rarely any family history of the condition. Where both parents are carriers there is a one in four chance of a child being affected (homozygote). There is a one in two chance that a child would also be a carrier (heterozygote) and a one in four chance that a child would not carry the gene at all.

There are several reasons why the mode of inheritance of most of the conditions described in this chapter are autosomal recessive. The main reason is that in autosomal recessive diseases selective pressures are minimal because most of the genes are carried by asymptomatic heterozygotes who are unlikely to be aware that they are liable to pass the gene on to their offspring. Dominant disorders, on the other hand, are selected against, because the carriers of the gene show clinical symptoms. Severe dominant conditions are often the results of fresh mutations. Some are incompatible with normal life and therefore are less likely to be passed on, whereas recessive conditions are maintained in the heterozygous carrier state. Similarly, X-linked recessive disorders are rare because, although the female heterozygotes carriers are generally normal, affected males are selected against. Most of the recessive disorders have a gene frequency of less than 1% and a disease frequency of less than 1 in 20 000. The specific diseases vary in each Jewish community based on their place of origin.

Gene drift and founder effect

Historically, Jews often lived in small secluded communities and therefore the chance of abnormal genes concentrating would have been increased due to the reduced level of gene drift (or gene flow). This would have been concentrated by founder effect, whereby a community which is relatively isolated for geographical, social or, more importantly in this case, for religious reasons and starting from a very small number of individuals has a different frequency of genes than the population from where they originated. The original small community might have included two individuals who carried genes for a rare disorder, or alternatively, the genetic diseases arose by fresh mutation in individuals living within very small genetically isolated communities. These communities did not intermarry with the non-Jews around them and they had relatively little contact with other Jewish communities. Each of these isolated communities grew rapidly and within only a few generations had grown quite substantially (founder effect). Ashkenazi communities in particular followed a repeated pattern over many centuries. They lived in small isolated communities which grew and then following persecution or economic pressures were forced to move on, possibly merging with other communities to form larger groups and then subsequently splitting up and restarting once again as small communities (gene drift), amplifying the founder effect.

Endogamy and consanguinity

Although marrying out of the faith has become much more widespread in recent times, numbers were extremely low until the nineteenth century, and in orthodox circles it is still rare. Thus all marriages were within the Jewish community (endogamy). In many Jewish communities there had long been a tradition of marriage between close relatives (consanguinity). Where communities were very small and isolated this was inevitable but even where the communities were relatively large, close family marriages were not uncommon. This consanguinity serves to bring carriers together increasing the number of carrier couples with the resulting increase in rare recessive disorders. Judaism permits marriage between first cousins and between uncles and nieces. In the time of the Patriarchs (*see* p 24) there were many consanguineous marriages and even today it is still quite common both in some Ashkenazi (especially Chassidic) and Sephardi (especially oriental) communities. Historically, in some Sephardi

Jewish communities, first cousin marriage rates were almost 20% and up to a third of marriages were with other close relatives. Rates among Ashkenazi communities were generally lower but were still rather higher than in non-Jewish groups. The rate of consanguineous marriages has fallen considerably in the last generation or so because with the increasing urbanisation of Jewish communities, Jews no longer live in small geographically isolated communities and there is a wider choice of partner. Uncle–niece marriages were in the past particularly common in Jewish circles; a relationship endorsed by rabbinic law (*Talmud* Yevomos 62b and *Shulchon Oruch* Even Ho'ezer 2: 6). Consanguinity does not cause or create gene mutations, but serves to bring them together as carrier couples; endogamy keeps the genes within the community. With the gradual breaking down of distinctions between the various different Jewish groups since the Holocaust both in the Diaspora and especially in Israel, the chances of marriage between two related heterozygotes is reducing.

Differences between Ashkenazim and Sephardim

The best known diseases found in excess in Jews are listed in the Appendix to this chapter (*see* p 179) and, where known, the genetic basis and approximate incidence is shown. The Ashkenazim are shown as one group whereas the Sephardim are subdivided into place of origin. Interestingly, whereas there are different diseases found in different Jewish populations coming from different geographical origins, there are more subdivisions amongst the Sephardim than amongst the Ashkenazim. The Sephardim have originated from many more isolated communities separated geographically for long periods, whereas the Ashkenazim seem to have been more mobile with much closer intermixing over the generations.

The main Jewish genetic diseases

There are many genetically transmitted conditions which, although of interest to geneticists and anthropologists, are of little if any clinical significance (e.g. essential pentosuria, an autosomal recessive condition found amongst Ashkenazim with a carriage rate of about 1 in 25, which is of no clinical significance but which may be mistakenly diagnosed as diabetes on urine testing). Many of these conditions are extremely rare, are outside the scope of this book and will not be detailed here. I will only list the best known and commonest conditions that are of pathological significance.

Genetic disorders found amongst Ashkenazi Jews

Tay-Sachs disease

Tay-Sachs disease is an inherited disorder of lipid metabolism (one of the gangliosidoses), due to an inherited deficiency of the enzyme hexosaminidase A. Lipids (GM_2 gangliosides) build up in the central nervous system and peripheral nerves. After initial normal development, an affected infant begins to regress developmentally and fails to thrive from about the age of six months when both mental retardation and motor deterioration become evident. There is progressive dementia, weakness and blindness due to retinal degeneration. A characteristic cherry red spot is evident at the macula. Epileptic fits become progressively frequent and sustained and generalised spasticity develops in the terminal stages. Death is inevitable within the first three to four years of life.

The mode of inheritance is autosomal recessive, which means that both parents must carry the gene for a child to be affected. The gene is carried in about 1 in 25 members of the Ashkenazi community. Carriers themselves are completely normal, they are perfectly fit and healthy and would not know that they are carriers. Where both parents are carriers there is a one in four chance of a child being affected. There is a one in two chance that a child would also be a carrier and a one in four chance that a child would not inherit a Tay-Sachs gene at all.

A screening test is available to test for heterozygous carriage of the gene for Tay-Sachs disease (*see* 'Genetic screening', p 175).

Tay-Sachs screening

Mr and Mrs Gross were considering the suggestion that Brucha their oldest daughter be introduced to Meir for the purpose of marriage. Meir's parents wanted to know if she was a Tay-Sachs carrier before they met. They consulted their GP to arrange for testing. She suggested that both parents be tested, so that if neither were carriers they could be certain that none of their children were.

Gaucher's disease
(familial splenic anaemia)

This lysosomal storage disorder is due to a deficiency in glucocerebrosidase which results in an accumulation of glucosylceramide in the lysosomes of the reticuloendothelial system, particularly in the bone marrow, spleen and liver. It has a particularly high incidence in Ashkenazi Jews. There are various forms of Gaucher's disease but it is mainly type I, the chronic non-cerebral adult form, which affects Ashkenazi Jews. It is recessively inherited with a carrier rate of about 1 in 25 and the incidence is about 1 in 2500 births. Anaemia is due to a combination of hypersplenism, bone marrow replacement and thrombocytopenia associated haemorrhage. Fractures due to bone involvement are common. Splenectomy may become necessary in patients with gross hypersplenism and bone marrow transplant may be life saving in patients with large marrow infiltrates. Life span may be normal. Treatment with enzyme replacement therapy has recently started to be used and the results are encouraging.

Riley-Day syndrome
(familial dysautonomia)

This is a disease which primarily affects the autonomic nervous system and is largely confined to Ashkenazi Jewish families. The mode of inheritance is also autonomic recessive and the carriage rate in the Ashkenazi population in the UK is in the region of 1 in 30. There are a large number of symptoms which vary somewhat between affected children. The following are some of the most obvious ones and which are found to some extent in all affected children. An absence of tears (necessitating the frequent application of lubricants), which can cause corneal abrasions and poor vision; poor temperature control, which can be life threatening; poor blood pressure control; reduced perception of pain; inco-ordination of limbs with an unsteady gait; poor growth and scoliosis. Swallowing difficulties are common and uncontrollable vomiting bouts can lead to nutritional deficiencies. Children may succumb to inhalation pneumonia precipitated by the dysphagia. Intelligence is normal but emotional instability with wide mood swings is common.

A screening test to detect carriers has recently become available and screening programmes will soon include testing for familial dysautonomia along with testing for Tay-Sachs carriage (*see* 'Genetic screening', p 175).

Factor XI (plasma thromboplastin antecedent (PTA)) deficiency

This disorder of blood clotting is rare but is found in relatively higher frequency in Ashkenazi Jews of whom between 0.1 and 0.5% (depending on the specific Ashkenazi subgroup) are homozygous. The inheritance pattern is autosomal recessive. Heterozygotes have minimal, if any, problems but homozygotes may have bleeding problems which can range from very mild to quite marked, depending on the actual levels of factor XI present. Of particular relevance is the effect that this may have on clotting following a Jewish boy's *bris* (circumcision, *see* p 193), particularly where the diagnosis has not yet been made. Infants born into families with a known history of factor XI deficiency will need assessing shortly after birth and before a *bris* can be performed. Factor XI concentrate or fresh frozen plasma may have to be given before a *bris* where blood levels are known to be low. In cases of moderate deficiency, oral tranexamic acid may be recommended.

Canavan disease

Canavan disease is a disease characterised by spongy degeneration of the brain. It is transmitted in an autosomal recessive way and has a high prevalence in Ashkenazi Jews with a heterozygous carriage rate of 1 in 40. There is quite a wide variation in clinical severity. In babies with Canavan disease developmental delay starts from about three months of age. There is persistent hypotonia with head lag and macrocephaly may develop. As the child gets older severe developmental retardation becomes evident. Fits, optic atrophy and blindness progress with increasing age. Death occurs in the first or second decade of life. Treatment is supportive only. A genetic screening test for heterozygote carriage is available.

Fanconi's anaemia

This autosomal recessive inherited disorder causes aplastic anaemia and is associated with multiple developmental abnormalities particularly of the heart, skeleton and skin. The gene is carried by about 1 in 90 Ashkenazi Jews. Congenital abnormalities might be evident at birth, but otherwise the disease first manifests itself at about five years of age (or even later) commonly with bleeding due to pancytopenia. Skeletal and skin manifestations may only be evident later. The prognosis without treatment is poor and acute myeloid leukaemia is common (often as the presenting feature). Bone marrow transplant offers the only possible cure. A screening test for heterozygote carriage is available.

Rarer diseases

Other less commonly encountered genetically transmitted diseases found in Ashkenazim include Niemann-Pick disease (sphingomyelin lipidosis), lipid histiocytosis, abetalipoproteinaemia (Bassen-Kornzweig syndrome), primary torsion dystonia (dystonia musculorum deformans), spongy degeneration of the central nervous system, Bloom's syndrome, mucolipidosis type IV and pemphigus vulgaris.

Genetic disorders found amongst Sephardi Jews

Familial Mediterranean fever

Familial Mediterranean fever occurs predominantly in Sephardim of North African (especially Libyan) and Iraqi descent where the carriage rate is in the region of about 1 in 25. Although it is transmitted by autosomal recessive inheritance the disease is of variable penetrance and therefore there is quite a wide spectrum of clinical manifestations and severity. The condition is characterised by recurrent bouts of high fever, peritonitis, pleurisy and inflammatory arthritis. Renal amyloidosis can develop (with massive proteinuria) which can lead to renal failure and death unless treated by haemodialysis or renal transplant. Long-term treatment with colchicine may suppress the acute attacks in about two-thirds of patients and prevent the development of renal sarcoidosis.

Phenylketonuria (PKU)

Phenylketonuria, one of the group of disorders classified with the inborn errors of amino acid metabolism, is characterised by defective metabolism of the amino acid phenylalanine, a common constituent of proteins. The disease is relatively common in Yemenite Jews (about 1 in 5000) and it also occurs in Jews of North African origin (about 1 in 15 000). Untreated it inevitably causes severe mental retardation and early death. Treatment is by severely limiting dietary phenylalanine (protein) intake especially in the first few months of life.

Type III glycogen storage disease (Forbes/Cori's disease)

This is a rare disease which is almost entirely confined to Sephardi Jews of Moroccan decent. Infants present with hypoglycaemia, short stature and hepatomegaly. There may be a mild but progressive myopathy, neuropathy and occasionally hypertrophic cardiomyopathy. Treatment is aimed at maintaining normal glycaemic levels through nutritional therapy with forms of carbohydrate which are absorbed slowly and protein supplement as an alternative, non-carbohydrate source of energy.

Glucose-6-phosphate dehydrogenase (G6PD) deficiency

This X-linked inherited disorder in which red blood cells have a markedly decreased activity of the enzyme glucose-6-phosphate dehydrogenase (G6PD) can cause haemolytic anaemia. Although quite widespread in many other groups it is particularly commonly found in many Sephardi groups with, for instance, up to 60% of Kurdish Jews being affected. Clinical features include anaemia, jaundice and haemoglobinuria due to rapid intravascular haemolysis. Attacks of haemolytic anaemia can be precipitated by ingesting certain foods (the best known of which is fava beans) and certain drugs, some of which are in common use (listed in the *BNF*). Red cell transfusion may be required in severe haemolysis.

Beta-thalassaemia

Beta-thalassaemia is an inherited disorder in the production of the beta chains of haemoglobin. It is relatively common in some small Sephardi groups such as those of Kurdish origin and those from some Indian Jewish communities. Heterozygotes have thalassaemia minor (or trait), characterised by mild anaemia with little, if any, clinical manifestations. Homozygotes have thalassaemia major and are unable to synthesise much, if any, haemoglobin A, so that after the fourth month of life they start to develop a severe hypochromic anaemia with failure to thrive and recurrent bacterial infections. Extramedullary haemopoiesis leads to hepatosplenomegaly and bone expansion which in the skull produces the classic thalassaemic facies. Treatment is by blood transfusion (with concurrent desferrioxamine therapy to help prevent iron overload), splenectomy, folic acid supplement and ultimately bone marrow transplant.

Selective vitamin B_{12} malabsorption

This autosomal recessive condition, which is the commonest cause of megaloblastic anaemia due to vitamin B_{12} deficiency in childhood, has a particularly high prevalence amongst Jews of Tunisian origin.

Pseudocholinesterase deficiency

This enzyme deficiency is particularly common among Sephardi Jews of Iranian and Iraqi origin. As a result they metabolise the muscle relaxant suxamethonium used in surgical anaesthesia very slowly, resulting in prolonged muscle paralysis and apnoea. It would seem prudent to test this group for sensitivity to suxamethonium prior to surgery.

Other diseases

Rare conditions or those of less clinical significance include Dubin-Johnson syndrome (a benign disorder of bilirubin metabolism), hereditary deficiency of peroxidase and phospholids in eosinophilic granlocytes (Presentey's anomoly), ataxia-telangiectasia syndrome, congenital adrenal hyperplasia, cystinosis, cystinuria, familial deafness, Glanzmann, disease (thromasthenia), ichthyosis vulgaris, metachromic leukodystrophy, pituitary dwarfism (type II) and selective hypoaldosteronism (type II).

Diseases with a genetic susceptibility and found more frequently in Jews

There are a number of conditions found more frequently in Jewish patients than in surrounding populations of non-Jewish patients. They cluster in families but do not seem to follow an obvious genetic pattern of inheritance. Of these, perhaps the best known are inflammatory bowel disease (both Crohn's disease and ulcerative colitis, *see* below) in Ashkenazim and childhood celiac disease in some Sephardi groups. These and various other conditions with increased prevalence in Jewish patients are thought likely to be due to a complex interaction between genetic, environmental and other factors. Possibly a genetic predisposition combines in some complex way with various environmental factors (such as diet, lifestyle or occupation) to produce pathological change. This group of conditions includes diabetes (particularly type II or non-insulin dependent diabetes), ischaemic heart disease, auto-immune diseases (particularly the HLA-associated ones) and various malignancies (*see* next section). This last group, the malignancies, presents a particular challenge in trying to differentiate between genetic predisposition or environmental factors and the highly complex interaction of the two. The immigration of large groups of Jews to Israel from the Diaspora since the middle of the twentieth century has produced some research data which has tried to separate out environmental from genetic components. For example, Yemenite Jews had a very low incidence of coronary heart disease whilst living in Yemen where they had lived for millennia. However, when in the 1950s large groups of them emigrated to Israel it was noted that the incidence started to rise quite markedly. One possible explanation is that the diet of Yemenite Jews changed after moving to Israel to a more Westernised diet with much higher levels of saturated fat intake.

There is some evidence that there is an increased carriage rate of group A streptococcus in orthodox (Chassidic) Jews with the possibility of increased streptococcal-related diseases in this population group. There is some suggestion that Down syndrome may be somewhat more prevalent in Jews than in other populations. Here again it is hard to determine whether this is a genuinely genetic predisposition or whether the increased incidence is related to the higher number of births to older mothers and large family size.

My personal observations, corroborated by colleagues working in similar practices, is that there appears to be a disproportionate incidence of acute lower limb cellulitis (erysipelas) in Jewish patients, considerably in excess of that found in other patient groups. This is characteristically recurrent and in some patients can become chronic and disabling with permanently swollen legs, ulceration and pain. Although more common in obese patients it is not restricted to that group and does not seem to be age dependent. This increased incidence seems to be associated with a high prevalence of fungal infections of the feet (both athlete's foot and onychomycosis) in Jewish adults, which are often associated with secondary bacterial infections between the toes which cause ascending lymphangitis and cellulitis through breaches in the skin. One suggestion is that this increased incidence of fungal and secondary bacterial infection of the feet is associated with frequent attendance at the *mikveh*, but this seems unlikely to be the entire story as it seems improbable that this could explain the frequency and severity of the lower limb cellulitis found in this group. It is possible that other factors are involved and it has been speculated that, to some extent at least, this may be due to genetic variation in the vasculature or lymphatic drainage of the lower limb making Jews more susceptible to these problems. This would fit in with the observation that varicose veins seem to be more prevalent in Ashkenazi Jewish patients. Discussion with chiropodists working in areas with large numbers of Chassidic patients confirms the impression that there is a disproportionate incidence of ingrown toe nails particularly in young adults. The reason seems unclear but may be related to a combination of poor foot hygiene and ill fitting footwear of the type favoured by Chassidim.

Cancers

In the mid 1990s it was found that certain gene mutations (BRCA genes, from breast cancer) predispose to breast, ovarian and to a lesser extent prostate and possibly colorectal cancer. These mutant genes are carried in a much higher proportion of Ashkenazi Jews than in the general population and predispose them to an increased incidence of breast and ovarian cancer. It is estimated that 1 in 40 Ashkenazi Jews (2.5% compared to about 0.5% in the general population) carry one of the mutant genes (BRCA1-185delAG, BRCA1-5382insC or BRCA2-6174delT), so that about 75% of Ashkenazi Jewish women with familial breast cancer carry one of these mutations. Of Ashkenazi women who develop breast cancer before the age of 40, 30% carry one of these genes and of those over the age of 40, 10% carry one of these genes. At least half of Ashkenazi women with ovarian cancer have one of these mutations. Almost all Ashkenazi Jewish woman with both breast and ovarian cancer carry one of these genes.

Women with a mutation of the BRCA genes have about a 60% (50–85%) chance of developing breast cancer and an 18% (15–45%) chance of developing ovarian cancer before the age of 70. This risk must however be considered in the context of the overall risk of developing breast cancer, in that only about 10% of all breast cancers in Ashkenazi Jewish women are due to mutant BRCA genes.

When considering family histories of breast or ovarian cancer it is important to remember that the BRCA mutations can be inherited from the father or mother.

Studies in male carriers of BRCA1 have not given clear data but it seems likely that male carriers have about a 16% chance of developing prostate cancer by age 70. However the overall incidence of prostatic cancer is high in men anyway and the actual proportion of prostatic cancer in Ashkenazi men associated with these mutations is probably quite low.

Male carriers of BRCA2 have an increased risk of developing breast cancer although this is still a rare disease and the increased risk has not as yet been quantified. There is also some suggestion that carriers of BRCA1 of either sex may possibly have a slightly increased risk of developing colorectal cancer.

Several other gene mutations have also been identified in Ashkenazi Jews leading to increased incidence of bowel cancer. There is evidence that hereditary non-polyposis colorectal cancer (HNPCC), the most common form of hereditary colon cancer, is more common in Ashkenazim and it is also possible that the adenomatous polyposis coli gene mutation is present in around 6% of Ashkenazim. Several other gene mutations have been implicated in the increased incidence of bowel cancers in this group.

This is a rapidly developing area of medical research with major implications for the prevention and treatment of these diseases. Problems that will be encountered include the complex area of screening and prophylactic mastectomies or oophorectomies in high risk carriers or in carriers with a previously treated breast cancer. Contemporary rabbinic literature has begun to address these issues.

Inflammatory bowel disease

There is an increased incidence of inflammatory bowel disease, particularly Crohn's disease, in Ashkenazi Jews. In the UK this has been reported to be between two and five times that of the general population. In addition, it is well known that there is marked familial aggregation of cases of inflammatory bowel disease, particularly Crohn's disease, in Jewish families, an effect which is much more marked in Ashkenazi Jewish families. Furthermore, it seems clear that Ashkenazi Jews seem to have a predilection for unusually aggressive Crohn's disease, often with large numbers of members of extended families severely affected. Interestingly, studies from Israel suggest that the high incidence of inflammatory bowel disease might be due more to geographic, environmental, cultural and dietary factors rather than to genetic effects. This does not rule out a possible genetic predisposition to inflammatory bowel disease, although it has not been possible to demonstrate any obvious genetic pattern. The overall increase is likely to be due to a complex interaction and combination of environmental, cultural or other factors combined with a genetic predisposition.

Psychiatric illness/mental health

Although there is some suggestion that bipolar affective disorders might possibly be slightly more common in Jewish patients than in others, overall the incidence and prevalence of psychiatric problems and the spread of diagnoses seems to be broadly similar to that of the rest of the population. However, the symptomatology and presentation of mental health problems may reflect the patients' specific Jewish background. For example, a patient with obsessional-compulsive disorder (OCD) may present with behavioural mannerisms which are based on Jewish ritualistic practice. For instance, although it is normal practice for orthodox Jews to wash their hands before prayers and before eating, a patient with OCD might spend many hours doing this for fear that he is not sufficiently 'clean' to pray or eat.

Obsessional-compulsive disorder (OCD)

Steve and Helen both came from secular non-religious homes and met when they were both on a gap year in Israel. Whilst there, they found their religious roots and following their marriage set up a religiously observant home in a predominantly orthodox district in Manchester.

Their typical kosher kitchen had separate sections for dairy and meat foods in accordance with the halachic requirement to keep the two apart (*see* p 116). Steve started to become excessively concerned about the meat and milk laws worrying that they might become mixed together resulting in food and kitchen utensils becoming *treifah* (unkosher). He started to take things to extremes insisting on everyone washing hands before and after handling anything in the kitchen for fear of cross contamination. He worried that splashes from the washing up might carry right across the kitchen, wiping all surfaces several times afterwards. Steve spent several hours a day inspecting the kitchen surfaces, utensils and cutlery as well as wiping down sauce bottles and ingredient containers that might legitimately have been used for both meat and dairy cooking. His day ended with a final inspection of the kitchen. Helen, although also relatively new to *Kashrus* observance, realised that this was not normal behaviour but a manifestation of an obsessional disorder.

Steve's non-Jewish GP referred him to an orthodox Jewish clinical psychologist. However Steve was only really cured when, following a meeting with the psychologist and a respected rabbi, he agreed that all aspects of the *Kashrus* in the home should be exclusively Helen's responsibility, he was to trust her implicitly and the kitchen was to be her exclusive domain, placing all aspects of *Kashrus* observance in the home on her shoulders. In effect the kitchen became a no-go area for Steve. His role extended to helping with the shopping and purchase of kosher food.

Jewish patients with manic symptoms might display inappropriate ecstasy and fervour during prayer shouting out about how wonderful God is to them! A psychotic patient may present with specifically Jewish religious manifestations such as visions relating to prophecy and messianic revelations in which they have been selected to be special and different than anyone else. Alzheimer's disease or senile dementia may present in ways that might only be understood by other practising Jews, for example when a strictly *Shabbos* observant man starts to openly perform actions forbidden on *Shabbos* (*see* p 100), such as switching on electric lights, or when he performs religious rituals at inappropriate times, such as putting on his *tefillin* (phylacteries) in the evening. These actions are so inappropriate that they can only signify an abnormal mental state. Paranoid symptoms, particularly in older patients or increasingly in the children of Holocaust survivors, may manifest as feelings of anti-Semitism, and this can be particularly difficult for non-Jewish medical or nursing staff to deal with.

Divine Revelation

Hershey was always a bit of a loner and when he left *yeshiva*, aged 22, he moved into a flat on his own, becoming somewhat of a hermit. To his few close confidants he whispered that he was 'The Chosen One' and that when the time was right he would be 'revealed'. And revealed he was, when one evening he walked through his predominantly Jewish neighbourhood stark naked distributing leaflets informing the world that *Moshiach* (the Messiah) had arrived.

> A period of compulsory hospital admission confirmed his views that all non-Jews, everyone, doctors, nurses and the ward domestic staff, were all anti-Semitic Nazis preventing *Moshiach*'s mission to save the world.
>
> He had several such admissions over the years but eventually his schizophrenia burnt out. An organisation caring for orthodox Jewish patients with mental health problems took an interest in Hershey and eventually he moved into one of their group accommodation homes where he seemed content and, although always quiet, took his turn helping with domestic duties and caused no problems.

In these situations it is essential that the patient, especially if from one of the more orthodox or Chassidic groups, sees a practitioner who understands their religious practices and cultural environment in context. Such a practitioner will be in a position initially to understand the symptoms and recognise them as being examples of aberrant practice, rather than normal behaviour, and more importantly can relate to the patient and establish a therapeutic relationship in which he/she can be helped. It is therefore essential that in areas with large Jewish communities that there are psychiatrists, community psychiatric nurses, counsellors, marital and other therapists, who have an understanding of, and are sympathetic to, their Jewish patients and their religious practices. In the ultra orthodox community there is considerable opposition to therapies where the medium is essentially some form of 'talking treatment' such as counselling, clinical psychology, psychotherapy or similar modalities. There is suspicion of the methods employed, which it is felt involve techniques that are contrary to traditional Jewish beliefs. Some will go so far as to say that it makes no difference if the therapist him/herself is an orthodox practising Jew, as the training undergone and the methods used are intrinsically un-Jewish and therefore forbidden. For advice, they would rather go to a rabbi; doctors are for medication. Attitudes are changing slowly but in the strictly orthodox Chassidic community antagonism to counsellors and therapists is quite strong and it will take a long time to make any really acceptable differences. On those occasions where strictly orthodox patients do need to see a counsellor or psychologist the patient might be accompanied by a close family confidant or rabbi who may wish to stay in during the consultation, as the patient's advocate or facilitator (culture-broker, *see* Greenberg and Witztum in the Bibliography at the back of the book). This third party might be able to help the therapist by explaining aspects of the patient's problems and symptoms in the context of what might be normal for someone of his/her background, as well as helping with interpretation. Ideally, in areas with Chassidic communities there should be Yiddish speaking mental health professionals.

Jews have always placed considerable emphasis on academic attainment, and pressure to achieve from schools, parents and the pupils themselves can carry with it some degree of psychiatric morbidity, particular in adolescents. My discussions with colleagues serving similar communities seems to confirm my observation that the incidence of teenagers who crack under the pressure to attain seems to be rather higher in Jewish adolescents than in the general population.

As discussed previously (*see* p 88), psychiatric illness carries considerable stigma in strictly orthodox circles and sufferers and their families might go to great lengths to hide it. Denial is particularly powerful, which unfortunately may delay presentation and diagnosis. Patients with mental health problems are at risk of becoming socially isolated. It may be difficult for patients and their carers to recognise and accept psychological problems, whether as presenting problems in their own right or as part of other conditions. Frequently, patients or their relatives will hide behind a pragmatic medical model of illness, denying a psychiatric or psychological component, and may look for a purely medical cure involving medication to treat and 'cure' the illness. As discussed above, there is, particularly in strictly orthodox groups, considerable reluctance to accept forms of counselling or psychotherapy. Parents of children with learning difficulties or disabilities may expend considerable resources in their unrealistic hunt for the elusive 'nothing short of a total cure' and be reluctant to accept that there is no cure as such, thereby delaying the start of special educational help and other forms of treatment. Where in-patient treatment in a psychiatric unit or hospital is required, strictly orthodox Jewish patients, who may not have mixed socially with non-Jews and who may have led quite isolated lifestyles, might find the environment totally alien and very intimidating. Caring for Jewish patients with psychiatric illness is challenging in itself, but caring for the strictly orthodox with mental health problems is so much more so.

Genetic counselling

Although the basic principles of genetic counselling are no different for Jewish patients than anyone else they will predominantly relate to those conditions found more frequently in Jewish patients. This is especially the case in areas with smaller isolated communities who have a high rate of consanguinity and might therefore present with rare recessive syndromes. There are, however, some specific points worth considering when dealing with Jewish patients.

When counselling Jewish couples, it is essential at the outset to ascertain the level of observance of the family before starting any counselling session. They may be completely secularised, ultra-orthodox or somewhere in between these extremes. This might help the counsellor to assess what their attitude might be to contraception, prenatal screening, termination of pregnancy, artificial insemination, IVF or even surrogacy. Here, as always, it is preferable not to assume but to ask. For instance some Jews might accept artificial insemination by donor (some might specify that the donor must be non-Jewish so as to reduce the risk of consanguinity; the child would still be Jewish as Judaism is determined matrilineally, *see* p 138). Similarly, having an insight into the pressures on strictly orthodox couples to start a family and for them to have many children (*see* p 136) will enable counselling appropriate to their culture. Following a stillbirth or a neonatal death it might not be possible to obtain information from a post-mortem examination, as parents might be reluctant to give consent unless there is a very strong reason for it to be done. If there is reason to believe that information obtained from an autopsy would help to enable the couple to have other healthy children then it might be possible to obtain consent for at least a limited examination. Discussion with the family's rabbinic adviser and/or a rabbi with specific expertise in this field might be required before a decision can be made.

The acceptability of prenatal testing and diagnosis will vary between different groups and for different conditions (*see* p 132). Here too it is best not to assume, for even in cases where parents would refuse any intervention they may wish to have the various tests, particularly non-invasive ones, performed if only to be forewarned and prepared for the probability of having an abnormal baby. Because rabbinical advice might need to be obtained and this might cause some delay, prenatal testing should, where appropriate, be offered as early as possible during pregnancy especially in the rare cases where a termination might be permitted, for according to some halachic authorities the earlier in pregnancy that it is performed the more likely it is to be permitted.

Orthodox Jewish couples and families may have their own support networks and might not avail themselves of those offered by genetic counselling services outside of their own community. There might nevertheless have to be some secondary contact between the family's supporters and the genetic counselling service, if only for the provision of factual information and for advice on the specialised expertise required in this area. Less orthodox families might be more comfortable using the counselling services of the local genetic counselling clinics.

Genetic counselling

Suzi, aged 25, consults her GP in a distressed state. She is one of five children and has just heard that one of her sisters, who lives in Israel, has a baby of seven months who has just been diagnosed as having Tay-Sachs disease. She wants to know all about the condition and the chances that she might pass it on to her children. She asks the GP what she should tell her fiancé.

Genetic screening

Screening tests are available for a number of the Jewish genetically transmitted diseases. Testing for Tay-Sachs disease carriage is well established, has been available for several decades and blood testing is routinely available at hospitals in areas with large Jewish populations. Screening programmes for detection of Tay-Sachs carriage have been run regularly in most Jewish communities for many years. More recently, a screening test to detect carriers of Riley-Day syndrome (familial dysautonomia) has become available and screening programmes will soon include testing for this condition in addition to testing for Tay-Sachs carriage. Screening tests are also available for Canavan disease and Fanconi's anaemia and occasionally these may also be requested. There are various testing programmes organised regularly through synagogues and Jewish community organisations as well as at Jewish schools, colleges and youth groups. Testing to see if individuals are carriers should be considered for all members of the Ashkenazi Jewish community well before engagement and marriage plans are made. Testing married couples may present some halachic problems, for if they are both found to be carriers there may be issues relating to future pregnancies, particularly since abortion may not be acceptable. A decision by a couple who do not yet have any children not to have any at all is not an option acceptable to many orthodox halachic authorities. Similarly, although it may be possible to test a foetus in early pregnancy to see if it has Tay-Sachs disease, this may also lead to problems surrounding the permissibility of terminating a pregnancy. Pre-implantation genetic diagnosis is a possibility during IVF treatment and is acceptable to most halachic authorities. For families who have children but who have yet to complete their family, although the testing of both parents is the most logical way of screening the entire family, this may be problematic for the reasons discussed above. For all these reasons, testing is best carried out on older teenagers, before marriage and pregnancy is contemplated. Therefore the screening programmes that are organised in Jewish schools, colleges and clubs are generally targeted at teenagers and adolescents. Occasionally, someone may request to be screened urgently, for instance when an engagement is imminent but where only one party has been tested and insists on screening of the other prior to finalising arrangements.

An ingenious screening programme for the main Jewish genetically transmitted diseases was developed by an organisation called Dor-Yeshorim in the ultra-orthodox Satmar Chassidic community in New York. Dor-Yeshorim now operate on a world-wide basis. This scheme is particularly suitable for those groups who rely on the *shidduch* system of arranged introductions before a young couple meet with a view to finding a marriage partner (*see* p 124). The Dor-Yeshorim organisation arranges screening programmes for teenagers through schools and colleges well before the age that a *shidduch* might be suggested. Those tested are not given their results, but these are stored on a central database instead. Participants are issued with a unique number relating to their entry on the database. When a *shidduch* is suggested, the *shadchan* (or the parents) would be given both parties' numbers even before the couple have been told about the *shidduch*. The *shadchan* (or parents) then contacts the database with both numbers. If both parties are carriers the *shadchan* will be told that the couple are incompatible and the *shidduch* will not even be suggested to the young couple. In this way heterozygotes should never find out that they are carriers. This system involves total anonymity and is based on the belief that carriers would be upset and feel stigmatised if they knew that they carry genes for serious illnesses. The scheme works best in communities where couples do not meet by chance but only by introduction through a *shidduch*. The scheme has been well publicised and is particularly popular within the Chassidic community where it has been endorsed by many *rebbes*. In addition to their original test for Tay-Sachs disease, Dor-Yeshorim have added an increasing range of Jewish genetic conditions to their screening profile including Canavan disease, Fanconi's anaemia and shortly Riley-Day syndrome will also be added.

Conclusion

Although most of the diseases discussed in this chapter are individually relatively rare, collectively they cause much morbidity and mortality. A doctor working in areas with a significant proportion of Jewish patients needs to have an increased awareness of the possibility that these conditions may present, an understanding of the issues of carrier testing and genetic counselling, and the dilemmas that are associated with them. With the rapid advances in molecular biology and the increasing understanding of the basis of genetic mechanisms, early diagnosis of diseases and the detection of carrier status will become all the more important, and patients may increasingly consult requesting screening investigations. Local clinical genetic services should be able to provide up-to-date specific advice.

Summary

- Some diseases are more common in Jews than in non-Jews; many have a clearly defined genetic pattern and of these most are autosomal recessive.
- Reasons for this include the fact that historically Jews lived in small isolated communities with much inbreeding and high levels of consanguinity.
- The best known are Tay-Sachs disease, Gaucher's disease and Riley-Day syndrome.
- The pattern of diseases is different in Ashkenazim and Sephardim and varies considerably in Sephardim from different regions.
- There are a number of conditions without a clear genetic pattern (such as inflammatory bowel disease); the increased incidence is due to a complex interaction between genetic and environmental factors.
- It is possible to screen patients for heterozygous carriage for some conditions; screening programmes are directed mainly at teenagers and young adults.
- Genetic counselling needs to take account of Jewish patients' values and beliefs.

Further reading

Allen R *et al.* (eds) (1997) *Inflammatory Bowel Disease* (3e). Churchill Livingstone, London, pp 13, 648.

Bleich JD (1988) *Bioethical Dilemmas: a Jewish perspective*. Ktav, New York.

Bonné-Tamair B and Avinoam A (eds) (1992) *Genetic Diversity Among Jews; disease and markers at the DNA level*. Oxford University Press, New York.

Feldman E and Wolowelsky JB (1997) *Jewish Law and the New Reproductive Technologies*. Ktav, New Jersey.

Feuer J and Spiera H (1997) Acute rheumatic fever in adults: a resurgence in the Hasidic Jewish community. *J Rheumatol.* **24**(2): 337–40.

Fisher NL (ed.) (1996) *Cultural and Ethnic Diversity – a guide for genetics professionals.* Johns Hopkins University Press, Baltimore.

Forbes A (2001) *Clinicians' Guide to Inflammatory Bowel Disease* (2e). Arnold, London, pp 4, 72.

Goodman RM (1975) Genetic disorders among the Jewish people. In: AEH Emery (ed.) *Modern Trends in Human Genetics* (2e). Butterworth, London.

Goodman RM (1979) *Genetic Disorders Among the Jewish People.* Johns Hopkins University Press, Baltimore.

Harper PS (1988) *Practical Genetic Counselling* (5e). Oxford University Press, Oxford.

Karlinger K *et al.* (2000) The epidemiology and pathogenesis of inflammatory bowel disease. *Eur J Radiol.* **35**(3): 154–67.

King RA, Rotter JI and Motulsky AG (1992) *The Genetic Basis of Common Diseases.* Oxford University Press, Oxford.

Marteau T (1992) Screening ethics and the law. *BMJ.* **305**: 1433–4.

Marteau T and Richards M (1999) *The Troubled Helix: social and psychological implications of the new human.* Cambridge University Press, Cambridge.

Mayberry JF, Judd D, Smart H *et al.* (1986) Crohn's disease in Jewish people – an epidemiological study in south-east Wales. *Digestion.* **35**: 237–40.

Mourant AE, Kopec AC and Domaniewska-Sobczak K (1978) *The Genetics of the Jews.* Clarendon Press, Oxford.

Roth NP *et al.* (1989) Familial empirical risk estimates of inflammatory bowel disease in Ashkenazi Jews. *Gastroenterology.* **96**: 1016–20.

Spitzer J, Hennessy E and Neville L (2001) High group A streptococcal carriage in the Orthodox Jewish community of north Hackney. *Br J General Practice.* **51**: 101–5.

Wahrman J and Fried K (1970) The Jerusalem prospective newborn survey of mongolism. *Ann NY Acad SCI.* **171**: 341.

Zoltogora J *et al.* (1991) Prevalence of inflammatory bowel disease in family members of Jewish Crohn's disease patients in Israel. *Dig Dis Sci.* **36**(4): 471–5.

Appendix

Table 13.1: Disorders with a relatively high incidence in Jews

	Mode of inheritance	Approximate frequency
All Jewish groups		
lactose intolerance	autosomal recessive	
Ashkenazim		
abetalipoproteinaemia	autosomal recessive	rare
adrenal hyperplasia III (non-classical 21-OH deficiency)	autosomal recessive	1:27
Bloom's syndrome	autosomal recessive	1:100 000
coronary heart disease	multifactorial	
diabetes (type 2, NIDDM)	multifactorial	
dystonia musculorum deformans	autosomal dominant	1:23 000
familial dysautonomia (Riley-Day syndrome)	autosomal recessive	1:3700
Fanconi's anaemia	autosomal recessive	1:30 000
Gaucher's disease type 1	autosomal recessive	1:2500
mucolipidosis IV	autosomal recessive	1:30 000
Niemann-Pick disease	autosomal recessive	1:60 000
pentosuria	autosomal recessive	1:5000
PTA deficiency (factor XI deficiency)	autosomal recessive	1:175
regional enteritis (Crohn's disease)	multifactorial	
spongy degeneration of central nervous system (Canavan disease)	autosomal recessive	1:10 000
Tay-Sachs disease:		
infantile	autosomal recessive	1:2500
adult	autosomal recessive	1:65 000
ulcerative colitis	multifactorial	
Sephardim		
Oriental		
India (Cochin, Kerala):		
keratosis palmoplantaris with periodontopathia and onychogryphosis	autosomal recessive	?
Kurdistan:		
alpha thalassaemia	autosomal recessive	1:80 carriers
beta thalassaemia	autosomal recessive	1:160
G6PD deficiency	X-linked recessive	1:1.6 males

	Mode of inheritance	Approximate frequency
Yemenite		
Yemen:		
alpha thalassaemia	autosomal recessive	1 : 5 carriers
celiac disease	multifactorial	
chronic familial neutropaenia	autosomal dominant	1 : 50
metachromatic leukodystrophy, late infantile (Habbanite Jews)	autosomal recessive	1 : 75
phenylketonuria	autosomal recessive	1 : 5000
pituitary dwarfism II (Laron)	autosomal recessive	?
Middle Eastern		
combined factor V & VIII deficiency	autosomal recessive	1 : 100 000
Egypt (Karaites):		
Huntington's disease	autosomal dominant	?
spinal muscular atrophy 1	autosomal recessive	1 : 400
Turkey:		
familial Mediterranean fever	autosomal recessive	1 : 1000
Iran:		
aldosterone deficiency (18 hydroxysteroid dehydrogenase)	autosomal recessive	1 : 4000
G6PD deficiency	X-linked recessive	1 : 7 males
hyperbilirubinaemia II (Dubin-Johnson syndrome)	autosomal recessive	1 : 1300
myasthenia gravis, infantile	autosomal recessive	?
pituitary dwarfism II (Laron)	autosomal recessive	?
polyglandular deficiency syndrome	autosomal recessive	?
pseudocholinesterase deficiency (E1)	autosomal dominant	1 : 9
Iraq:		
familial Mediterranean fever	autosomal recessive	1 : 2000
G6PD deficiency	X-linked recessive	1 : 4 males
myasthenia gravis, infantile	autosomal recessive	?
optic atrophy, movement disorder and spastic paraplegia	autosomal recessive	1 : 10 000
pituitary dwarfism II (Laron)	autosomal recessive	?
pseudocholinesterase deficiency (E1)	autosomal dominant	1 : 11
thrombasthaenia (Glanzmann)	autosomal recessive	1 : 7700
North African		
celiac disease	multifactorial	
combined factor V & VIII deficiency	autosomal recessive	1 : 100 000
phenylketonuria	autosomal recessive	1 : 15 000
Algeria:		
familial Mediterranean fever	autosomal recessive	1 : 700

	Mode of inheritance	Approximate frequency
Ethiopia:		
chronic familial neutropaenia	autosomal dominant	?
Libya:		
Creutzfeld-Jakob disease	autosomal dominant	1:24 000
cystinuria	autosomal recessive	1:2500
familial Mediterranean fever	autosomal recessive	1:250
muscular dystrophy 1	autosomal recessive	1:1000
Morocco:		
adrenal hyperplasia IV	autosomal recessive	1:5000
(II-betahydroxylase deficiency)		
ataxia telangiectasia	autosomal recessive	1:8000
cerebrotendinous xanthomatosis	autosomal recessive	1:10 000
cystinosis	autosomal recessive	
familial Mediterranean fever	autosomal recessive	1:700
glycogen storage disease type III	autosomal recessive	1:5000
Tunisia:		
brittle cornea syndrome	autosomal recessive	
familial Mediterranean fever	autosomal recessive	1:700
selective vitamin B_{12} malabsorption	autosomal recessive	1:1600

Based on various sources including Bonné-Tamair and Avinoam (1992) and Goodman (1975 and 1979), *see* Further reading in this chapter.

Judaism's attitude to genetic engineering
(permitted or possibly even required but with caution)

The *Midrash*[1] records a debate between Rabbi Akiva and the Roman general Turnus Rufus, who challenged him to defend the Jewish practice of circumcision, which he saw as the apparent mutilation of the finished work of the Creator. He reasoned that if God wanted men to be circumcised they would emerge from the womb already circumcised. Rabbi Akiva demonstrated to Turnus Rufus that man had to complete God's work by comparing ears of wheat as created by God with bread produced by man. Man has to add the finishing touches to complete the unfinished works of the Creator. Man is permitted, and sometimes commanded, to alter nature in order to perfect the works of the Creator.

Nevertheless, while Jewish tradition assigns man the God-given right and even obligation to manipulate nature in order to bring benefit to man and the world, it also recognises that man, through inappropriate use of his freewill, can negatively interfere with the creation to the point of destroying himself and the natural world, as is expressed in the following *Midrash*:[2] 'When God created the first Man he took him and showed him all the trees of the Garden of Eden and said to him "See my works, how beautiful and praiseworthy they are. And everything that I created, I created it for you. Be careful not to spoil or destroy my world – for if you do, there will be nobody after you to repair it".'

Judaism's attitude to IVF

Rabbi Menachem Meiri (1249–1306) discusses the importance of scientific breakthroughs and the ability to take advantage of technological advances. In his commentary to the *Talmud* (Sanhedrin 67b) he writes:

What is the difference between witchcraft (sorcery) from which the *Torah* forbids one to benefit and science which the *Torah* welcomes?

---

[1] *Midrash Tanchuma* Tazriah 19.
[2] Koheles Raba 7: 13.

Any advances achieved through natural science are not considered magic (which is prohibited). There will come a time when science will know how to create human beings without the natural intimate act. This is explained in science books and is not an impossibility. It is permitted to be involved in such procedures for they are considered to be within the order of nature and not in the category of (forbidden) magic. This is similar to the statement that anything achieved through the science of medicine is not considered *darkei emori* (witchcraft or sorcery, which is forbidden) (and is therefore permitted).

Haemophilia, genetics, the *Talmud* and rabbinic law[3]

The first description of haemophilia and its mode of transmission to be published in the medical literature was that of John Conrad Otto published in 1803 (Medical Repository 6: 1). The *Talmud*, written over 1500 years earlier, discusses (Yevomos 64b) the problem of a woman, two of whose sons die as a result of circumcision. It rules that subsequent sons are exempt from circumcision. Maimonides (twelfth century), in his codification of Jewish law (*Mishne Torah*, Ahava, Laws of Circumcision 1:18), states that this applies even if the sons are from different fathers. (Incidentally, in this context he stated the all-important principle of Jewish law, that 'danger to life overrides every other consideration; it is possible to delay circumcision, but it is impossible to restore a single (deceased) life'). Rabbi Yossef Caro (sixteenth century) in his code of Jewish law rules that if two sisters each have a son who has died as a result of circumcision then not only are their subsequent sons exempt from circumcision but the sons of any other sisters that they may have are also exempt. Rabbi Moishe Isserles (sixteenth century) in his notes on *Shulchon Oruch* (Yoreh Deah 263:2) implies that although it is only males that are afflicted with haemophilia, it is transmitted only by females.

It is evident that the rabbis of the *Talmud* and subsequent generations had a clear understanding of the mode of inheritance of haemophilia and applied this to the practical application of Jewish law long before it had been described in medical literature.

---

[3] Based on Rosner (1969), *see* the Bibliography at the end of the book.

CHAPTER 14

Miscellaneous health related topics

Good health is something Jews pray for constantly

... and you shall return it to him (Deuteronomy 22: 2). *This is written in relation to returning a lost object to its owner. The rabbis interpret this verse to include the obligation to help restore an invalid's lost good health, obliging a surgeon to practise his skills, a physician to provide his expert advice and a wealthy person to supply funds, in order to 'return that which has been lost', i.e. to help return him to full health.*

Talmud Sanhedrin 73a

Shimon the Righteous used to say: 'The world stands on three things, on Torah, worship of God and performing acts of kindness'.

Avos 1: 2

Preventive medicine

Jews are required to look after their health and this includes making use of preventive medicine where appropriate. Preventive medicine, or looking after one's health, includes leading a healthy lifestyle with plenty of exercise and following a sensible diet. One might have thought, therefore, that the more observant Jews are, the more fit and healthy they would be. Unfortunately the reverse seems to be the case. Whereas there are many sports clubs and teams amongst the less strictly observant sections of the community (as evidenced by the lively sports section of the Anglo-Jewish national weekly newspaper *The Jewish Chronicle*), the more orthodox community seem to lead rather sedentary and generally unhealthy lifestyles (*see* p 86). As stated previously some orthodox and all Chassidic families do not have televisions, many have no radios, and most do not read the national press, so they may be unaware of national healthcare campaigns such as immunisation, health promotion, or preventive medicine programmes such as cervical cytology screening. Important health information or advice, such as might need to be provided during epidemics, should be publicised in the orthodox Jewish press.

Cervical screening, immunisation and infectious diseases

It is well known that the incidence of cervical carcinoma is low in Jewish women. The uptake of cervical smear screening amongst orthodox Jewish women is somewhat poor, possibly a reflection of the very low incidence of cervical carcinoma in this group and possibly also due to the worry that taking a smear may cause some cervical bleeding resulting in *niddah* problems (*see* p 140).

Infant immunisation rates in Jewish children were generally quite high but, particularly in orthodox groups, uptake seems to be even more sensitive to falls prompted by periodic immunisation scares than in the rest of the population and also seems to take longer to recover afterwards. At the end of the twentieth century there was considerable adverse publicity about infant immunisation, particularly about the combined MMR vaccine. Following this, there was an considerable drop in take up rate which was especially marked in orthodox Jewish children. Of the 29 ethnic groups recorded as living in the City and Hackney area of east London, orthodox Jews had the lowest uptake of infant vaccination in 2001 (less than 50%).

From time to time there are outbreaks or epidemics of infectious diseases (such as hepatitis A, salmonella or chicken pox) which can spread quite dramatically through the orthodox community. This is possibly a reflection of the closeness of the community, with people mixing socially with friends and neighbours, at home, in the synagogues and in schools. Friends and extended families live in close proximity and families are in and out of each other's homes and often share meals prepared in each other's kitchens. Other possible contributory factors are the relatively large family sizes, the cramped housing and the early age at which children start nursery school or play-group.

Harmful behaviour

Jewish law strictly forbids individuals to indulge in harmful behaviour or to put others at risk or expose them to risk. This is based on the premise that a person's body is not his to do what he wants with it; it belongs to God and must be treated with respect (*see* p 95). Self harm and hence suicide is strictly forbidden; smoking, drinking excessive amounts of alcohol and the use of dangerous recreational drugs would all be included in the prohibition on self harm and are therefore not permitted.

Smoking

Although Jewish law does not expressly forbid smoking, it is certainly not approved, and exposing third parties to one's smoke (i.e. passive smoking) is definitely forbidden. With the increasing awareness of the harmful effects of smoking, and the religious obligation to avoid activities damaging to health, the number of smokers in the Jewish community has plummeted, particularly so in the orthodox community although the rate is still rather high amongst Chassidic men. Smoking rates amongst Jewish women are low and it is exceedingly rare for orthodox women to smoke.

Alcohol

Although drinking alcohol is permitted, it is usually consumed in small quantities at times of celebration. Wine is used sacramentally as part of some religious ceremonies, such as *Shabbos* and *Yom-Tov kiddush* services and even then in small amounts. Four cups of wine are drunk as part of the *Pessach Seder* service (*see* p 107). Whenever wine is required for sacramental purposes, non-alcoholic grape juice may be substituted. Once a year, as part of the *Purim* celebrations, some men may become slightly drunk, but this is a once-a-year exception! Alcoholism is relatively rare amongst Jews and is almost unheard of within the orthodox Jewish community.

Drug abuse

Illicit drug use is strictly forbidden by Jewish law for various reasons, including the ban of self harm and the injunction on all Jews to uphold the laws of the land in which they live. However, as in all branches of modern society, drug use has crept into contemporary Jewish society, particularly amongst adolescents and young adults. Although not a major problem, it is becoming of increasing concern, to the extent that there are drug agencies working within the Jewish community (Chabad Drugsline) giving support to addicts and their families, as well as giving advice to young people and educating them about the dangers. Although not unheard of, the incidence of drug and substance abuse within the orthodox Jewish community is still extremely low. The level of parental and social control both at home and in school is such that most orthodox teenagers do not have the opportunity to experiment with drugs or similar substances.

Care and support within the community

Helping others is regarded as a great *mitzvah* (a divine commandment or good deed) and encompasses the very important concepts of *tzedoka* (of being charitable and helping others) and *chessed* (acts of kindness, generosity and selflessness) from which no-one is exempt. This helping of others is very fundamental to the Jewish way of life and performing *tzedoka* and *chessed* encompasses all forms of charity in the very broadest sense, not merely by giving monetary donations but by voluntarily giving something of oneself, be it time, skills or expertise so as to help others. It includes all forms of helping others, and everyone will do something, no matter how little, so as to help others within the community. As a result, there is a good support system operating within the Jewish community both on an informal and on a more organised basis. All Jews are required to give 10% of their income to charity (*tzedoka*).

Historically all Jewish communities made provision for the poor, the sick and the elderly, and by medieval times this had become well organised. Each town, large or small, had charitable societies to organise and manage care for the needy. At various points in Jewish history, some communities had the power to levy taxes and in many communities the care networks were quite sophisticated with hostels, hospitals, orphanages and residential facilities for the elderly. The Sephardi settlers who came to London when

Oliver Cromwell permitted Jews to resettle in Britain in 1656 brought these traditions with them. Indeed one of the conditions made by Oliver Cromwell was that the Jewish community would not be a drain on the state and that they would take responsibility for their own poor. Thus a well-developed support system of welfare and social services has been in place for several centuries. These are comprised of all types of organisations both large and small, many of them registered charities, providing some form of support or care, literally from cradle to grave. With the growth of the Anglo-Jewish community these charitable organisations have become diversified and new ones established. Today there are some two thousand independent Jewish voluntary organisations in the UK (Institute for Jewish Policy Research 2000) ranging in size from small family trusts to large multi-million pound organisations.

There are charitable organisations which provide services to all sections of the Jewish community, whereas others are targeted at specific groups within the community. For instance, as the orthodox and Chassidic communities have grown, a number of care and support organisations specific to their needs have developed. In the last decade or two, support organisations have mushroomed and many new groups have been set up. Most of these are voluntary bodies and encompass a very wide range of activities. There are organisations which provide support for the sick, for the housebound, for the poor, for the mentally ill, for those with physical handicap and for a wide variety of other problems such as providing help with transport to hospitals, the loan of cots and medical equipment etc. to needy families, or the provision of home helps for the elderly or infirm, to list but a few. There are residential homes for physically and mentally disabled adults (those organisations catering specifically for the strictly orthodox have separate homes for males and females). One of the best known and largest Jewish charitable organisations is Jewish Care which provides a broad spectrum of caring social services. Jewish Care 'Anglo-Jewry's Social Service Organisation' has over 50 centres spread mainly throughout London and south-east England. They offer 'a network of services for elderly, mentally ill, physically disabled and visually impaired people, as well as those who are unemployed and survivors of the Holocaust'. Services include a chain of care homes providing residential and nursing care, mainly for the frail and elderly but for others in need as well, such as the young physically disabled and the visually impaired. They also have a number of warden assisted sheltered housing schemes. Included in Jewish Care's extensive services are day care centres, support services for families and carers, home care services with carers being able to visit three times a day seven days a week where necessary, and an unemployment resource centre. Overall, Jewish Care provides a full range of social services for Jewish adults drawing on the resources of some 2000 professionals and

2500 volunteers. A similarly comprehensive service for Jewish children is provided by the charitable organisation Norwood (still named after its nineteenth-century place of origin) which provides wide-ranging services to families and children, including residential homes and accommodation for respite care for physically and learning disabled children. In the Stamford Hill area and in the Salford area of Manchester there are residential homes for the orthodox run by the Agudas Israel Housing Association, who also have a Mother and Baby home (called *Beis Brucha*) in north London where mothers can stay for a while following their discharge from the hospital maternity department (*see* p 135).

There are many support groups covering different parts of the Jewish community providing for a diverse range of problems; examples of these organisations include support for psychiatrically ill patients and their carers, for couples with infertility problems, and for providing kosher meals for the disabled. There are several confidential telephone help lines for a wide variety of problems such as those for children's behavioural problems, bereavement and the general stress of life. Some of these organisations may receive funding, but many are entirely voluntary with helpers giving of their own time.

A feature unique to Jewish communities are the *gemachs* (a word derived from the contracted form of the Hebrew phrase *gemilus chassodim*, meaning 'performing acts of kindness'). These are organisations, some small, others quite large, that loan items for a variety of needs at minimal or no cost. The variety of *gemachs* is quite wide-ranging, from those that provide interest free loans to those in need, to those for the loan of highchairs or cots. There are *gemachs* for the loan of medical equipment such as nebulisers, equipment for the disabled such as wheelchairs, tablecloths and cutlery for families making a *bris* or *Bar-mitzvah*, wedding dresses and even toys. In addition there are many charities that provide basic necessities for the needy either free of charge or at cost price. Examples of these charities include those providing for needy brides to assist with making a wedding and setting up home by providing basic necessities, those providing the basic requirements for Passover (*Pesach*) such as *matzos*, those sending children who would not otherwise get a break away for a summer holiday, or those helping with educational bursaries.

There are also a number of official organisations operating within the Jewish community, which provide a wide range of services, including many of those generally provided by the statutory social services, which in some areas have devolved their statutory roles to the Jewish equivalent organisations. The Agudas Israel Community Services (London and Manchester) provides a wide range of services particularly to the orthodox sector. Their broad range of services includes an employment bureau and a housing association providing low cost housing within the geographical location of the community. AJEX, the Association of Jewish Ex-Servicemen and Women, has sheltered accommodation for its elderly members. The Lubavitch movement (London and Manchester) also provides a similar range of services, as does Hackney Jewish Family Services in association with the Norwood (for children's services) and Jewish Care (adult services) organisations. Obviously there is a need for liaison between these organisations and the statutory bodies, and great strides have been made in recent years to achieve this goal.

There are a number of well established organisations within the community providing for children and adults with special needs and learning difficulties. These include for example Kisharon (for children and adults with learning difficulties), Side-by-Side (an integrated school where children with special needs are educated together with main stream children), Binoh (an educational advisory service) and Yad Voezer (residential homes for adults with learning and mental health difficulties). However, no matter how many places there are available there is always demand for more. Almost all the facilities are independently funded, albeit together with some statutory funding. This places a considerable financial burden on the community, but this provision is seen as being an important part of *chessed* and a valuable use of *tzedoka* or charitable funds.

A project of which the orthodox Jewish community in Hackney is justifiably proud is the Schonfeld Square development. Within the development there is a residential home for the elderly, sheltered accommodation and flats for the disabled as well as small and large family units. They are integrated on one site around a quiet square. A small synagogue has been included and there is space for children to play in the pleasantly landscaped grounds. This development exemplifies the communal extension of the family concept which is so central to the orthodox Jewish way of life, where all ages and generations live together in one community.

Visiting the sick (*bikur cholim*) is considered to be a *mitzvah* (a divine commandment or good deed) and families or friends may make arrangements for someone to be at an invalid's bedside possibly even right round the clock. There may be times when there are rather too many visitors present for the patient's own good or for the efficient running of a hospital ward or intensive care unit. This excess and constant attendance of visitors must be understood in the context of the friends' and relatives' good intentions and it is not meant to result in nuisance or inconvenience. A judicious word to a relative might ensure a more even distribution of visitors! For those who have no immediate family or friends to visit them, there is a Visitation Committee which will organise visits to Jewish patients in hospital (tel: 020 8343 8989).

Whilst discussing the topic of hospital visiting it is worth noting that when admitted to hospital some ultra-orthodox patients, having led rather insular lives, might feel quite vulnerable in what is to them an alien, frightening and possibly even intimidating environment. They might find that they have little in common with their fellow patients, they dress differently, their spoken English may be poor and they may have few subjects of common interest to talk about to other patients (they don't read the newspapers, don't watch TV, and often have little knowledge of sports affairs).

As discussed previously (*see* p 144), elderly or seriously ill patients and their families might feel that the staff have little regard for their quality of life and may not care for them actively, leaving them to fade away and die. Whether or not this is realistic, many families will be reluctant to leave ill or elderly patients unattended and will organise company around the clock. Indeed even when patients are not particularly seriously ill but are just in hospital for routine surgery or investigations they may be reluctant to be left alone (especially over *Shabbos*) in what they may perceive as being an environment run and inhabited by people who have a totally different set of values to their own. Sometimes there is also some element of distrust and fear which staff should attempt to allay sympathetically rather than confront antagonistically.

In discussing all the above mentioned facilities provided by the many organisations serving the Jewish community one might well wonder why it provides so much for itself instead of making use of the services provided for the public at large. Part of the answer at least lies in the fact that the needs of the community do not necessarily match the services available (such as the need for breast pumps or additional practical home care for mothers). However the full answer lies in the theme underlying this entire book, that Jewish patients need facilities in which they can feel comfortable, bearing in mind their cultural and religious needs. A place where the food is kosher, where the *Shabbos* and festivals are observed and where there are facilities for prayer; in essence, somewhere they can feel comfortable being Jewish. Provision of these facilities is seen not as a luxury, but as an absolute essential and there is an obligation on the community to establish and maintain them, whatever the cost in human and economic resources. This does have a negative side to it, for when it comes to applying for funding for projects from sources outside the community when all the various different ethnic and other religious groups are competing for funds, it is not unusual to hear comments to the effect that the Jewish community are capable of looking after themselves and thus they may lose out on provision of much needed resources. Furthermore, because the Jewish community has a rich communal life with all groups participating in communal activities irrespective of financial status, the levels of need and financial deprivation may not be immediately apparent particularly in the more orthodox and ultra-orthodox groups where families of widely differing financial status live and worship side by side.

Hatzolah

Hatzolah (the Hebrew word approximating to 'rescue') is a rapid response first-aid organisation run by orthodox volunteers with branches in the main Jewish residential areas both in this country and around the world. Hatzolah teams consist of trained, skilled first-aiders as well as dedicated switchboard staff, all of whom are volunteers and provide cover on a 24 hour rota basis. There is a team of volunteer doctors available on-call to deal with major emergencies.

Members carry two-way radios and Hatzolah prides itself on its very rapid response time to call outs, being able to arrive within minutes, long before an ambulance would arrive (in fact one of the reasons that Hatzolah was started was because of the poor ambulance response time). The volunteers all carry basic equipment and oxygen and have access to a defibrillator. Hatzolah volunteers are able to deal with most minor injuries themselves and all members receive regular retraining in cardiopulmonary resuscitation. Hatzolah liaises and works together with other local emergency services such as the ambulance service, the paramedics and the local hospital accident and emergency services. Some branches of Hatzolah have their own ambulances.

Circumcision (*bris*)

A fundamental and very basic principle of Judaism is that all males are circumcised. This is performed on the eighth day of life unless the baby is not well enough, when it is delayed until after the baby has recovered. The commonest cause for delay is jaundice, as Jewish law forbids circumcision in the presence of jaundice, even physiological jaundice. Low birth weight, feeding difficulties or sticky eyes are other common causes for postponement. Babies should have had vitamin K before the *bris*. The procedure is performed by a *mohel*. In the UK orthodox *mohelim* are licensed by The Initiation Society and are trained to a very high professional standard, not only in surgical techniques and hygiene but also in Jewish law. Most *mohelim* are rabbis or laymen who have been specially trained, however there are also a number of medically qualified *mohelim*. Not only does the *mohel* perform the *bris*, the actual circumcision, but he will provide a full aftercare service and visit the baby on several occasions over the following days, giving the mother precise instructions as to the aftercare both by way of explanation and written notes. A competent registered *mohel* would always be happy to liaise with other healthcare workers involved with the child's welfare. The non-orthodox synagogues also have their own organisation, The Association of Reform and Liberal Mohalim, supervising their own *mohelim*. Incidentally, some *mohelim* are prepared to perform non-religious circumcisions on non-Jewish children such as Muslims, West Africans, North Americans and Australians who are used to having their babies routinely circumcised in infancy, as this procedure is not generally available through the NHS when required for religious or cultural reasons and where it is not clinically indicated.

The surgical procedure involves the foreskin being pulled up over the penile glans and a safety shield being applied above the glans so as to prevent any damage to it. The foreskin is then cut off above the safety shield with a single cut. The mucus membrane layer is then folded back and a bandage applied. The bandage is removed next day and the wound heals rapidly. The actual procedure takes only a few minutes.

Because of the requirement for the infant to be fit and healthy prior to a *bris* being performed and the desirability for the *bris* to take place on the eighth day or as soon as possible thereafter, medical practitioners may be put under pressure to see a baby at very short notice, possibly to decide if he is fit for the procedure which is due to take place within a few minutes and for which a large crowd has gathered! If the *mohel* has any doubts about the health of the baby, he might recommend that the parents seek advice from the family's GP or possibly a paediatrician before he would feel prepared to perform the *bris*. Problems that could delay a *bris* include jaundice (even physiological jaundice), poor weight gain, feeding difficulties or anything giving rise to concerns about the overall general health of the infant.

Circumcision 1

The community midwife who visits Mrs Stobbman and her five day old baby boy mentions that the baby has physiological jaundice and reassures her that this is normal and should clear up in due course. Mrs Stobbman asks her to get a serum bilirubin assay as she needs to know what the level is because under Jewish law the *bris*, which normally takes place on the eighth day, must be deferred in the presence of jaundice. This is especially important because she would like her father to come from Israel to be present at the ceremony as this is his first grandchild. The pathologist questions the need for this blood test.

Apart from being a surgical procedure, circumcision is a religious ceremony. It can only be performed during the day, after sunrise and before sunset. It is customary to have at least ten men present (a *minyan*) at the ceremony and a *bris* is usually performed at home or in the synagogue. There may be occasions when a mother is still in hospital on the eighth day and then every consideration should be given to enable the *bris* to be performed in hospital.

Circumcision 2

Mr Silver is an orthopaedic in-patient when his first grandson is due to have his *bris*. His son-in-law would like him to hold the baby during the circumcision, something which is considered to be a great honour. He asks the ward sister if the *bris* could be performed in the ward day room, with a *minyan* (quorum of ten men) present.

A *bris* is a time of great family celebration. Following the actual *bris* itself, the baby is given his Hebrew name. The ceremony is followed by a festive meal. A *bris* can be an emotional or anxious time particularly for a mother and she may need extra understanding and support at this time. Some woman may find the gathering of family and friends at this early stage of new motherhood a bit daunting, whereas others will welcome it. Many couples, even those who have only tenuous religious affiliations, find the time spiritually meaningful and comforting, giving them a sense of connection with previous generations of Jews throughout the millennia reaching back to the days of Abraham.

A male convert (*ger*) has to be circumcised as part of his conversion process. If he has already been circumcised then a drop of blood is taken from the point of circumcision as a symbolic representation of the *bris*.

There is no female equivalent to a *bris* in Judaism, but girls are traditionally given their names in the synagogue, usually on the *Shabbos* after their birth, often followed by a reception (*kiddush*) after the service. Some Sephardi communities have a girl naming ceremony and celebration known as *zeved habas* (the gift of a daughter) at seven days (or in some communities at 30 days) old. The rabbi blesses the baby and there is a celebratory meal. In recent years the concept of having a special girl naming celebration has spread to many other parts of the Jewish community and in many congregations it is becoming the accepted norm.

Pidyon ha'ben

The Bible states (Exodus 13: 11–16) that every first-born son belongs to God and requires a *pidyon ha'ben* (a redemption of the first born). This is performed at a ceremony on the child's 31st day of life, when the father 'redeems' his child from a *kohen* (a descendant of the priestly family of Aaron, who incidentally are themselves exempt from this rite). A *pidyon ha'ben* ceremony is a joyous occasion and is accompanied by a festive celebratory meal.

Of clinical relevance is that *pidyon ha'ben* only applies where the first-born male child is born vaginally, not by caesarean section, and where there has been no previous late miscarriage or stillbirth. This might increase some primiparous women's reluctance to have a caesarean section (*see* p 132), although Jewish law would support a clinician's decision not to deliver vaginally where there is even the slightest possibility of increased risk to mother or infant. Occasionally, a Jewish woman may bring a piece of tissue expelled vaginally to her GP or gynaecologist, requesting that it be examined to see if it contains products of conception and if so, to try to establish the gestational age of the foetus. The same request might be made by a woman who has had a surgical evacuation of products of conception performed in a hospital.

Adoption and fostering

The *Talmud* says 'he who raises someone else's child is regarded as though he had actually brought him physically into the world' (Sanhedrin 19b) and giving a child a loving supportive home is regarded as a great *mitzvah* (meritorious act or good deed) and is regarded as one of the highest forms of charity. Because Jewish law does not see children as property, it does not recognise adoption in its literal sense, that is the legal transfer of ownership to others other than the natural parents. For these reasons couples, particularly orthodox ones, might be more willing to foster than adopt. Nevertheless, both adoption and fostering is encouraged, particularly as Jews would want Jewish children to be cared for and brought up only in a Jewish environment and would strongly oppose a Jewish child being placed with a non-Jewish family. With the recent trend away from institutionalised care for children with special needs and the modern emphasis on community care, there are a often a small number of children with special needs who are available for adoption or fostering. Orthodox Jewish couples will usually only want to adopt a child who is Jewish by birth, but unfortunately for them there are not many of these available. There is however always a need for orthodox Jewish foster parents. Adopting a non-Jewish child would not make that child Jewish, and orthodox Jewish rabbinic courts (*Beis Din*) would discourage conversions of children for the sake of adoption, preferring to wait until the child is old enough to choose for itself to convert. Non-orthodox rabbis might be more flexible and accept the conversion of adopted children.

Adoption or fostering

Whoever brings up an orphan in his home, is considered as if he had fathered him.

Talmud Sanhedrin 19b

Summary

- Although Jews are required to look after their health, in practice health promotion measures are largely ignored.
- Cervical cancer incidence in Jewish women is relatively low; screening rates are reasonable but could be better.
- Due to large family size and overcrowding, particularly in the strictly orthodox community, it is vital to achieve high immunisation rates.
- Smoking rates are dropping in all sections of the Jewish community; alcoholism is very rare.
- There are a large number of care and support organisations serving the Jewish community; participating in charitable work is central to Judaism.
- Circumcision of all males is an absolute basic essential of Judaism; this is done on the eighth day of life unless delayed for health reasons.
- Judaism regards fostering and adoption as highly commendable.

Further reading

Abbott S (2002) *Health Visiting and the Orthodox Jewish Community*. City University, London.

Amsel A (1969) *Judaism and Psychology*. Feldheim, New York.

Amsel A (1976) *Rational Irrational Man*. Feldheim, Jerusalem/New York.

Ganzfried S (1961) *Kitzur Sulchan Aruch: code of Jewish law* (trans H Goldin). Hebrew Publishing Co, New York.

Greenberg D and Witztum E (2001) *Sanity and Sanctity – mental health work among the ultra-orthodox of Jerusalem*. Yale University Press, New Haven.

Holman C (2001) *Orthodox Jewish Housing Needs in Stamford Hill*. Agudas Israel Housing Association, London.

Holman C and Holman N (2002) *Torah, Worship and Acts of Loving Kindness: baseline indicators for the charedi community in Stamford Hill*. Interlink Foundation, London.

Jacobson B (1990) *Investigation and Control of an Epidemic of Hepatitis in a Strictly Orthodox Religious Community*. Faculty of Public Health Medicine, Royal College of Physicians UK, London.

Qreshi B (1989) *Transcultural Medicine*. Kluwer, London.

Rabinowitz A (1999) *Judaism and Psychology: meeting points*. Aronson, New Jersey.

Spero MH (1980) *Judaism and Psychology: halachic perspectives*. Ketav, New York.

Spero MH (1986) *Handbook of Psychotherapy and Jewish Ethics*. Feldheim, Jerusalem/New York.

Spitzer J (1996) *The Surgery of Bris Milah (Jewish Religious Circumcision)*. Initiation Society, London.

Spitzer J (2002) *A Guide to the Orthodox Jewish Way of Life for Healthcare Professionals* (3e). J Spitzer, London.

Wein B (2002) *Living Jewish: values, practices and traditions*. Artscroll, New York.

CHAPTER 15

Jews as patients

One aspect of the challenge of practising in a multicultural society

The uniqueness of each individual:

> *The reason that Adam was created alone (as opposed to Adam and Eve being created together) is to teach that whoever destroys a single human being is considered by the Torah as if he had destroyed the entire world; and whoever preserves a single human life it is considered by the Torah as though he has kept the entire world alive. ... another reason why Adam was created singly, is to foster peace between man so that no one can say to another 'my father was greater than your father'. ... and also to teach the greatness of the Holy One Blessed is He; for when man mints many coins from a single mould all the coins are identical, but the King of Kings minted all men from the mould of Adam and yet no man is like any other.*

Based on *Talmud* Sanhedrin 37a

Introduction

When practising medicine in the UK today, doctors and healthcare professionals will come into contact with patients from a wide range of cultures, ethnic backgrounds and religions. The key to helping all patients lies in trying to understand them and their backgrounds and to deal with differences in an understanding, non-judgemental or prejudicial way. Jewish patients have their own particular characteristics, some relating to the culture of their places of recent origin or at least the place of origin of their parents or grandparents. Other characteristics relate to their inherent Jewishness and are based on the fundamentals of religious law, religious practice and degree of observance. Whereas the former are likely to change with the environment and over time, the latter are by definition unchangeable and will only become lost through assimilation and dilution of religious identity. Jewish characteristics, independent of the degree of religious observance, are the material beloved of comedians and do indeed exist, although perhaps not in such exaggerated stereotypical form! In this last chapter I will look at two aspects of caring for Jewish patients. First, looking at the characteristics of Jews as patients in the consultation, and then dealing with Jewish patients in the practice, describing a few organisational aspects of practices in areas with large Jewish populations, particularly if strictly orthodox. Of course there is huge variation in Jewish patients and in writing this chapter I am aware of the risk of being accused of stereotyping, but I feel that it is a risk that I can safely take, being an orthodox Jew myself and having practised for many years in a practice with a very high proportion of orthodox Jewish patients. I feel that my observations based on first hand and long personal experience may be of value to colleagues.

Jews as patients

There are certain characteristics in the consultation behaviour of Jewish patients, especially orthodox ones, which although not exclusive to them seem to be particularly prevalent in Jewish patients and I will describe some of them here. (Readers might recognise some as being characteristic of other minority groups as well.)

Jewish patients as a rule, and orthodox ones especially, are quite likely to question a doctor's decision and may want to know the basis on which it has been made. Often they will want to consider management options in detail, weighing up the pros and cons of the various alternatives at some length. Consultations may include the frequent use of both open and closed questions by the patient; to some extent this is a learned behaviour characteristic of orthodox Jews and is based (not necessarily consciously) on the traditional (talmudic) style of discussion with almost every conversation being in question and answer format. This is a style particularly typical of Yiddish speaking patients (and often mimicked by comedians). For those unused to this form of speech it can be quite unsettling, until it is realised that the patient is not necessarily being inquisitorial but is merely using a culturally specific form of speech. Although this is more common in those who speak Yiddish as a first language, it may nevertheless apply even to those with a good command of the English language. Similarly, use of Yiddish sentence construction may make a patient's questions and requests sound rather more demanding or assertive than intended. For example instead of 'will you be able to see my mother this evening?', the question might be phrased 'you will be seeing my mother this evening?', with the question being implied in the intonation rather than the wording. Another linguistic characteristic of Yiddish speaking patients is the use of (repeated) superlatives in a way unfamiliar to the English ear, as for example 'my baby is really, really ill with the worst cold I have ever, ever seen'.

Another unfamiliar form of speech that a healthcare professional might encounter is the practice of addressing and talking to someone (particularly figures of authority) in the third person. For example when talking to the doctor they might say 'does the doctor think that ...' rather than 'would you think that ...'. This has all but disappeared in English usage where it is considered archaic, but is still common in everyday Yiddish and Hebrew, and speakers from backgrounds where those languages are spoken might well use it when speaking in English. These are but a few examples where an understanding of linguistic variation (as with other cultures and languages) helps to facilitate communication with patients. Yiddish speaking men may sometimes bring their wives (or less commonly, their mothers) with them to the doctor or nurse because, on balance, Chassidic women tend to speak English better than the men.

I have already mentioned the propensity for seeking more than one opinion and requests for referrals for this purpose and the reasons behind this behaviour (looking for the right *shaliach* or agent, *see* pp 69 and 86). Therefore although doctors may sometimes feel slighted by requests for a further opinion, a request from an orthodox Jewish patient need not necessarily imply any offence. However, because of the linguistic nuances described above the request might be couched in what sounds like assertive or demanding terms, compounding the doctor's feelings even though no actual offence is intended. If a non-Jewish doctor with whom they are unfamiliar is consulted, it is quite common for orthodox patients to telephone their usual (Jewish) practitioner to corroborate the advice given. This applies both to other medical practitioners or to other healthcare professionals particularly for example where a (non-Jewish) dentist might have given the patient a prescription and the patient might want to know from his usual (Jewish) practitioner if it is all right to be taken. Similarly they might phone a Jewish pharmacist to enquire about the *Kashrus* of medication. In the holiday season patients might telephone their own doctor at home, having seen a doctor somewhere else, possibly even calling from overseas.

Because many orthodox families are quite large and have a large age spread it is not unusual for older siblings to accompany younger ones to the surgery in place of a parent or even for relatively young children to attend unaccompanied. Sisters or other members of an extended family may help each other out by bringing each other's children to the doctor.

Large busy families may find compliance with demanding medication regimens difficult and it is not unusual to be asked to give medications, particularly for children in once, or at maximum twice, daily doses.

Another characteristic feature of communities living closely in large extended family units is for there to be consultations involving family groupings not often found in the general population. For instance, a mother might attend together with her daughter and son-in-law (especially, but not exclusively, if they married at quite a young age) where, for example, he has recently been diagnosed as suffering from infectious mononucleosis. This has implications for confidentiality, although the patients and their families might not understand this concept in the conventional way familiar to medical practitioners, insisting that 'we have no secrets in our family'. The above has to balanced against the apparent paradox where, for the various reasons discussed previously (*see* p 88), illness, particularly chronic or serious ones, will be kept hidden and secret even from close family and friends. This paradoxical behaviour can understandably lead to conflict within families.

Family medicine

When Mr Eli Milim, who had been married for under a year, came for his appointment he entered the consulting room together with his young wife and his mother-in-law. It was the mother-in-law who opened the consultation, saying that Eli had recently had an MRI scan as part of the investigations into several neurological episodes and that she understood that the results had come back; did they confirm the suspected diagnosis of multiple sclerosis and if so, what was the next step in his management? The doctor sensed that Eli was uncomfortable and asked him directly if he was happy for both his wife and mother-in-law to be present during the discussion. Before Eli could answer, his wife said 'we are all one family, we have no secrets and you can tell all of us!'

In the context of understanding the concept of medical confidentiality and its implications, I have previously mentioned (*see* p 88) that doctors caring for strictly orthodox families might receive enquiries about the state of health of a prospective party to a *shidduch* for whom he/she has provided medical care and for whom he/she holds medical records. The concept of a patient's entitlement to total confidentiality may not be fully appreciated and has to be explained to the enquirer who needs to be told that no information can be disclosed without the patient's specific consent. Parents making enquiries on behalf of their child (even when adult) may not appreciate that their child is entitled to his/her medical details being kept strictly confidential, that any information is available to the patient alone and can not be disclosed or discussed with a third party without the patient's consent. Where appropriate, practitioners who get involved in these matters are best advised to get written consent from all parties before disclosing any confidential information.

Because many orthodox Jews live in insular communities they may be unaware of events in the wider world including the dates of Bank Holidays and other national holidays, and expect normal services to be available. Indeed in these communities it is not unusual for life to continue as normal and some Chassidic schools may even be open on 25 December. Patients of practices in areas with large orthodox Jewish populations may expect them to be open on these days and may express surprise if they are closed (particularly where the doctors are themselves Jewish).

Jewish patients in the practice

A medical practice which has a large number of Jewish patients, particularly strictly orthodox ones, might wish to consider some aspects of practice organisation to help make their patients feel more comfortable. Some of these topics have been covered elsewhere in this book but are mentioned again here for completeness sake.

Although they would not expect practice staff to dress like them, strictly orthodox patients might feel uncomfortable when confronted by receptionists, doctors or other healthcare workers wearing sleeveless or revealing tops. The wearing of long sleeves, skirts covering the knees and high necklines demonstrates a degree of sensitivity to the patients' feelings and will be appreciated.

Mention has been made previously (*see* p 59) that because of the restriction on physical contact, some members of the strictly orthodox community may not even pass objects directly to a member of the opposite sex, but will put them down first. This should not cause offence in situations such as when reception staff hand prescriptions to patients or when giving change.

Many strictly orthodox patients might avoid direct eye contact, particularly prolonged eye contact, with members of the opposite sex. Healthcare workers used to working with the general population may find this quite disconcerting at first, but they must remember that this is a cultural behaviour and not intended in any way as an insult.

There are some ultra-orthodox patients of either sex who when being examined might only uncover small areas (less than a handbreadth) of the body at any one time. This is not just due to their being coy but is part of their way of life, only undressing fully in the bathroom or bedroom. It is something that doctors, nurses or midwives might find difficult to cope with initially, but this behaviour should be respected or accepted and asking them or attempting to undress the patient further might make them feel so uncomfortable as to render the examination of little clinical value. Of course screens, blankets or gowns should always be provided where appropriate.

In an area with a high proportion of ultra-orthodox patients the provision of separate waiting areas for patients of both sexes might be welcomed and is something worth considering when designing new premises.

The reading material provided in the waiting room should reflect the interests of the practice population. Many strictly orthodox Jews might be offended by magazines containing pictures of scantily dressed people and articles with any sexual content, such as found in most modern women's magazines and the photo news magazines. A supply of more conservative magazines or books in Hebrew such as bibles, psalms and prayer books would be greatly appreciated. Pictures on health information posters or leaflets in waiting areas might similarly cause offence if deemed 'unsuitable' and 'offending' material might occasionally be removed without permission.

A secluded area where mothers can breast feed their babies would be appreciated by both mothers and other patients who may feel uncomfortable about breast feeding in company, particularly mixed company.

Hand washing after the toilet is a requirement of Jewish law and many orthodox Jews do so meticulously. Many are particular that the washing facilities are not in the same room as the actual lavatory and where the sink is in the same room as the toilet, they might want to at least dry their hands outside. When designing new facilities it would be appreciated if the sink and drying facilities were to be separated. Some patients may be particular to use a cup for hand washing and a supply near the sink would be appreciated; a disposable cup dispenser fitted to the wall near the sink is ideal. Many strictly observant Jews may also wish to wash their hands after touching parts of their body that are usually kept covered or after touching their shoes. After being examined and redressing, patients may ask to wash and dry their hands.

The variation in workload in relation to the Jewish calendar has been described in some detail (*see* p 111) and a practice with a high Jewish population would do well to plan for these variations possibly by having extra consultation sessions available on Friday mornings, around the festival times and by opening on Sunday mornings.

Because of the restrictions on using electrical equipment on the *Shabbos* and *Yom-Tov* (festivals), alternative arrangements for access to surgery buildings which have door entry phones or electric doors might need to be organised, to enable strictly observant patients to get in without violating Jewish law (*see* p 101).

Conclusion

Caring for patients from different ethnic, cultural or religious groups can be challenging. To make it rewarding one has to make the effort to try to understand what makes these patients different and how it makes them different; this insight will enable the well informed practitioner to provide sensitive and appropriate care. Caring for Jewish patients is no exception.

The parting handshake

Benny Stein was admitted to A&E with acute abdominal pain. Ms Lorna Cole the on-call surgical specialist registrar was called to assess him. After taking a full history she examined him thoroughly including palpating his hernial orifices, his scrotum (to rule out testicular torsion) and performed a rectal examination. Having completed her physical examination she discussed her findings with Benny and advised that he be admitted for observation. As she turned to leave she leaned forward to shake Benny's hand, but he shrunk back and said 'sorry, but as an Orthodox Jew I'm not able to shake hands with a member of the opposite sex!' Ms Cole was bemused – she had just examined him thoroughly, quite intimately in fact, yet he now refused to take her hand. Sensing her confusion, Benny tried to explain that whereas physical contact for professional medical reasons was perfectly acceptable, social contact, even a handshake, was forbidden! As she left the room she made a mental note to sign up for a course on 'Caring for Patients in a Multicultural Society' she had seen advertised on the mess notice board!

Summary

- Jewish patients, especially Yiddish speaking ones, may use unfamiliar nuances of speech during consultations.
- Questioning is part of the Jewish personality; so is shopping around for second opinions. No offence is intended.
- Certain aspects of practice organisation and surgery design might help Jewish patients feel more comfortable, for example, putting culturally sensitive reading material in the waiting room and separating toilet from hand washing and drying facilities.
- Practices with a high proportion of observant patients may need to take the Jewish calendar into account when considering their workload.
- Caring for patients of different cultures is more rewarding if efforts have been made to try to understand them.

Further reading

Abbott S (2002) *Health Visiting and the Orthodox Jewish Community*. City University, London.

Fuller JHS and Toon PD (1988) *Medical Practice in a Multicultural Society*. Heinemann, Oxford.

Qreshi B (1989) *Transcultural Medicine*. Kluwer, London.

Spitzer J (2002) *A Guide to the Orthodox Jewish Way of Life for Healthcare Professionals* (3e). J Spitzer, London.

In conclusion, when all has been considered; fear God and keep his commandment for that is man's sole purpose.

Ecclesiastes 12: 13

Bibliography

Jews have often been called 'The People of the Book' referring not only to the *Torah* (the Bible), but attesting also to the fact that so much time is spent studying. Jewish Hebrew literature is truly vast, especially as old and even ancient works are rarely seen as going out of date; newer works are additional to previous writings and are not seen as superseding previous works but enhancing and adding to them. Most of the Jewish halachic sources are to be found in the Jewish legal codes which are written in Hebrew. This bibliography is confined to readily available works in the English language. Inclusion of a title on the list does not imply my personal endorsement of the work.

The most comprehensive (and continuously growing) series of translated classic Hebrew texts is published by Artscroll-Mesorah Publications, New York (www.ArtScroll.com). These are generally in the format of having the original Hebrew text alongside a modern English translation with English notes or commentary. Publications in this format include the *Chumash* (Pentateuch or Five Books of Moses) in several formats, the *Tenach* (the entire Old Testament) again in several formats, the *Mishna* and the *Talmud* (a monumental work in progress which will comprise some 72 volumes when completed). Mesorah publications also include educational works, biographies, histories and novels.

Other major publishers of Judaica include:

- CIS Publishers, Lakewood, New Jersey
- Feldheim Publishers, New York and Jerusalem (www.feldheim.com)
- Jason Aronson, Northvale, New Jersey (www.aronson.com)
- Judaica Press, Brooklyn, New York (www.judaicapress.com)
- Ktav, Hoboken, New Jersey (www.ktav.com)
- Soncino Press, Brooklyn, New York (www.soncino.com)
- Targum Press, Jerusalem (www.targum.com).

One of the largest stockists and wholesalers of Judaica in the UK is Lehmanns (email: info@lehmanns.co.uk).

Aronson A (2000) *The Foundation of Judaism* (2e). Targum/Feldheim, New York.
Abbott S (2002) *Health Visiting and the Orthodox Jewish Community*. City University, London.

Abraham SA (1980) *Medical Halacha for Everyone: a comprehensive guide to Jewish medical law in sickness and health*. Feldheim, Jerusalem/New York.

Abraham SA (1990) *The Comprehensive Guide to Medical Halacha*. Feldheim, New York.

Abraham SA (2000/2002) *Nishmat Avraham: medical halachah for doctors, nurses, health-care personnel and patients* (vols 1/2). Artscroll, New York.

Adler A and Spiro MD (1986) *Medicines and Kashrus: a practical guide to the Kashrus of medicines* (with regular updates). Gateshead.

Aiken L (1996) *Why Me, God?: a Jewish guide for coping with suffering*. Aronson, New Jersey.

Allen R *et al.* (ed.) (1997) *Inflammatory Bowel Disease* (3e). Churchill Livingstone, London.

Amsel A (1969) *Judaism and Psychology*. Feldheim, New York.

Amsel A (1976) *Rational Irrational Man*. Feldheim, Jerusalem/New York.

Bisset RAL *et al.* (2002) Postmortem examinations using magnetic resonance imaging: four year review of a working service. *BMJ*. **324**: 1423–4.

Blech B (1999) *The Complete Idiot's Guide to Jewish History and Culture*. Alpha Books, Indianapolis.

Blech B (1999) *The Complete Idiot's Guide to Understanding Judaism*. Alpha Books, Indianapolis.

Bleich JD (1977/1981/1989/1995) *Contemporary Halakhic Problems* (vols 1–4). Ktav, New York.

Bleich JD (1981) *Judaism and Healing: halachic perspectives*. Ktav, New York.

Bleich JD (1991) *Time of Death in Jewish Law*. Z Berman Publishing Co, New York.

Bleich JD (1998) *Bioethical Dilemmas: a Jewish perspective*. Ktav, New York.

Bonné-Tamair B and Avinoam A (eds) (1992) *Genetic Diversity Among Jews: disease and markers at the DNA level*. Oxford University Press, New York.

Carmell A (1991) *Masterplan, Judaism: its program, meaning, goals*. Feldheim, Jerusalem/New York.

Carmell A and Domb C (1988) *Challenge: Torah views on science and its problems*. Feldheim, Jerusalem/New York.

Cohen J (2002) *The Bedside Companion for Jewish Patients*. Genisa, Stanmore.

Cohen SB (1992) *The Shabbos Kitchen*. Artscroll, New York.

Cohn-Sherbok L and Cohn-Sherbok D (1994) *A Short History of Judaism*. Oneworld, Oxford.

Cohn-Sherbok L and Cohn-Sherbok D (1997) *A Popular Dictionary of Judaism*. Curzon, Richmond.

Cohn-Sherbok L and Cohn-Sherbok D (1998) *A Concise Encyclopaedia of Judaism*. Oneworld, Oxford.

Cohn-Sherbok L and Cohn-Sherbok D (1999) *A Short Reader in Judaism*. Oneworld, Oxford.

Dorff E (1998) *Matters of Life and Death*. Jewish Publication Society of Philadelphia, Philadelphia.

Feldman D (1974) *Marital Relations, Birth Control and Abortion in Jewish Law* (3e). New York University Press, New York.

Feldman DM (1995) *Birth Control in Jewish Law*. University of London Press, London.

Feldman E and Wolowelsky JB (1997) *Jewish Law and the New Reproductive Technologies*. Ktav, New Jersey.

Feuer J and Spiera H (1977) Acute rheumatic fever in adults: a resurgence in the Hasidic Jewish community. *J Rheumatol.* **24** (2): 337–40.

Finkel AY (1995) *In My Flesh I See God: a treasury of rabbinic insight about human anatomy.* Aronson, New Jersey.

Fisher NL (ed.) (1996) *Cultural and Ethnic Diversity – a guide for genetics professionals.* Johns Hopkins University Press, Baltimore.

Flancbaum L (2001) *'... And You Shall Live By Them' – contemporary Jewish approaches to medical ethics.* Mirkov Publications, Pittsburgh.

Forbes A (2001) *Clinicians' Guide to Inflammatory Bowel Disease* (2e). Arnold, London.

Forst B (1993) *The Laws of Kashrus: a comprehensive exposition of their underlying concepts and applications.* Artscroll, New York.

Forta A (1995) *Judaism.* Heinemann, Oxford.

Forta A (1996) *Judaism: a dictionary.* Nelson Thornes, Cheltenham.

Freudenthal G (ed.) (1998) *AIDS in Jewish Thought and Law.* Ktav, New Jersey.

Friedenwald H (1944) *The Jews and Medicine.* Johns Hopkins University Press, Baltimore.

Fuller JHS and Toon PD (1988) *Medical Practice in a Multicultural Society.* Heinemann, Oxford.

Ganzfried S (1961) *Kitzur Sulchan Aruch: code of Jewish law* (trans H Goldin). Hebrew Publishing Co, New York.

Gilbert M (1987) *The Holocaust: the Jewish tragedy.* HarperCollins, London.

Gilbert M (1993) *Atlas of Jewish History* (5e). Routledge, London.

Gilbert M (2002) *Letters to Aunt Fori: the 5000-year history of the Jewish people and their faith.* Weidenfeld & Nicolson, London.

Goodman RM (1975) Genetic disorders among the Jewish people. In: AEH Emery (ed.) *Modern Trends in Human Genetics* (vol 2). Butterworth, London.

Goodman RM (1979) *Genetic Disorders Among the Jewish People.* Johns Hopkins University Press, Baltimore.

Grazi RV (1994) *Be Fruitful and Multiply: fertility therapy and the Jewish tradition.* Genesis Jerusalem Press, Jerusalem.

Greenberg D and Witztum E (2001) *Sanity and Sanctity – mental health work among the ultra-orthodox of Jerusalem.* Yale University Press, New Haven.

Grunfeld I (1989) *The Jewish Dietary Laws.* Soncino Press, London, Jerusalem & New York.

Grunfeld I (1986) *The Shabbos: a guide to its understanding and observance.* Feldheim, Jerusalem/New York.

Hakohol. The annual magazine of The Union of Orthodox Hebrew Congregations (140 Stamford Hill, London N16 6QT) published before Passover and containing a list of kosher/non-kosher medication and preparations suitable for Passover.

HaLevi J (1964) *The Kuzari: an argument for the faith of Israel* (trans H Hirschfeld). Schocken Books, New York.

Harper PS (1998) *Practical Genetic Counselling* (5e). Oxford University Press, Oxford.

Heynick F (2002) *Jews and Medicine: an epic saga.* Ktav, New York.

Hirsch SR (1962) *Horeb: a philosophy of Jewish laws and observances* (trans I Grunfeld). Soncino Press, New York.

Hirsch SR (1994) *The Nineteen Letters on Judaism.* Feldheim, Spring Valley.

Holman C (2001) *Orthodox Jewish Housing Needs in Stamford Hill.* Agudas Israel Housing Association, London.

Holman C and Holman N (2002) *Torah, Worship and Acts of Loving Kindness: baseline indicators for the charedi community in Stamford Hill.* Interlink Foundation, London.

Isaacs RH (1998) *Judaism, Medicine and Healing.* Aronson, New Jersey.

Jacobson B (1990) *Investigation and Control of an Epidemic of Hepatitis in a Strictly Orthodox Religious Community.* Faculty of Public Health Medicine, Royal College of Physicians UK, London.

Jakobovits I (1975) *Jewish Medical Ethics.* Bloch Publishing Company, New York.

Kaplan A (1992) *The Handbook of Jewish Thought.* Maznaim Press, New York/Jerusalem.

Karlinger K *et al.* (2000) The epidemiology and pathogenesis of inflammatory bowel disease. *Eur J Radiol.* **35** (3): 154–67.

Katz M (1982) *Menucha v'Simcha: a guide to the basic laws of Shabbos and Yom Tov.* Feldheim, New York.

King RA, Rotter JI and Motulsky AG (1992) *The Genetic Basis of Common Diseases.* Oxford University Press, Oxford.

Koenigsberg M (1997) *Halacha and Medicine Today: experts discuss the application of Halachah to contemporary medical practice.* Feldheim, New York.

Lamb N (1969) *The Jewish Way in Death and Mourning.* Jonathan David Publishers, New York.

Levin F (1987) *Halacha, Medical Science and Technology: perspectives on contemporary Halacha issues.* Maznaim, Jerusalem.

Marteau T (1992) Screening ethics and the law. *BMJ.* **305**: 1433–4.

Marteau T and Richards M (1999) *The Troubled Helix: social and psychological implications of the new human.* Cambridge University Press, Cambridge.

Mayberry JF, Judd D, Smart H *et al.* (1986) Crohn's disease in Jewish people – an epidemiological study in south-east Wales. *Digestion.* **35**: 237–40.

Meier L (1991) *Jewish Values in Health and Medicine.* Lanham, New York/London.

Mourant AE, Kopec AC and Domaniewska-Sobczak K (1978) *The Genetics of the Jews.* Clarendon Press, Oxford.

Munk E (1963) *The World of Prayer.* Feldheim Publishers, New York.

Ozarowski JS (1998) *To Walk in God's Name: Jewish pastoral perspectives on illness and bereavement.* Aronson, New Jersey.

Pick E (1975) *Guide to Shabbos Observance.* Targum Press, Southfield, MI.

Preuss J (1994) *Julius Preuss' Biblical and Talmudic Medicine* (trans F Rosner). Aronson, New Jersey.

Qreshi B (1989) *Transcultural Medicine.* Kluwer, London.

Rabinowitz A (1999) *Judaism and Psychology: meeting points.* Aronson, New Jersey.

Robinson G (2000) *Essential Judaism – a complete guide to beliefs, customs and rituals.* Pocket Books, New York.

Rosner F (1969) Hemophilia in the Talmud and Rabbinic Writings. *Annals of Internal Medicine.* **70**(4): 833–7.

Rosner F (1977) *Medicine in the Bible and Talmud.* Ktav, New York.

Rosner F (1984) *Maimonides Medical Writings* (series of several volumes published from 1984). Maimonides Research Institute, Haifa.

Rosner F (1984) *Medicine in the Mishneh Torah of Maimonides*. Ktav, New York.

Rosner F (1991) *Modern Medicine and Jewish Ethics*. Ktav, New York.

Rosner F (1995) *Maimonides' Introduction to His Commentary on the Mishnah*. Aronson, New Jersey.

Rosner F (1997) *Pioneers in Jewish Medical Ethics*. Aronson, New Jersey.

Rosner F (2000) *Encyclopaedia of Medicine in the Bible and the Talmud*. Aronson, New Jersey.

Rosner F (2001) *Biomedical Ethics and Jewish Law*. Ktav, New York.

Rosner F and Bleich JD (2000) *Jewish Bioethics*. Ktav, New York.

Rosner F and Kottek SS (1993) *Moses Maimonides: physician scientist and philosopher*. Aronson, New Jersey.

Rosner F and Tendler MD (1997) *Practical Medical Halacha*. Aronson, New Jersey.

Roth MP *et al.* (1989) Familial empirical risk estimates of inflammatory bowel disease in Ashkenazi Jews. *Gastroenterology*. **96**: 1016–20.

Roth C (1942) *A History of the Jews in England*. Oxford University Press, Oxford.

Roth C (ed.) (1972) *Encyclopaedia Judaica*. Keter, Jerusalem: 16 vols (also single vol concise edn and junior edn) with yearbook and decennial updates.

Rottenberg G and Spitzer L (2001) *Maternity Issues and Halcha*. Norwood Children & Family Services, London.

Sacks J (2000) *Radical Then, Radical Now: the legacy of the world's oldest religion*. HarperCollins, London.

Schott J and Henley A (1996) *Culture, Religion and Childbearing in a Multicultural Society: a handbook for health professionals*. Butterworth-Heinemann, Oxford.

Schur TG (1987) *Illness and Crisis, Coping the Jewish Way*. NSCY/Orthodox Union, New York.

Segal MZ (1959) *The Complete Book of Ben Sira* (2e). Bialik Institute, Jerusalem.

Shulman NE (1998) *Jewish Answers to Medical Ethical Questions*. Aronson, New Jersey.

Sinclair DB (1989) *Tradition and the Biological Revolution: an application of Jewish law to the treatment of the critically ill*. Edinburgh University Press, Edinburgh.

Solomon N (1996) *Judaism – a very short introduction*. Oxford University Press, Oxford.

Spero MH (1980) *Judaism and Psychology: halachic perspectives*. Ktav, New York.

Spero MH (1986) *Handbook of Psychotherapy and Jewish Ethics*. Feldheim, Jerusalem/ New York.

Spitzer J (1996) *The Surgery of Bris Milah (Jewish Religious Circumcision)*. Initiation Society, London.

Spitzer J (2002) *A Guide to the Orthodox Jewish Way of Life for Healthcare Professionals* (3e). J Spitzer, London.

Spitzer J, Hennessy E and Neville L (2001) High group A streptococcal carriage in the Orthodox Jewish community of north Hackney. *Br J General Practice*. **51**: 101–5.

Steinberg A (1980) *Jewish Medical Law*. Gefen Publishing, Jerusalem/California.

Swirsky M (1996) *At the Threshold: Jewish mediations on death*. Aronson, New Jersey.

Telushkin J (1991) *Jewish Literacy: the most important things to know about the Jewish religion, its people and its history.* William Morrow & Co, New York.

Wagschal S (1993) *Care of Children on Shabbos and Festivals.* Feldheim, New York.

Wagschal S (1993) *The Practical Guide to Childbirth on Shabbos and Yom Tov.* Feldheim, New York.

Wagschal S (1997) *The Practical Guide to Kashruth.* Feldheim, New York.

Wahrman J and Fried K (1970) The Jerusalem prospective newborn survey of mongolism. *Ann NY Acad Sci.* **171**: 341.

Webster YD (1997) *The Halachos of Pregnancy and Childbirth.* CIS Publishers, Lakewood.

Wein B (1990) *Triumph of Survival – the history of the Jews in the modern era 1640–1990.* Shar Press, New York.

Wein B (1993) *Herald of Destiny – the story of the Jews 750–1650.* Shar Press, New York.

Wein B (1995) *Echoes of Glory – the story of the Jews in the classical era 350BCE–750CE.* Shar Press, New York.

Wein B (2001) *Faith and Fate – the story of the Jews in the twentieth century.* Shar Press, New York.

Wein B (2002) *Living Jewish: values, practices and traditions.* Artscroll, New York.

Weiner Y (1995) *Ye Shall Surely Heal: medical ethics from a halachic perspective.* Jerusalem Centre for Research, Jerusalem.

Wouk H (1992) *This is My God – the Jewish way of life.* Souvenir Press, London.

Wouk H (2000) *The Will to Live On: this is our heritage.* HarperCollins, New York.

Zohar NJ (1997) *Alternatives in Jewish Bioethics.* State University of New York, New York.

Zoltogora J *et al.* (1991) Prevalence of inflammatory bowel disease in family members of Jewish Crohn's disease patients in Israel. *Dig Dis Sci.* **36** (4): 471–5.

Glossary[1]

Acharonim: (lit. 'the Later Ones') the rabbinic leaders of Judaism from c. 1450 CE onwards.

Ashkenazi: (pl. *Ashkenazim*) Jew(s) of European origin.

Av Beis Din: head of the *Beis Din* (rabbinic court) or of the *Sanhedrin*.

Bar-mitzvah: male adult aged over 13 years, required to keep the *mitzvos*.

Bas-mitzvah: female equivalent of *Bar-mitzvah* but from 12 years.

Beis Din: (or *Beth Din*) rabbinical court, also rabbinic administrative organisation and *Kashrus* supervisory body.

Bekishe: the long black shiny jacket worn by Chassidic men on *Shabbos*, *Yom-Tov* and festive occasions.

Bikur cholim: visiting the sick.

Bris: circumcision.

Brochoh: a blessing, typically recited before eating.

Chanukah: Festival of Lights in mid winter.

Charedi: term used to denote Jews who are strictly religiously observant, often used as alternative to 'orthodox' or 'ultra-orthodox'.

Chassid: (lit. 'the Righteous Ones') Jews of Eastern European origin belonging to the movement founded by Ba'al Shem Tov (BeShT) in the eighteenth century (alt. spelling *Hassid*, pl. *Hassidim*).

Chatzitzah: substance on skin (preventing *mikveh* water from coming into direct contact with the body).

Cheder: Jewish school.

Chessed: kindness, generosity; a selfless act.

Chevra kadisha: burial society.

Chol Hamoed: the middle days of the *Succos* and *Pesach* festivals.

Chometz: leavened foods forbidden on *Pesach*.

Chumash: (lit. 'the five') Pentateuch, the Five Books of Moses.

Dayan: (lit. 'judge', pl. *dayanim*) a member(s) of a rabbinical court (*Beis Din*).

Eretz Yisroel: the (biblical) land of Israel.

Esrog: citron, a lemon-like fruit used together with the *lulov* as part of the *Succos* service.

Gemach: charitable organisation (derived from the Hebrew phrase *gemilus chassodim*).

---

[1] For a more detailed listing *see* Cohn-Sherbok and Cohn-Sherbok (1997) in the Bibliography. Note: 'ch' is guttural (as in the Scottish 'loch').

Gemilus chassodim: performing acts of kindness.

Geonim: (lit. 'The Brilliant (or Majestic) Ones') the rabbinic leaders of Judaism, based in Babylon c. 690–1040 CE.

Ger: a convert to Judaism.

Halochoh: Jewish religious law.

Hashem: (lit. 'the name') one of several words substituted for God's name in daily conversation, to avoid the prohibition of using God's name in vain.

Haskalah: the secular enlightenment of the eighteenth and nineteenth centuries.

Hassid: alt. spelling of *Chassid*, pl. *Hassidim*.

Havdolah: ceremonial prayer said over a cup of wine at the end of *Shabbos* and *Yom-Tov*.

Hechsher: certificate that a product is kosher, often seen in the form of a small symbol or logo on food packaging.

Kabbolah: Jewish mysticism, much of which has been incorporated into Chassidic philosophy.

Kaddish: prayer recited by the bereaved, as part of the synagogue prayer services, during the mourning period and on anniversary of a death.

Kappel: (syn. *yarmulke* or *kippah*) skullcap worn constantly by men.

Kashrus/Kashruth: the Jewish dietary laws, the kosher rules.

Kavonoh: sincerity, devotion, concentration and understanding as in performing the commandments and in prayer.

Kesuvim: Books of the Holy Writings.

Kiddush: ceremonial prayer said over a cup of wine on *Shabbos* and *Yom-Tov*; hence a reception held in the synagogue on *Shabbos* morning after the service at which *kiddush* is recited.

Kippah: alternate name for *kappel*.

Kohen: a 'Priest', a descendant of the priestly family of Aaron (also, Cohen).

Kollel: institute of advanced rabbinical and talmudic studies.

Kosher: food complying with the Jewish dietary laws.

Lulov: palm branch used in *Succos* service.

Matzoh: (alt. *matza*) unrisen wheat flour crackers eaten on *Pesach*.

Medrash/Midrash: various collections of rabbinic writings compiled between the first and tenth centuries CE. Very wide ranging contents, including explanations of the Bible and Jewish law, stories of the rabbis, parables, moral lessons and theological ideas.

Melochoh: any type of activity forbidden on *Shabbos*.

Mezuzoh: parchment scroll fixed to door posts, often encased in wood, plastic or metal.

Mikveh: ritual bath (house).

Minyan: prayer quorum of ten males over the age of *Bar-mitzvah* (13 years old).

Mishne: the first written summary of rabbinic law completed around 188 CE which forms the basis of the written law and the *Talmud*.

Mishne Torah: (lit. 'repetition of the *Torah*') the title of the monumental work by Maimonides (1135–1204), codifying all talmudic law.

Misnagdim: (lit. 'the opponents') that group of Ashkenazi Jews who originally opposed the rise of the Chassidic movement and who do not share all their philosophical views.

Mitzvah: (pl. *mitzvos*) divine commandment; good deed.

Mohel: (pl. *mohelim*) man who performs a *bris* (circumcision).

Morror: bitter herbs eaten at the *Pesach seder* service, in commemoration of the bitterness of the slavery in Egypt.

Moshiach: the Messiah, for whose coming Jews pray constantly.

Neshoma: the soul.

Nevi'im: the Prophets (and their writings, as in The Books of the *Nevi'im*).

Niddah: the term used to describe the status of a woman who has had uterine bleeding (e.g. menstruation or labour) until she has immersed herself in the *mikveh*.

Nosi: (lit. 'prince') leader of the *Sanhedrin*, the Supreme Court of the Second Temple period.

Parev: neutral foods, i.e. neither meat nor dairy.

Payos: locks of hair worn by Chassidic men, at the sides of the head.

Pesach: festival of Passover in the spring, lasts for eight days.

Pidyon ha'ben: Redemption of the Firstborn, a ceremony held on a firstborn male infant's 31st day of life.

Pikuach nefesh: the saving or preserving of life, the principle whereby almost all halachic restrictions or requirements are set aside where there is a risk to life or health.

Purim: one-day joyous festival in early spring.

Rabbonim: plural of rabbi.

Reb: Mr.

Rebbe: spiritual leader of a group of *Chassidim*.

Rishonim: (lit. 'The First Ones') the rabbinic leaders of Judaism c. 1000–1450 CE.

Rosh Hashona: New Year, two-day (solemn) holyday festival in autumn.

Sanhedrin: the Supreme Court, the highest rabbinical court, ruled the Jews especially during the second Temple era.

Savoraim: (lit. 'The Ponderers') the rabbinic leaders of Judaism (based in Babylon) c. 500–700 CE.

Seder: ceremonial *Pesach* night meal to commemorate and discuss the exodus from Egypt.

Sephardi/Sefardi: (pl. *Sephardim/Sefardim*) Jews of Oriental, Middle Eastern and North African origin (i.e. non-Ashkenazi).

Shabbos: Sabbath (from Friday evening to Saturday night).

Shaliach: (lit. messenger) the concept that a doctor is God's messenger or intermediary in effecting cure.

Shavuos: festival of Pentecost (early summer), lasts for two days.

Shema: declaration of faith said three times a day and also written on the small parchment scrolls inside *tefillin* and *mezuzos*.

Shemini Atzeres: festival appended to *Succos*.

Shemirah: 'guarding' or 'watching' used in several senses, e.g. supervision of the manufacture of kosher products or watching over a corpse.

Shidduch/Shadchan: an arranged introduction (*shidduch*) between a couple for the purpose of marriage (arranged by a *shadchan*).

Shiur: (pl. *shiurim*) lecture(s) or study session(s).

Shiva: seven-day period of mourning for a close relative.

Shofar: ram's horn used during the *Rosh Hashona* service.

Shomer: noun, the person who does *shemirah*.

Shtiebel: small synagogue (prayer room).

Shtreimel: the round fur hats worn by married Chassidic men on *Shabbos*, *Yom-Tov* and festive occasions.

Shul: synagogue (Yiddish).

Shulchon Oruch: Code of Jewish Law, compiled by Rabbi Yossef Caro (1488–1575), standard text book of *Halochoh*.

Simchas **Torah**: Rejoicing of the *Torah*, a one-day festival following on from *Shemini Atzeres* which itself is appended to *Succos*.

Succah: tabernacle, a temporary (outdoor) structure where meals are eaten on *Succos*.

Succos: Tabernacles, festival in autumn, lasts for seven days.

Tallis: white or cream coloured prayer shawl with *tzitzis* on the four corners, worn during the morning service.

Tallis koton: small *tallis* with *tzitzis* on each corner worn by men at all times under or over their shirts.

Talmud: encyclopaedic work of Jewish law and practice (main source of post-biblical rabbinic law, contained in 20 or so large tomes, which is studied in depth).

Tefillin: (translated into English as 'phylacteries') small black leather boxes containing scriptural passages, worn by men during the morning service, strapped to the head and arm with long black leather straps.

Tehillim: psalms, often recited (in Hebrew) by invalids or their carers.

Tenach: the entire Old Testament.

Tisha B'av: ninth of Av, fast day in late midsummer.

Torah: (lit. 'The Law') The Five Books of Moses (Pentateuch); but also used in the much broader sense encompassing all Jewish religious teaching, knowledge and laws contained in the Oral and the Written Law.

Treif(a): non-kosher food.

Tzedoka: charity, performing charitable acts, helping others.

Tzitzis: tassels on each of the four corners of a *tallis* or *tallis koton*, often worn dangling over the trousers.

Viddui: confession, especially in context of death bed confession.

Yahrzeit: anniversary of a death, observed by next of kin.

Yarmulke: (syn. *kappel*) skullcap worn constantly by men.

Yeshiva: talmudical college for young men.

Yiddish: language originally spoken by Jews throughout Eastern Europe, based on early medieval German, written in Hebrew characters; the main language spoken by many *Chassidim* today.

Yom Kippur: Day of Atonement, solemn fast day, occurring ten days after *Rosh Hashona*.

Yomim Noraim: (lit. 'days of awe') the High Holydays consisting of *Rosh Hashona*, *Yom Kippur* and the week in between.

Yom-Tov: festival, holyday.

Zeved habas: 'the gift of a daughter', girl naming ceremony and celebration.

Zugos: 'the Pairs', the joint heads of the *Sanhedrin* who were the rabbinic leaders during the latter 300 years of the second Temple era.

Index